CHEFFES DE CUISINE

CHEFFES DE CUISINE

Women and Work in the Professional French Kitchen

RACHEL E. BLACK

UNIVERSITY OF ILLINOIS PRESS
Urbana, Chicago, and Springfield

1 2 3 4 5 C P 5 4 3 2 1
∞ This book is printed on acid-free paper.

Cataloging data available from the Library of Congress
ISBN 978-0-252-04400-7 (cloth)
ISBN 978-0-252-08605-2 (paperback)
ISBN 978-0-252-05293-4 (ebook)

In memory of my grandmothers
Lois "Otis" Black (1927–1996)
and
Barbara Jessel (1924–2016)

CONTENTS

ACKNOWLEDGMENTS

Throughout my career, Carole Counihan has been my tireless mentor and supporter. I want to thank Carole for never giving up on me, particularly in moments when I was ready to give up on myself. Carole was there to push my thinking as I originally outlined my ideas for this book. She encouraged me as I confronted the challenges of motherhood, research, writing, and my academic career. She inspired me with her own example. Carole read and commented on versions of this manuscript and helped me to think further about the central themes of this work. The only way I know how to pay my debt to Carole is by paying it forward to the next generation of anthropology and food scholars.

Barbara Rotger, thank you for your support during the formative moment when this project was just getting underway. Your friendship has brought much light and joy into my life particularly during difficult times. This book probably would not have happened if it were not for a few fateful conversations with Jean-Jacques Paimblanc in my office at Boston University. I am grateful for the many people I met at BU through the Gastronomy Program who inspired me to pursue this research.

There have been so many people who have weighed in on aspects of this project all along the way. Thank you to Psyche Williams Forson,

David Beriss, Jim Taggart, and Amy Trubek for your input. Thanks to my Association for the Study of Food and Society family who listened to my conference presentations, responded to my probing emails, and gave me feedback and support all along this journey. Alice Julier, I am grateful for your guidance and advice at a particularly challenging moment when I came back from the field discouraged. You talked me off the edge and brought to light new opportunities and directions for my work. Fabio Parasecoli, thank for your friendship. It is a grounding force and source of great joy. Thank you, Netta Davis, Beth Forrest, Greg de St. Maurice, Jon Deutsch, Scott Barton, and Warren Belasco.

Thank you to my Society for the Anthropology of Food and Nutrition family. Ryan Adams, I feel like we have been on a journey together. I appreciate your support. Janet Chrzan, thank you for your friendship over the years. Leslie Carlin, I appreciate your constant friendship and support. Penny Van Esterik, from academic to breastfeeding advice, you have been there for me as a friend and mentor. Joan Gross, Deborah Heath, Michael Di Giovine, Heather Paxson, and Melissa Caldwell, I am grateful for your support of my career and for your inspiring scholarship. Valeria Siniscalchi (Franco and Adriano), thank you for taking me under your wing while I was in France and for your continued friendship.

When I arrived at the Connecticut College Anthropology Department, I knew I had found my academic home. I am so grateful for my colleagues, who have provided me with the best work environment a person could want. You are my role models, you have given me your support, and best of all has been your friendship. Thank you, Joyce Bennett, Anthony Graesch, Catherine Benoît, Chris Steiner, Jeff Cole, and Sufia Udin. I have also benefitted from discussions with my students about this project, and I am thankful to have so many bright young minds in my life.

There are many others at Connecticut College who have shown me care and support throughout the writing of this book. Particularly, I am grateful for all of my writing group friends. Mónika López Anuarbe, you are an inspiration and a ray of light. Afshan Jafar, Karen Gonzalez Rice, Priya Kohli, Luis Gonzalez, and Ari Rotramel, you all helped keep this project on track. It was good to know I was not the only one juggling family, teaching, and writing. I am grateful for your kind words of support each day.

Thanks to Nancy Lewandowski, Ellen Maloney, and Rosa Woodhams for your support. You are three of the most competent people I have ever met. From cake-decorating tips to compiling my tenure file, you made my life better in so many thoughtful ways. Andrew Lopez, Aartee Hosanee, and Melissa Avilez Lopez, I am grateful for your help with the bibliography.

Michelle Neely, your scholarship is an inspiration and your friendship and support have been invaluable for keeping up my spirits while completing this project. To the rest of my *maman*/academic/professional gang, Mariko Moher, Ginny Anderson, and Nora Leech, your comradery and friendship are truly special gifts. Thank you for being there.

I am grateful for the initial funding from the Culinary Trust and the Julia Child Foundation, which helped get my research off the ground. I also want to thank the Collegium de Lyon for the generous funding and support that made my year of fieldwork in Lyon possible. I am grateful for the 2014–15 fellows: Erik Bleich, Demyan Belyaev, Raffaele Carbone, Alistair Cole, Antonella del Prete, Spike Gildea, Massimo Leone, Nelle Schmitz, Pinar Selek, Michael Sonenscher, Michel Tissier, and Przemyslaw Urbanczyk. Your feedback on this project and your friendship over many cafeteria lunches and paper presentations was appreciated.

Many people helped me in the field and became friends over the years that it took me to complete this book. My culinary school classmates shared that formative experience with me. Jacotte Brazier took me under her wing and shared her family's history and her vision for women in the professional kitchen—the research behind this book is immeasurably richer because of her. Sonia Ezgulian pushed my thinking about the changes taking place in the culinary arts in France and helped me see that there are many ways to be a woman who cooks; her talent and passion are an inspiration. Emmanuel Auger generously shared his photography and vision of Lyon's culinary scene. Connie Zagora let me into her world, fed me delicious food, and provided friendship—I hope we will have many more moments at the table together. Lucy Vanel welcomed me into her home, taught me to make croissants, and shared her research and thoughts about the history of the *mères lyonnaises*. Clotilde Martin-Mathieu fed me and let me into her kitchen. Her experiences shaped my thinking about what it means to be a mother and also to cook and feed others for a living. Other participants in my research who did not consent to be named appear in this book by first name (pseudonym) only; you know who you are, and you have my continued gratitude.

To my old and new friends in Lyon, you made it hard for me to leave the field. Jaki and Gérard Martelin have been with me every step of the way: thank you for always being there for me. Clémence and Alex Plaisance, your friendship during our stay and beyond is a true gift.

Thank you to David Sutton and the anonymous reviewer of this book for encouraging me to find my voice. Your constructive, thoughtful feedback helped move my writing and thinking in a positive direction.

To the many editors I worked with at the University Illinois Press, I appreciate your patience and support throughout this project. Deborah Oliver, thank you for your careful reading, suggestions, and edits.

I am grateful for my entire family who has been there for me throughout the writing of this book. Thank you to my sons, Félix and Lucien, for making me a mother in the midst of putting this book together. You bring joy to each day. Last, but most important of all, I am indebted to my husband, Doug Cook, who believed in me, encouraged me, and made many sacrifices so I could write this book. Your love makes it all possible.

PROLOGUE

La mère Brazier: The Woman, the Chef

This story starts in La Tranclière (Ain), a small village near the provincial town of Bourg-en-Bresse, seventy kilometers from Lyon. On June 12, 1895, Eugénie Brazier, the main protagonist, was born here on a farm into a life of hard work with little leisure. This was also the case for the village's other 250 or so residents. At the end of the nineteenth century, the French countryside was changing; young people were leaving to find work in growing cities. Eugénie was about to be swept up in these changes. She was part of a historic moment and, although she did not know it, she was going to make history.

By the age of five, Eugénie's job was to watch the pigs. Everyone on the farm labored, and children only went to school when there was little work, which was rare. Like most French farmers, the Braziers rarely ate meat. They subsisted on broths made from water and vegetables that they ate with rustic bread or *gaudes,* a slow-cooked gruel made from cornmeal, which was a staple for most farm families in the Bresse area.

After Brazier's mother died when she was ten years old, social services sent her to work on a nearby farm. In her biography, Brazier recounts that she worked hard, but her wardens treated her kindly (Brazier 1992, 20–22). This tranquil country life abruptly came to an end when, at the age of nineteen, the unwed Brazier gave birth to a child. Shunned by her father and the local community, she left her son, Gaston, with a wet nurse and set out for Lyon in hopes of finding a way to support herself and Gaston.[1] In 1914, at the start of World War I, Eugénie Brazier arrived in Lyon. Who knows what this sturdy farm girl felt as she approached the Milliat villa, her new home and workplace.

Brazier's first job in the city involved feeding people—in this case, an infant. She was employed as a wet nurse working in the home of the Milliat family. Owners of a prosperous pasta factory, this family had made their fortune in the expanding industrial food sector in Lyon (Mesplède 2001, 9). Only the most well-to-do middle-class families could afford to hire a live-in wet nurse, but this was a popular entrée into urban life for country girls (Sussman 1975, 308). Most women did not stay in domestic service their entire careers; they saw it as a stepping-stone to a better life (Perrot 1978, 6). In the case of Brazier, Madame Milliat could see that this young woman had raw talent in the kitchen, and she encouraged her to learn more. Eventually, she introduced Eugénie Brazier to la mère Fillioux, who ran a small restaurant at 73 rue Duquesne in Lyon's Sixth Arrondissement. Monsieur and Madame Milliat were regular customers at la mère Fillioux's restaurant.

Fillioux's background was not so different from Brazier's: Françoise Fillioux (née Fayolle) was born in the countryside, Cunlhat in the Puy de Dôme. At a young age, she left her family home to work as a domestic servant in the house of a general in Grenoble. She did not stay long there. Moving on to Lyon, she found employment in Gaston Eymard's home. Eymard, the director of the insurance company La France, was a well-known gastronome. Fillioux worked in Eymard's kitchen for ten years, learning the finer points of *la cuisine bourgeoise.* During this time, she met a young wine merchant, Louis Fillioux, whom she married. The couple pooled their savings to buy a small bistro (Mesplède 2001, 11–15).[2] Françoise cooked and Louis worked the front of the house selling wine and socializing with the patrons (Varille 1928, 21–23). Fillioux was known for dishes such as her exquisite artichoke hearts with foie gras and her *poularde en demi-deuil* (lit., chicken in half mourning), which she carved at the table for her guests using a tiny knife.[3] The well-poached chickens nearly fell off the bone.

For businessmen working in the neighborhood and gamblers returning from the nearby racetrack, the restaurant Mère Fillioux became a popular place to gather. The food was seen as *bon rapport qualité prix* (good value for the money) and Fillioux's *plat phare* (best-known dish), the poularde en demi-deuil, which was always on the menu, kept her customers coming back for more. The steady flow of excellent Beaujolais wine also helped. Restaurant critics lauded and publicized 73 rue Duquesne in their guidebooks. From Curnonsky (1925) to Cousin (1927), the gastronomes loved la mère Fillioux: "The day when gastronomy becomes a religion with its own calendar, saints and confessors, its virgins and martyrs, the mère Fillioux will be canonized and will become one of the patron saints of French Cuisine" (Curnonsky in Mesplède 2001, 14).

An observant study, Eugénie learned Fillioux's techniques and recipes. However, Fillioux recognized Brazier's talent and felt threatened by her young understudy. Relations between the two women were fraught. Fillioux criticized Brazier at every opportunity until the young woman could take no more (Mesplède 2001, 16).

After working for la mère Fillioux, Brazier went on to build her reputation at the Dragon restaurant on the rue de la République. Fillioux's customers thought that the Dragon was her new venture because Brazier's cooking was so good and imitated her teacher so well. Fillioux was quick to rebuff with comments like: "How can she cook? She was a dishwasher when she worked with me" (Mesplède 2001, 17).

After a few years, Brazier was ready to strike out on her own. A small *épicerie-comptoir* (a combination of a corner store that also served drinks and simple dishes) in rue Royale was for sale in a street not far from her apartment. It was 1921 and for entrepreneurial women at the time buying a business was not as easy as it sounds—women were not allowed to hold property in their own names. It was husbands and male relatives whose names appeared on the deeds of women's businesses and properties. Eugénie was a *mère fille* (unwed mother), but she had a longtime male companion. Although she maintained control of all aspects of her business, it was through her companion that she was able to work around the administrative constraints that she faced. This did not mean she took a secondary role when it came to business. The mères Fillioux and Brazier were astute businesswomen, and there is little doubt in the historic record that they were in charge.

Brazier's establishment started off as a bar that she quickly transformed into a simple restaurant that served the artisans, workers, and business owners in the neighborhood. As the fame of her cooking grew, she expanded her restaurant, acquiring another apartment that she transformed into additional dining rooms. Her capital was so limited that she initially had to borrow chairs from neighbors and bought new chairs one at a time (Brazier 2009). While growing her business, Brazier also refined her cuisine. Working-class clients were no longer her target market as the economy in Lyon improved. By the mid-1930s, local politicians, business people, the rich bourgeois, and travelers flocked to mère Brazier's restaurant; her reputation for producing sumptuous but honest food reminded clients of an age when the bourgeoisie dined in luxury at home. Brazier's new fame was largely thanks to the growing genre of *littérature gastronomique* (gastronomic literature) and increased tourism—she was the darling of Curnonsky and other prominent writers of this new type of food writing.

Eugénie Brazier arrived at the pinnacle of her success in 1933 when the *Guide Michelin* awarded her three Michelin stars for her two restaurants (one in rue Royale in Lyon and the other at Col de la Luère in Pollionnay, just outside of Lyon). She remains the only woman in the history of French gastronomy to earn three stars for two restaurants at the same time. This recognition from the relatively new but widely respected national Guide Michelin cemented Brazier's fame and her place in Lyonnais and French culinary history.

Gaston, Brazier's son, had followed his mother into the kitchen. He went on to run the restaurant in rue Royale. After the war, relations broke down between Eugénie and her son and his wife. They remained on difficult terms until his death in 1974. Although cuisine bourgeoise and *cuisine des mères* fell out of fashion in the 1960s with the rise of nouvelle cuisine, Eugénie Brazier remained a prominent figure in Lyon even after her death in 1977.

La mère Brazier's achievements were exceptional. However, in many ways, Brazier's story is not so different from other women who cooked in restaurants in Lyon during the same period. These were women who came from the surrounding countryside, who worked in bourgeois households, and then went on to cook in restaurants, often small, family-run establishments—frequently bouchons lyonnais (see chapter 2). However, of the culinary professionals I spoke with, Brazier stands out as a symbolic mère: she embodied the most central traits of what it means to be a mère lyonnaise, from her cooking to her character. She had a strong personality, she was exacting, her cooking was true to the traditions of *cuisine bourgeoise,* and it was perfectly executed.

Although the mère Brazier is an important figure in Lyonnais gastronomic history, she is a less prominent person in the history of French cuisine. Even in Lyon, there is little public commemoration of Eugénie Brazier. While there are several murals featuring the famed local chef Paul Bocuse and a covered market that was renamed for him, there is almost no trace of the mères lyonnaises. As I began my research, I thought more about women's absence from the historic record of French gastronomic history. Had this lack of recognition played a part in women's continued underrepresentation in French cuisine? Where were the women who had fed so many people and who had played a role in shaping regional cuisines? Even if they were not celebrated, women had always been in professional kitchens. Eugénie Brazier's story was a door into this world of women cooking in Lyon.

Figure 0.1: Eugénie Brazier. (Photograph by Marcelle Vallet, 1950s, P0701 006BIS N2566, courtesy of Bibliothèque municipale de Lyon)

GLOSSARY

Apprenti (apprentice) is one of the lowest positions in the brigade system kitchen. This is where novice cooks start their hands-on learning of the culinary trades. This is generally an unpaid or low-paying position. In the past, apprentices were given room and board.

Bistronomie is a type of cooking that uses quality products, requires a high level of skill, but offers dishes that are not overly elaborate. The food is generally served in a bistro setting where tablecloths are eschewed.

Bobo means *bourgeois bohème*, a group of middle-class people with socialist political views. Bobo have been seen as responsible for gentrification in Paris and other large French cities. This term has become a common expression in the past twenty years (Gunther 2016).

Bouchon is a small restaurant that serves a canon of dishes that focus on tripe and pork. There are often red-and-white checked tablecloths on tables positioned close together. The décor is usually eclectic. These restaurants originally served travelers, silk workers (**canuts**), artisans, and business-people. Even today, these restaurants often serve the **mâchon**. After the economic downturn at the end of the nineteenth century, many women who worked in bourgeois households found employment in bouchons. The term *bouchon* comes from the old French *bousche*, a bundle of straw or branches used to brush horses. These bundles of straw or sticks placed on the signs or doors of these establishments designated them as places where wine and food could be purchased, and distinguish them from inns (Rouèche 2018, 38).

Canut is the name for Lyonnais silk weavers who mainly populated the Croix-Rousse hill. In 1831, 1834 and 1848, they famously revolted in protest of their working conditions. Their living and working quarters are still called canuts (Plessy and Challet 1988). A popular Lyonnais dish called *cervelle de canut*, literally silk weaver's brains, is made from fresh cheese, chives (sometimes other herbs), and garlic or shallots.

CAP (certificat d'aptitude professionnelle) is a vocational certificate that an individual is qualified to practice a specific vocation. There are CAP certificates in cooking, pastry, and baking, in addition to over two hundred other professions.

Chef de cuisine is the person in charge of the daily running of the kitchen. This person can be considered the manager in charge of making sure the kitchen staff work well together and is also in charge of the overall quality of the food. In cases where there is no executive chef, the chef de cuisine is also in charge of recipe development.

Cheffe is the feminized title for the person who leads the kitchen (or any other type of restaurant work). This is a term that the Académie française, the body that prescribes correct usage of the French language, approved in 2019.

Commis is one rank higher than **apprenti**. This is an entry-level position in the professional kitchen. In large kitchens, there are usually many commis who do the majority of the prep work and menial labor.

Cuisine gastronomique is high-end cooking that uses quality ingredients, which can be expensive and rare. The dishes are artfully presented and require a great deal of skill to prepare. In English, we often use the term "fine dining" to explain this style of cooking and eating out.

Dressage d'assiette is the plating of food. It is usually considered to be one of the more artful jobs in the kitchen.

Formation is a French term for training. It suggests both the acquisition of knowledge and skill, but there is also a connotation that the trainee is being shaped or transformed physically and/or intellectually in the process of learning.

Garde-manger is the position in charge of cold dishes. This is usually translated as "pantry chef."

Haute cuisine in France was historically the cuisine of kings and the noble classes. As Sidney Mintz (1996) suggests, haute cuisine is oriented more toward class than regional cuisine. The ingredients are expensive and often hard to procure. Seasonality is generally disregarded—having strawberries in winter was once considered a novelty. The amount of labor to produce dishes is extensive. In the twentieth century, haute cuisine came to signify the upper echelons of fine dining that was reserved for the rich.

Mâchon is a meal, often made up of tripe dishes and charcuterie, that is accompanied by a **pot** of Beaujolais or Mâconnais. Workers coming off of night shifts or who start work before dawn partake of this meal at small neighborhood restaurants.

Meilleur ouvrier de France (MOF) (Best worker in France) was first started in the early twentieth century to bring honor to and celebrate skilled trades and crafts. The MOF cuisine is one of the most publicized competitions, and those who achieve this honor are celebrated widely in France. This distinguished title is technically a diploma, whose recipients are the only chefs allowed to wear the French tricolor collar on their chef coats.

Métiers de bouche are occupations related to eating, such as cook, pastry chef, chocolatier, butcher, baker, sommelier, and cheesemonger. Literally, "crafts of the mouth."

Mise en place is the preparation and organization of ingredients that takes place before cooking.

Piano is the stove in a commercial kitchen.

Pots de vin are heavy, glass-bottomed 46 cl bottles that were originally given to workers as part of their wages. They are still used today, particularly in bars and **bouchons**, serving as a daily connection to the past.

Quenelle is a dish made from creamed fish (often pike) or other seafood and meats mixed with flour or bread crumbs and eggs. The name also denotes the egg-like shape. They are usually served with a decadent cream sauce.

Second is also referred to as the sous-chef. This person is in charge when the **chef de cuisine** is not in the kitchen. The seconde is the second in command.

Service refers to the dinner or lunch service.

Stage is a period of apprenticeship or some sort of practical experience that generally has a hands-on component that allows the trainee to gain practical experience.

CHEFFES DE CUISINE

INTRODUCTION

"Madame, there is no room for you here!" another apprentice shouted at me along the busy hot line. I pressed in closer to the *piano* so he could squeeze by me, my belly almost touching the hot flame. I knew I was a lot older and a little slower than the average seventeen-year-old apprenti. Addressing me as "madame" was already bad enough, but did he have to say that I did not belong in the kitchen? As I rode the metro home after a long shift in the small Parisian bistro, my feet ached, I felt exhausted, and my mind wandered back to the comment my coworker had lobbed at me in the middle of the *service.* I knew I was out of place in many ways, but perhaps my colleague had meant that I did not fit in a more literal sense. I was five months pregnant, and my belly was growing larger each day. It was getting harder for the other people in the kitchen to get past me to do their work in such a tight space. I was only just beginning to understand some of the challenges that women face in the culinary arts.

The Current Status of Women in Restaurant Kitchens

Women's presence in professional kitchens in France is growing. The French statistical agency DARES reports that from 2012 to 2014, 38 percent of all people employed as *cuisiniers* (cooks) were women

(Direction de l'animation 2016). That is up 8 percent from 30 percent in 1984. Statistics from the Ministère de l'éducation nationale et de la jeunesse show that women are entering secondary and postsecondary professional training in the culinary arts at higher rates than men and are also more successful in attaining their degrees.[1] However, of the few women who reach the highest ranks in the kitchen, not many are recognized for their skill and achievements. The prestigious Meilleur ouvrier de France (MOF) has only ever been awarded to two women in the cuisine category in its ninety-four-year history. The *2018 Guide Michelin* included a single female-led three-star restaurant, and only 17 of the 621 restaurants with stars are headed up by women (2.7 percent). Yet, if more women than ever are entering the profession, why are they so deeply underrepresented at the top ranks of the profession? This is one of the central questions of this book, and it is important for understanding how certain professions impede access to specific groups based on gender, nationality, sexual orientation, and race.

Women have limited upward mobility in the culinary arts in France. From my observations and interviews, a clear gender segregation happens in most kitchens (Bourelly 2010). These divisions of labor follow stereotypes that construct women as creative thinkers with artistic skill and finesse, but often also as less competent or not strong enough to stand the physical labor required of kitchen work. Specific kitchen tasks are coded as masculine or feminine (Harris and Giuffre 2015, 2). This sidelining of women through the segregation of work is one of the issues that keeps them from achieving in culinary professions.

While some studies have looked at women's lack of mobility in the restaurant industry in the United States (Druckman 2010; Harris and Giuffre 2015), little on this issue in France has been published (Marie 2014). Vérane Frédiani's documentary film *The Goddesses of Food* (2017) chronicles the dynamic and diverse lives of women working in the food industry across the globe and asks why there are so few women among the top ranks of professional chefs, an issue all over the world. This book focuses on the experiences of women working in France within the constructs of French culture. The cultural specificity of the French case became clearer to me in the past several years as I followed the #MeToo movement in the United States and how it has helped bring greater public scrutiny to the gender disparities and sexual abuse that happens in restaurants. What kinds of waves would #MeToo make elsewhere? I watched and waited to see what would happen in my French field sites. The movement has gained little traction in France, particularly in culinary professions, underlining a persistent aversion to dealing with issues of inequality and abuse. *Cheffes de Cuisine* seeks to place gender inequality in the culinary arts in cultural context and looks at how women in different groups live this experience. Lessons learned in professional kitchens can be applied in other male-dominated professions.

Lyon is a city with a long history of women cooking professionally. One of my central goals has been to understand whether this history has opened up possibilities for women today. Lyon is considered the gastronomic capital of France and it is an important place for both the maintenance of French culinary traditions and innovation. For these reasons, Lyon offers an opportunity to better understand the role that women have, and the obstacles they face, in both maintaining culinary heritage and innovating for the future.

Finding Women in Kitchens in the Past and the Present

Initially, I had set out to study *les mères lyonnaises*, a group of Lyonnais women who rose to prominence in the local restaurant scene in the 1930s. I first heard about these women when I was doing research on another food-related topic in Lyon in the 1990s, and I was curious about how a group of women had become legends in Lyonnais culinary history. I was intrigued but had no opportunity to do further research at that time. One afternoon in 2012, I was having tea with a chef instructor of the culinary arts program in the kitchen across the hall from my office at Boston University and we got to talking about France. It turns out that this chef's hometown is Lyon. I mentioned that I had lived there for three years and that while I was working and studying in Lyon a few people had told me the story of a group of famous women who cooked in Lyonnais restaurants between the two wars. Chef's ears perked up and a huge smile came across his face: "The mères lyonnaises! I apprenticed with the Mère Brazier." He went on to talk about his life as a young man, his apprenticeship experience, and how Brazier had shaped not only his learning but also his future as a chef. He lamented the fact that there are few mères left and that it was a shame that no one had written anything about them. A few days later, he deposited a tattered shoebox on my desk. It was full of memorabilia—menus, postcards, and photos—from his early days as an apprenti at la mère Brazier's restaurant at Col de Luère. I took this as a sign that it was time to return to the gastronomic capital to explore the story of the mères lyonnaises.

In the summer of 2013, I arrived in Lyon ready to dig into the archives and chase leads on people who had apprenticed with various mères in and around Lyon. My enthusiasm was met with some early disappointments. The municipal archives and library held scant materials about the women I was trying to find: I located just a few dossiers with newspaper clippings and photos of the best-known mères. I tried to figure out how many women had owned their own restaurants in the 1930s, but I kept coming up short: very few restaurants were registered in women's names, probably because this was still at a time when women could not hold their own bank accounts. Finding paper traces of the mères proved to be extremely challenging, so I turned to oral histories to try to fill in the gaps. The original mères from the 1930s had all passed, so I interviewed family members, former apprentices, local culinary historians, gastronomic writers, and critics. What quickly became apparent was that I was not going to be able to produce a rigorously documented history of the mères lyonnaises. Women's histories are often oral histories because of what society deemed important to record (P. Thompson and Bornat 2017, 6–7) and, specifically in this case, the types of work that women were doing in kitchens left a scant paper trail beyond a few photos, chatty newspaper articles, and menus. Where were all the recipes? Why had no one written a memoir? I quickly learned that most mères did not write down their recipes: techniques and dishes were learned through apprenticeship and passed on from one cook to the next. Although France had mandatory primary education in the twentieth century, not everyone was proficiently literate. This is particularly true for children in the countryside and from the working classes, for whom earning one's keep was more important than going to school. If women could write, most did not have the time to take notes. The only people who write memoirs are those with the time and those who think their thoughts and experiences are worth memorializing. After much frustration, I came to realize that uncovering the history of the mères lyonnaises was not going to tell me much about who these women actually were and what their lives had been like. Later, I would learn that I was not the first person to find the archival unearthing of the mères to be a hopelessly incomplete project: in 2018, journalist Catherine Simon published *Mangées: Une histoire des mères lyonnaises*, a fictional story about the mères lyonnaises based on extensive archival research.[2] I took Simon's book as another sign that there were just too many holes in the data to be able to publish a definitive history of these women who only in retrospect became associated as a group or a movement.

While carefully examining books about Lyon's culinary scene in the early twentieth century, it dawned on me that men had authored most of what had been written about the mères lyonnaises. Historical sources I could find about these women were secondhand accounts from the burgeoning field of gastronomic writing. In *La France gastronomique: Lyon et le Lyonnais* (1925), Curnonsky and Rouff wrote glowing accounts of meals eaten chez la mère Filloux and la mère Brazier. They lauded the mères as the keepers of regional culinary traditions at a time when regional identities were important for constructing a sense of a strong but diverse nation (Goodfellow 2009). If I were going to look to these early gastronomic writings as the main source for understanding the centrality of women in Lyonnais cuisine in the early twentieth century, I had to deal with the fact that men were almost entirely responsible for constructing the memory of these women and their cuisine. What are the implications of men representing women in the historical record? From my reading of these texts it seemed that these male gastronomes needed the mères to be maternal, constant, and comforting. In what ways does this muffle the much more complex realities of these women's lives and their work in the tiny, stuffy kitchens of Lyonnais restaurants? The construction of a historical record and memory of public individuals as a gendered process (Spongberg 2002, 5–6) is explored further in chapter 1. In addition to thinking about the influences of these men's writings, I consider the specific political moment of this ethnography: it is a time when women are speaking out against inequality and injustice in the workplace. This has shaped my construction of a new telling of the story of the mères lyonnaises and women in kitchens. I came to realize I also needed the mères to be something specific—strong, trail-blazing mavericks. I had to keep my own bias and desires in check.

Methods

After my initial archival research and collection of oral histories, I decided to do fieldwork with contemporary female chefs in Lyon to better understand the lived reality of working in a restaurant kitchen. I wanted to know what the specific challenges are for different groups of women, what the factors are that cause women to drop out of the profession, and what keeps them from rising to the top if they decide to stay. Rather than simply conducting interviews and observing from the sidelines of kitchens, I felt it was necessary to embody kitchen work for myself and in order to gain rapport with the people I wanted to learn more about. I needed to gain culinary skills and learn the language of the kitchen.

In the summer of 2014, I started my year of fieldwork in culinary school. My initiation into the professional world of cooking taught me the technical and insider language that would become invaluable for understanding restaurant kitchen cultures. Being familiar with professional parlance also illuminated the ways in which language reinforces the hierarchy of the kitchen, how it is gendered, and how language is used to include and exclude certain groups, particularly women, minorities and immigrants. I observed that if you could not speak French, you were relegated to one of the lowest positions in the kitchen, most often washing dishes and other disagreeable cleaning duties. Without a specialized French vocabulary, I knew I too would be excluded from fully participating in kitchen work. This is a topic I explore further when I discuss my training and apprenticeship in chapter 3.

My culinary training helped me understand the embodied realities that women can experience in the kitchen—physical challenges, pain, and fulfillment. My time in kitchens gave me an opportunity to develop specific techniques of the body and think about Marcel Mauss's (2002) notion of how these techniques could extend to the gendering of the body through work. Joanna Brewis's work on the female body at work echoes this need to consider the material reality of bodies at work and how experience is shaped not only by the physical nature of work but also the dominant discourses around organization, gender, age, and ethnicity or origins (2000, 166). Kitchen work gave me plenty of opportunities to reflect on how the culture of schooling and apprenticeship shapes movement and sediments into the body differently depending on gender, race, and ethnicity. This is a topic I also dive into more deeply in chapter 3. This base of professional culinary knowledge allowed me to understand firsthand the challenges of being a woman in a kitchen from the start of my schooling to working the hot line during the dinner rush in a small bistro.

When I arrived in Lyon, my culinary training enabled me to carry out participant observations in kitchens without getting in the way—I could integrate into the kitchen and experience the dynamics of various workplaces. In addition to working in kitchens, I conducted interviews with twenty-seven female culinary professionals ranging from cooks in bistros to culinary instructors. I used guidebooks, newspaper articles, and snowball sampling to locate female culinary professionals.[3] Jacotte Brazier, the granddaughter of Eugénie Brazier, was a key participant who connected me with culinary professionals and restaurant critics. Brazier's ongoing work to encourage young women to enter the culinary professions has helped her maintain a robust network in Lyon and at a national level.

In addition to female culinary professionals, I interviewed restaurant critics, renowned Lyonnais chefs, and family members of mères lyonnaises. I transcribed these interviews and analyzed the formal and informal discussions I had with culinary professionals in the kitchen and at the table using qualitative data analysis software. Through this systematic analysis, I was able to define the central themes that emerged from these conversations. From municipal and personal archives, I scanned photographs, postcards, letters, newspaper clippings, restaurant guides, and gastronomic writings from the 1930s and the present. Once I had coded all of these documents, what emerged was a striking discourse of how the past informed the present for many women working in Lyonnais kitchens. With this book, I weave together a narrative that gives voice to women in the past, people currently working in restaurant kitchens, and my own experience in French kitchens in order to contribute to the debate on women's underrepresentation in male-dominated professions and workplaces.

Speaking Out against Misconduct in the Kitchen, or Not

While writing this book, the #MeToo movement in the United States began to gain traction in 2017–18. Along with Hollywood, the restaurant industry has become a focal point in which women are speaking out about sexual harassment and abuse. Celebrity chefs Mario Batali and John Besh stepped down from their culinary empires after allegations of sexual misconduct.

#BalanceTonPorc ("rat out your pig"), the French movement inspired by #MeToo, has given some women courage to speak out against harassment. However, in a culture that finds Americans rather moralistic about sex, it took the outing of American sexual harassment cases to bring French women into the spotlight (Donadio 2018). Not all French women were on board. Most notably, actor Catherine Deneuve and other popular figures denounced the #MeToo movement as the end of intimacy and a totalitarian attack on men (Safronova 2018). Despite a few news articles about the problem of sexual harassment in the French restaurant industry, there have been no specific cases of high-profile chefs being taken to task for sexual misconduct. This does not mean that abuses do not occur in French kitchens. On the contrary, the tightknit and insular nature of the restaurant industry in France is probably the reason for women's continued silence. Women know that if they decry sexual misconduct, it is likely they cannot be hired at another restaurant. Despite this grim reality, there is hope as a younger generation of culinary professionals have begun to throw off the patriarchal hierarchies of the kitchen. Part of this has come from a broader sea change in the cultures of some kitchens. Whether headed up by a woman or not, there are now restaurant kitchens that have more collaborative organizations where all members of the team are seen as valuable actors, and where apprenticeship is not seen as a painful rite of passage. My research with young chefs, male and female, confirmed this trend.

While anthropology seeks to generalize from the specific, my research showed me that it is also important to maintain diversity and heterogeneity when studying a phenomenon. Not all cases fit into one mold, concept, or cohesive idea. The voices in this book seek to capture the diversity of experiences when it comes to navigating the professional kitchen. Being a woman does not mean that a person is a member of a homogeneous social group—lumping all women together is counterproductive because of different lived experiences and the complexity of women's identities. Being a woman is only one part of the equation for many of the chefs with whom I worked. Age, class, regional, sexual orientation, and ethnic origin were also powerful forces shaping my participants' worldviews and experiences.

Understanding the Structures of Inequality

While journalists have worked to expose the uneven power relations in restaurants, there are not many systematic scholarly studies to help us better understand the deeper reasons for the abuses that are just coming to light. Deborah A. Harris and Patti Giuffre's *Taking the Heat: Women Chefs and Gender Inequality in the Professional Kitchen* (2015) is one of the few qualitative studies that gives a closer look at the back of the house in the U.S. restaurant industry. The statistical data of women's participation in the restaurant industry is only one side of the story; women's narratives fill in the blanks as to why restaurant kitchens remain incredibly hostile toward women. Harris and Giuffre focus on how the media legitimates the role of men and undermines women's competency in the professional kitchen. Eli Revelle Yano Wilson's *Front of the House, Back of the House: Race and Inequality in the Lives of Restaurant Workers* (2021) is an intimate look at racial inequality in U.S. restaurant kitchens, but it focuses almost entirely on men. In the context of France, Patricia Marie's monograph on apprenticeship and the transmission of culinary knowledge also looks at the role of the French media in perpetuating the image of the chef de cuisine as a man. Marie considers the historic reasons for women's exclusion from formal culinary training and the profession: in particular, she focuses on access to training and the ways in which the labor market for chefs has remained closed to women in France (2014). This topic is discussed further in chapter 4.

When breaking down the experiences of training and workplace routines, it is necessary to look at how social relations lie at the center of gender inequality and its persistence. It is through everyday relations, actions and words, that people define themselves and negotiate their identities. Ridgeway makes the point that "societal patterns of gender inequality are actually enacted through social relations" (2011, 7). She goes on to argue that most people use sex and gender as an initial cultural tool for organizing social relational accounts. When gender is used as a framing device, it spreads gendered meanings, which are embedded with notions of inequality. Although Ridgeway's explanation for the persistence of gender inequality in the United States is useful for understanding many of the biases that women experience in kitchens, it is limiting when considering the agency of female actors. The narratives of female culinary professionals in Lyon echo this persistence of bias against women, but there is also a story here where women are confronting implicit bias and changing the discourse at a relational level.

This book creates a deeper understanding of the structural issues at play in the creation of gender inequality in the culinary professions. In particular, this research focuses on the importance of role models, both contemporary and historic. If the dominant representation of a chef de cuisine is always a man, how can women imagine themselves at the head of a kitchen? The history and current embodiments of the mères lyonnaises legend offer examples of alternate role models that are important to women in Lyon. It helps to expand notions of what it means to be a chef and a woman in the kitchen. In addition, changing media representations of women who cook are helping to normalize women's presence in the professional kitchen.

However, the structures that have contributed to keeping women in secondary roles are at the root of this problem of their underrepresentation. In particular, culinary education and apprenticeship offer insights into the ways in which training is a deeply gendered and exclusive process that places women at a disadvantage. In French, culinary training is called *formation* (training). Here there is a notion of shaping or molding the student into the ideal worker. From my own culinary school experience, I concluded that this formation is very much about shaping male bodies and minds (Lamamra, Fassa, and Chaponnière 2014). As demonstrated in the opening vignette from my apprenticeship, the female body is sometimes even incongruent to the space of the kitchen.

There is a lot to learn from women who succeed in culinary school and who make their way through apprenticeships. How does their training shape them and how do they also push back to make room for their ways of doing and being that may not fit the prescribed objectives of training programs? Women's agency in creating alternative models for restaurant work is an important part of many success stories. Many of the female chefs I interviewed and worked with had succeeded in creating more egalitarian kitchen structures, whether in restaurants, culinary schools, or catering kitchens (Gvion and Leedon 2019). There were also those who owned their own restaurants and could operate with opening hours that allowed for a better work-life balance than the usual restaurant split shift. Conversely, I try to capture the other side of the narrative: I listened to the reasons that women gave me for dropping out of culinary school or for leaving conventional restaurant kitchens. The diversity of women's experiences is represented through individual narratives that speak to themes of both exclusion and empowerment.

Food, Cooking, and Feminism

Feminist scholars have had a love-hate relationship with women's food production activities. The main focus of feminist research has been on women cooking in the home. Second-wave feminism in particular gave women a way to critique domestic work that they felt was inequitable and a burden (M. Shapiro, Ingols, and Blake-Beard 2008). In the *Feminine Mystique* (1963), Betty Friedan goes so far as to argue that domestic work was contrary to the aims of feminism. Cairns and Johnston remark that working-class women and women of color made it possible for privileged women to have formal employment (2015, 9); this was not a feminist liberation from domestic drudgery for everyone.

Avakian and Haber have been critical of women's studies' neglect of women's food work until recently (2005). However, there has also been a strong movement on the part of feminist scholars to see the power and agency that women possess in maintaining control over home cooking. In *Around the Tuscan Table* (2004), Counihan considers the ways in which cooking gives Italian women power over the family finances. In *A Tortilla Is Like Life* (2009), through food-centered life histories, Counihan shows how women in Antonito, Colorado, contribute to the well-being of their families and to their own importance. Similarly, Abarca looks at women's food voices through *charlas culinarias* (culinary chats) to show how women express their agency and creativity through cooking at home and in public kitchens (2006, 2007). Adapon (2008) distinguishes between home cooking and other forms of domestic work in an attempt to bring value to women's culinary work: "cooking is complex and artistic practice, different from other kinds of housework because of the creative component involved" (71). In Mexico, paid and unpaid domestic and extra-domestic work is acknowledged and valued (73). In France, there has not been the same interest in the study of women's reproductive work or a valuing of domestic labor (Dussuet 2017).

Third-wave feminism has also reconsidered women's engagement with the domestic sphere, but not without its contradictions and issues. "New domestics" (Matchar 2013) and "feminivores" (Orenstein 2010) can be seen as a critique of capitalist economies and an attempt to revalue homemaking (Hayes 2010). At the same time, this movement is also deeply problematic because it does not address the uneven distribution of domestic labor and the double burden many women face as they work in both the public sphere and at home. These neo-domestic movements in France and the United States tend to be predominantly White and middle class.

While women's reproductive labor in the domestic sphere has been the focus of many works, the productive labor of women in professional kitchens has had little scrutiny on the part of feminist scholars (Harris and Giuffre 2015). Nonetheless, there is a well-developed scholarship in gender and organization studies (Acker 1990; Britton 2000; Kelan 2009). In this area, Lewis (2014) and R. Gill, Kelan, and Scharff (2017) have popularized the use of a postfeminist sensibility in order to understand gender relations in the workplace. Postfeminism itself has many contradictory interpretations and some scholars have described it as a break from feminism, and for others it is seen as the continuation of a different feminist project (Gill, Kelan, and Scharff 2017, 227). Postfeminism focuses on individual agency and downplays the necessity for a feminist movement, seeing women as already liberated. The postfeminist sensibility that Gill defines is "an analytical category designed to capture empirical regularities in the world" (2016, 216). When used in this way, postfeminism can help identify cultural norms and how they shape the subjectivities of the individuals who work within them (Lewis et al. 2017, 214).

Applying postfeminist sensibility to culinary work as a critical concept has allowed me to analyze what kinds of subjects men and women become in culinary professions (Lewis 2014). In what ways do gender norms dictate how men and women are expected to act, interact, and work in the professional kitchen? In turn, how do these expected gendered norms produce and reproduce equality or inequality in this workplace? Expectations about what it means to be a man or a woman in the kitchen are tied to broader cultural norms, but they take on specific meanings in the context of work.

All work is gendered. Acker (1990) has shown that organizations are not gender neutral and that masculine norms are structural aspects of organizations. Modeled after the French military, there is no doubt that the brigade system seeks to shape, train, and establish a hierarchy of male bodies. Although some chefs told me that feminine attention to detail and creativity were prized in their kitchens, it was clear that these stereotypes about the way that women work were also used to sideline women into secondary positions. What are described as women's talents are often seen as a naturalized ability that does not have the same value as the skilled, trained performances of men (Adkins 2001). This is an example of the ways in which cultural discourses about culinary work shape, and are shaped by, our thinking about gender, femininity, and ability in this workplace. In some interviews, these discourses about femininity were essentializing: some participants attempted to lump all women together into a single category with universal attributes. It is here that a postfeminist framework is useful for bringing to light the heterogeneity and multiplicity of identities and experiences of women working in kitchens in Lyon.

An Intersectional Approach Faces France's Denial of Racism

The accounts of the people I worked with are not just about being a woman or a man: gender is only one part of these people's identities. Although I have chosen to focus on women, I do not want to create an essentialized category—exactly what the participants in my research were trying to avoid. Many women I worked with repeatedly expressed a desire to work on an even playing field with men. "Why should my work be judged differently just because I am a woman?" one chef asked me as we sat down after a busy lunch service. Early on in my research, I understood that this would not be a simple story of women being excluded from a boys' club: there was more going on here. I heard very clearly from the women I worked with that they did not want to be put into a separate gender category; this would invalidate their goals of being the best chefs possible.

In understanding how the French culinary world is constructed, it is important to look at the internal forces that create and police a specific gastronomic field and how popular culture reinforces these boundaries. Harris and Giuffre elaborate on Ferguson's concept of a gastronomic field in their *Taking the Heat* (2015). Using Bourdieu's notion of a field in which industry professionals, culinary schools, training, and established chefs police access to resources and legitimacy, Harris and Giuffre introduce Acker's gendered organizations theory to "explain how the rules of a field are developed and enacted in ways that can disadvantage women and how women can challenge or bypass certain rules of the game in order to win and succeed as a chef" (7). In this research, I use the framework of a gastronomic field to analyze the ways in which women both challenge and work within the structures that police professionalism in the culinary arts in France.

I consider people's experiences of oppression and resistance at the axes of systems of exclusion. The voices of the female chefs interviewed for this book express the unique lived experiences and the multidimensional and relational social locations that these women navigate in their work as culinary professionals. Drawing on Crenshaw's intersectional approach, I create a more nuanced exploration of working women's experiences in kitchens in Lyon. While women are my focus, their experiences and political identities are diverse (Williams-Forson and Wilkerson 2011). This is important to keep in mind in order to avoid the pitfall of conflating or ignoring intragroup differences (Crenshaw 1995). The challenges and successes that female culinary professionals in Lyon often face are not related only to their gender but also to class, sexual orientation, migrant status, and life stage. It is through understanding how the intersections of their diverse identities play out that I bring to light new perspectives on women's underrepresentation in the culinary arts.

Applying an intersectional approach to the study of French society offers some specific challenges. The notion of race in France cannot be compared to that in other European countries or the United States. There are no official statistics in France on race because French law prohibits the government from making any distinction among citizens based on race or religion. This is partly due to the founding myth of the Republic that emphasizes the unitarian, universalist, and inclusive nature of the Republic. This myth was cemented into law through the Déclaration des droits de l'homme (Declaration of the Rights of Man). Bleich (2001) points out that the issue of race is extremely taboo for the French and that for many it is a reminder of the atrocities of Nazi Germany and Vichy France's complicity in deporting Jews. The French government maintains a "color-blind" approach to public policy: it uses geographic and class-based criteria to address issues of social inequality. However, this does not mean that notions of race do not exist in France; they have their own colonial and postcolonial frameworks.

In Lamont's study of racial boundaries among French workers, she found that White native French workers (blue and white collar) drew the strongest boundaries toward North Africans. Lamont shows that the workers use three central arguments about North Africans: they lack a strong work ethic and they abuse public resources; they are culturally incompatible; and they are unable to assimilate (Lamont 2004, 143). A French colony for 130 years, Algeria played an important role in France's colonial empire. Decolonization was gradual in most French colonies. This was not the case with Algeria where the process was violent and fraught. The French Algerian War (1952–64), which killed 600,000 people, left a painful legacy on both sides (Smith 1975). It is not only Algerians who experience discrimination in France. In the construction of Otherness, there is little distinction between Algerians, Tunisians, and Moroccans. They are lumped together into categories such as North Africans, Arabs, and Maghrebis (Lamont 2004, 148).

Lamont found that workers' boundaries toward Blacks was not as strong as it was toward North Africans. She attributes this to the fact that race in France has been decoupled from Blackness. Blacks in

France are generally not recent migrants, and they are a culturally and religiously heterogenous group hailing from a variety of Dom-Toms (*domaines et territoires d'Outre-Mer*, French-held territories outside of Metropolitan France). Lamont also attributes a culture of republicanism to the downplaying of the boundaries against Blacks (150). Racism in France may not be publicly condoned or acknowledge in and of itself, but it is certainly present in mainstream society, particularly in politics and the structures that organize life in France.

The right-wing political party Rassemblement national (formerly FN, the Front National) is one of France's most contentious political parties because of its openly anti-Semitic and anti-immigrant stance. The FN reached the pinnacle of its success in 2015 during the regional elections when the party won 27.7 percent of the popular vote. The popularity of far-right political parties, which have openly racist platforms, is a strong indicator of the racist and xenophobic unrest in France today. Starting in the later 1990s, the French government has begun to address issues of racism through a series of antidiscrimination laws, although these have had limited success (Hargreaves 2004).

When we take an intersectional approach to the study of French social issues, race, as an intersectional point, needs to be considered within the French frameworks and logics of difference and identity politics. Although most of the participants in my research did not explicitly talk about race, I tried to consider at what moments and for what reasons they experienced discrimination or unequal treatment on the basis of race, gender, class, or age in their professional lives. Little literature explores how intersections between race, ethnicity, and gender play out in French employment practices and the workplace (Pailhé 2008). This book helps fill this gap.

Due to the predominantly White nature of the French culinary world, race was not a central intersection that the participants in this study articulated as a point of exclusion. However, I do question the lack of racial and ethnic diversity in French kitchens—there is a broader story of exclusion here. The narratives of French women in kitchens became just as much about who is cooking as much as who is not. Why are certain groups underrepresented, particularly at the higher levels of the kitchen hierarchy? I encountered only one Black female chef de cuisine at a small bistro in Lyon, and among Michelin-starred restaurants there is nearly a complete lack of racial and ethnic diversity. In the restaurant where I apprenticed, the only person of color was an Indian man who had a limited command of French and who worked as a dishwasher. The only group that has made headway is a small number of foreign-born Japanese men who are highly educated and have managed to rise through the ranks and who have their own restaurants.

When thinking about the various layers of identity and intersectional points of analysis of the participants in this research, class and life stage were two prominent intersections where patriarchy and exclusion presented themselves. Status as a migrant was also an interesting point that did not necessarily mean that a woman was discriminated against or excluded for not being of French origin. In many cases, being a foreigner or outsider allowed women to operate beyond the structures that reproduce exclusion and oppression in the kitchen. However, immigrant status combined with race could also be grounds for exclusion and racism. This was the experience of Marcus Samuelsson, an award-winning Black American chef who was born in Ethiopia and raised in Sweden, when he tried to land an entry-level position at a prominent hotel restaurant in Nice. After writing a letter to the head chef, he was encouraged to come try out. When Samuelsson presented himself in person, he was immediately turned away (2012, 105). Samuelsson also remarks that *negre,* which translates roughly as "black," is the term used in French kitchen for low-level jobs, such as dishwashing (169). These are generally the only positions accessible to people of color. In French restaurants, racial discrimination is alive and well.

This study is particularly relevant in the context of contemporary France because it raises broader issues about the underrepresentation of women and people of color in certain professions. French cuisine is a crucial topic in which to consider women's exclusion because it is an important cultural form that has been held up high as a point of national pride. However, with the encroachment of fast food and foreign cuisines, the media has portrayed male chefs as the defenders of French culture and identity. The media, specifically food writing, no longer see women as the guardians of regional culinary traditions. Popular depictions of women paint them as selling out their families to the frozen-food aisles in favor of a focus on careers and life outside of the home, despite the slow middle-class acceptance of upscale frozen foods (Murphy 2018). In French popular culture, women's double bind of domestic and salaried work outside the home has placed them in a position where media representations goad them for their lack of attention to domestic duties and their inability to earn the same salaries as men (Devetter and Rousseau 2011).

Chapter Overviews

This book does not unfold strictly chronologically, but it does begin in the past at a time when women's presence in professional kitchens in Lyon was reaching a point of critical mass and acclaim. The past permeates the lived experiences of many of the contemporary women who spoke with me. After attempting to uncover the history of the original mères lyonnaises, this book delves into the present with the women who, at first glance, most resemble the mères of the early twentieth century. Upon further exploration, it becomes apparent there is not just one way to be a mère and that past representations are part of present lived realities. Although there are various attempts to protect the memory of these women, their iconic dishes, and a certain style of restaurant, it becomes clear that there is not one *cuisine lyonnaise.* Understanding what is at stake in accepting this culinary plurality is at the heart of this book. Lyon first defined itself as the gastronomic capital of France in order to create value around a cultural form, cuisine, that represented the city and its region. This book aims to show that the city's identity has been particularly in flux in the twenty-first century. In turn, this has meant new culinary forms.

While the cuisine des mères and the bouchon lyonnais are categories in which certain types of women are well represented, there are many struggles for young women beginning their careers. The mères lyonnaises did not completely pave the way for women of generations to follow. A closer look at culinary training and apprenticeship reveals the structural gender biases that are reproduced in these formative settings. Few women survive the brutal early years of their career to go on to reach the pinnacles of the profession. However, those who do are important symbols of what women can achieve. At the same time, other women are quietly remaking culinary work in their own image—one of collaboration and creativity. Lyon offers an exceptional case study for understand what the future might look like for a more egalitarian workplace, where men and women's labor is equally valuable.

The first chapter, "*Cuisine des mères lyonnaises*: Making Sense of Women's Culinary Work," places the mères lyonnaises, the first generation of acclaimed female chefs in Lyon, in historic context and then delves into how the Lyonnais created a legend around these women's memory. Starting with the movement of female cooks in Lyon's bourgeois households to work in restaurant kitchens in the public sphere at the start of the twentieth century, this chapter looks at how women navigated the move from the domestic to the professional kitchen. From a historic perspective, this chapter explores the contribution of the mères lyonnaises to the construction of a distinguished regional cuisine that brought Lyon to the forefront of French gastronomy during the interwar years (Csergo 1996, 2008). The rise of women like Eugénie Brazier to three-star Michelin fame was tied to the development of gastronomic literature, tourism, and a broader regionalist movement. In addition to archival sources, oral histories with former apprentices to the mères lyonnaises and interviews with culinary experts offer perspectives on the centrality of the mères lyonnaises in Lyon's culinary cultures. Ethnographic accounts uncover how this legend plays an active part in legitimating and framing the lived reality of women in Lyonnais kitchens today. The legend of the mères lyonnaises allows women to straddle domestic and professional worlds. At the same time, the legend also risks limiting women's culinary work to a specific type of cuisine and way of being in a kitchen.

The bouchon lyonnais acts as a backdrop for the performance of many mères lyonnaises. These historic restaurants are the focus for chapter 2, "*Des femmes avec du caractère:* Performing Gender and Authenticity in the *bouchon lyonnais*," which explores the bouchon as a gendered space of reproduction, consumption, and work. Bouchons started out as working-class eateries that served all the people of their neighborhoods—from silk workers to the businessmen. The food and wine served in these establishments aimed to sustain hungry working bodies. In most bouchons, a man would serve wine at a bar while a woman, usually the man's wife, would prepare simple dishes in a makeshift kitchen. In this gendered division of labor, the husband and wife perform mother and father roles that create a familial atmosphere. Still today, this gender division and reproduction of domesticity can be found in some bouchons lyonnais. This chapter looks at the continuation of the gendered division of labor, and it investigates how women's cooking lends legitimacy and authenticity to bouchon fare today within the context of tourism and the construction of Lyon's culinary identity.

As a popular tourist destination, the bouchon is a perfect place to explore the construction of culinary authenticity and the commodification of Lyonnais cuisine. Chapter 2 considers contemporary notions of regional cuisine and the ways in which women's culinary traditions have been resurrected to create a cuisine and dining experience that restaurants present as authentic. Here the struggle to maintain and validate authenticity among the city's many bouchons offers an interesting example of how local associations and the municipal government police memory and locality in order to retain value and an official cultural identity through food. This can be challenging when knowledge is not codified in texts.

Preparing *cuisine bourgeoise* was knowledge that was passed down from one woman to the next. Most women cooking professionally did not write down recipes or use cookbooks. Apprenticeship was at the heart of learning to be a cook—watching, tasting, and doing in the same kitchen as a more expert cook. Modern culinary education now includes textbooks and written recipes, but apprenticeship remains an important part of learning to cook professionally. Chapter 3, "*Apprentie*: Reproducing and Challenging Gender through Culinary Education," investigates the culinary school and apprenticeship experiences of young women today. This chapter outlines changes to French culinary education from the nineteenth century to the present and considers the gender implications of professional culinary education. Following the winners of the Eugénie Brazier scholarship, which supports and encourages women's participation in the culinary arts, chapter 3 looks at these young women's motivations for choosing this work and at their experiences at culinary school and during their apprenticeships. These young cooks' narratives show how they subvert and reproduce gender norms during culinary training. My own experience of attending culinary school and apprenticeship provides additional perspectives on the embodied nature of professional cooking and the inner workings of culinary training in France.

Drawing on Amy Trubek's work (2000) and that of French sociologist Patricia Marie (2014), chapter 3 investigates the ways in which gender norms and discrimination are woven into the basic educational structures of culinary school. Despite these structural impositions that often lead to a reproduction of gender-based subordination, interviews and participant observation seek to better understand the hopes, challenges, and successes of young women entering culinary professions today. How do the two institutions of culinary school and formal apprenticeship shape the experience of women and the ways in which culinary professions are gender biased to privilege men? How do women negotiate and challenge these institutions? If the restaurant industry in France is going to face its gender gap in the back of the house, culinary school is a logical place to look for roots of gender disparity and make changes.

When a woman graduates from culinary school and completes her apprenticeship, it is not a given that she will go on to actually practice her profession. Many women drop out early on in their culinary careers because of the harshness of their work environments and a lack of support. For those women who do continue, there are few who reach the highest level of the profession. Nonetheless, the few female success stories are important role models for young women coming up through the ranks. Chapter 4, "Stars in Their Eyes: Ambition and Bias in the Kitchen," considers the women who are competing for the top rankings in guidebooks and in culinary competitions.

There is currently only one female Michelin three-star chef in France, Anne-Sophie Pic, and two female MOFs en cuisine (in cooking), Andrée Rosier (2007), and Virginie Basselot (2015). Symbols of excellence in the French culinary world, these two titles remain almost entirely male dominated. Chapter 4 looks at the challenges for women cooking cuisine gastronomique and haute cuisine in Lyon, their career trajectories, successes, and challenges. Participant observations bring readers into the everyday work of the kitchen and its realities for these accomplished women working in Lyonnais kitchens.

The French media have started to focus on women cooking at the highest levels, an important part of constructing the image of the female culinary professional. Television shows like *Top Chef France* have given female chefs greater attention compared with traditional forms of food media such as magazines and guidebooks. Ethnographic interviews with young chefs and statistical data show that this media focus has led to an increase in enrollment of women in culinary training and growing participation in the industry. New media representations of women who cook are changing popular images of culinary professions, and imagining chefs as female (Hansen 2008). In addition, women have started participating in the shaping of media's construction of the culinary arts through blogs, television appearances, and restaurant reviews. This has meant that women play a more prominent role in taste-making and they showcase women in culinary professions (Johnston and Bauman 2010). There is still work to be done to overcome the underrepresentation of women in the media and to create opportunities for them to compete on a level playing field in the culinary arts. The exclusion of women also begs the question of the general exclusion of minorities from restaurant kitchens and media representations.

While there are women who seek to compete with men in an arena that is defined by norms of masculinity, there are other women who re-envision the professional kitchen and culinary work. Chapter 5, "*Cheffe de cuisine*: Redefining the Kitchen and Labor," considers women who are creating new models outside of the dominant patriarchy of most professional French kitchens. Paulette Castaing (1950–80s), Sonia Ezgulian (1990–present), and Connie Zagora (2000s–present) are women whose careers as cooks and chefs demonstrate that it is possible to cook and run a kitchen outside of the masculine gender norms. The male-dominated kitchen is one where subordination is generally maintained through humiliation (Bourelly 2010), where physical strength and speed are admired, and where creativity is reserved for only those at the top of the hierarchy. Reordering the kitchen, breaking down hierarchies, and changing ways of learning and doing are all part of this subversion of work in the professional kitchen. While some women seek to take on male roles and espouse masculine stereotypes in the kitchen (Swinbank 2002), there are those who have sought to reimagine this workplace. These changes are reflected not only in the organization of labor and space but also through the types of cuisine prepared. Through the story of three women, chapter 5 looks at female culinary traditions in Lyon and current realities that contest traditional masculine norms in the kitchen.

The case of women working in the culinary arts in Lyon relates to broader structural issues of gender disparity that exist in other professions and activities in France. The case of women as culinary professionals needs to be placed in the broader context of women's work and place in French society in order to address the complexities of exclusion and how they relate to issues of class, race, national origin and life stage. This book concludes by making a call for structural change to address gender bias and discrimination in the kitchen and beyond.

1

CUISINE DES MÈRES LYONNAISES

Making Sense of Women's Culinary Work

At Paul Bocuse's celebrated restaurant L'Auberge du Pont de Collonges are a series of murals that depict the history of French cuisine. Among these trompe l'oeils of culinary history is a scene devoted to the mères lyonnaises (fig. 1.1), sandwiched into this display of the male-dominated pantheon of French culinary history. Although these beautiful paintings adorn many buildings in the center of Lyon, this is the only one to feature the mères lyonnaises or indeed any of the city's female culinary heroes. Although these women are not visible, people still talk about them.

In fact, I was struck by how many of the people I interviewed, men and women, would start by telling me the story of the mères lyonnaises. This narrative framed the interview or was at least some part of a personal story. I began to realize that creating a connection with the mères lyonnaises was many women's way of telling me about their own lives in the kitchen. The similarity of the stories and how they make sense of each cook's unique experience got me thinking about the role of defining narratives in the experience of women in professional kitchens. This framing device legitimates, roots, and empowers women in a profession that has sought to marginalize and delegitimize female labor. Rather than seeing gender as a burden or a limitation, I could see how women use the legend of the mères lyonnaises to give meaning and value to their work.

Figure 1.1: Mural at Auberge du Pont de Collonge features la mère Brazier and la mère Fillioux. The men in the image (Édouard Herriot, far left, and Brazier's son, Gaston, background) are both secondary figures. (Mural by Cité de la Création, 1993)

Women Finding Meaning in the Legend of the Mères Lyonnaises

Historians have privileged written records that are usually produced by men. When it came to getting a better grasp on Lyon's gastronomic past, I needed to challenge this culinary history that reproduced men's prominent place in the culinary arts. Thus I looked to oral histories and living memories in order to hear women's voices more clearly. The archives pushed me out into kitchens to find new angles to the history of the mères lyonnaises. Ethnography gave me an understanding of the ways in which the past gives meaning to the present-day experiences of women in Lyon's kitchens. As I talked and worked next to women, I tried to make sense of why they kept insisting on telling me the story of the mères lyonnaises. I began to see how these stories, and particularly that of Eugénie Brazier, had become codified—a legend of sorts.

How had the mère Brazier become a legend, and what did this mean? First, I turned to learning more about legends and their social and cultural functions. Folklorists generally agree that a legend should be constructed from reality in a believable way: "it makes allusions to verifiable topographic features or historical personages" (Tangherlini 1990, 378). William Bascom defines legends as "prose narratives which, like myths, are regarded as true by the narrator and his audience, but they are set in a period considered less remote, when the world was much as it is today. Legends are more often secular than sacred, and their principal characters are human" (1965, 4). In the case of the legend of the mères lyonnaises, I am using the term "legend" to indicate a narrative that is accepted as true and which is retold in similar ways. The function of this legend is to memorate, to reproduce a personal experience, and in the process give meaning and context to these experiences (Von Sydow in Dégh and Vázsonyi 1974, 225). Although few of the people who I worked with and interviewed had firsthand experience of working with the mères in the 1930s, they were recounting their own experiences through this historical narrative. One of the functions of legends is to "reiterate and reinforce belief" (Tangherlini 1990, 379). This was notable in the way in which the women I worked with used the legend of the mères lyonnaises to legitimate their place in male-dominated professional kitchens.

The story of the mères lyonnaises has undergone a process of localized codification; it has come to fit the cultural situation of chefs and people in Lyon who are interested in cuisine (Tangherlini 1990, 377–78). The more times I heard people tell me Brazier's story, the more interested I became in the ways women cooking professionally in Lyon activate and shape this legend to construct a narrative that gives meaning and coherence to their professional activities. This is important at a time when women face challenges running their own establishments or when trying to work their way up through the brigade system in restaurants.

Women use the legend of the mères lyonnaises in many ways, but three themes became apparent. First, they engaged with this historical narrative to talk about their roles as defenders of local culinary traditions. Second, they used the legend to explain how motherhood is compatible with a professional culinary career and how the attributes of mothering could even be seen as positive in light of feeding people as a sort of care work not all that dissimilar from the domestic work of many mothers. Third, there was a group of women who saw the mères lyonnaises as important role models in a profession where few women have made it to the top ranks. Sitting down to analyze my interviews, I quickly realized that the mères are important for female culinary professionals. But I was still not much closer to understanding who the original mères were.

The Other Lyonnais Culinary Legend: Paul Bocuse

The larger-than-life figure of Paul Bocuse, Lyon's most famous chef, overshadowed nearly all of my attempts to understand who the mères lyonnaises were and what their place was in the local culinary scene. I resisted giving too much space to Bocuse in this book because he and other male chefs have so often taken away from women's contributions in the kitchen. Bocuse, like Mathieu Viannay, the current chef owner of the restaurant La Mère Brazier, and the Michelin-starred MOF Christian Têtedoie, the owner of La Mère Léa and other restaurants, carefully nod in respect to the mères, but this acknowledgment works to relegate these women to a dusty corner of history. Bill Buford mentions the mères several times in his recent memoir, *Dirt: Adventures in Lyon as a Chef in Training, Father, and Sleuth Looking for the Secret of French Cooking* (2020). The writer even apprentices at La Mère Brazier, but in the end he largely reinforces the idea that Lyonnais cuisine is the business of men. There is little investment of substance on the part of male Lyonnais chefs to acknowledge women's contributions to the culinary arts and the role that women play in making the city a gastronomic hub.

Paul Bocuse is a man who is everywhere in Lyon, even after his death in 2018. His image and name grace buildings, there is a culinary school named after him, and the Bocuse d'Or is one of the world's most prestigious culinary competitions in the world. I knew from the start that Bocuse had to be part of this story. That is why, bright and early on a chilly June morning, I took the number 40 bus from Lyon out to Collonges au Mont d'Or, where I was deposited at the side of the busy road not far from Bocuse's iconic three-starred restaurant. Walking across the bridge over the Saône River, I noted that the bridge was the Pont Paul Bocuse. I felt nervous. I was showing up without an appointment in an attempt to have a chitchat with France's most iconic chef. I knew it was nearly impossible to get an interview with Monsieur Paul, so I took the advice of Jacotte Brazier: "put on a nice dress and show up at the restaurant around 10:30 a.m. Bocuse will be there. You are a pretty woman. He will agree to see you." I was not feeling very good or confident about this plan, but I was hopeful that talking to Bocuse would reveal something new about the mères lyonnaises and Eugénie Brazier, with whom he had apprenticed.

The impression of opulence and excess of the garishly painted green-and-red building was a visual shock when I came upon it. I carefully threw my weight into opening the gleaming brass and glass door. I felt as if I were entering a temple. I stood awkwardly in the entranceway, and an employee quickly intercepted me. He sharply asked, "Madame, can I help you?" To which I replied, "I would like to speak to Paul Bocuse." The man volleyed back, "Do you have an appointment?" At this, I unabashedly dropped Jacotte's name, gave him my card, and hoped for the best. Even though the man was not pleased to be taken from his work and openly expressed his displeasure that I had no appointment, he plodded upstairs to see if Bocuse would receive me. He came back downstairs not long after and, much to my surprise, announced that Monsieur Paul had a few minutes for me. "Would you please take a seat in the lounge."

I nervously took out my notebook and pen. I triple-checked my recording device and flipped through my interview questions. I raised my eyes to see Paul Bocuse carefully navigating the lounge with his cane. He was still a formidable figure despite his age. Jacotte had told me that Parkinson's was taking its toll on him, and I should not wait to speak with him. Bocuse's look went from stern to a warm smile as I stood up to greet him. He asked me to take a seat and did so himself. I thanked him for his time and quickly explained who I was and that I was doing research on the cuisine des mères lyonnaises. Bocuse clearly had a soft spot for the mères.

Monsieur Paul launched into reciting the genealogy of the mères lyonnaises, starting with Fillioux. Then he told his story. Legend has it that seeing Paul Bocuse ride up to the restaurant at the Col de la Luère on his bike all the way from Collonges, Eugénie Brazier declared, "*Petit*, if you made it all the way here on a bicycle, you must be brave. You are hired." (Mesplède 2010, 108) This was in 1947 and Bocuse had already worked in his family's restaurant, but his life was about to change. He recounted his time as an apprentice under la mère Brazier at the Col de la Luère: "It was an excellent school of life. You had to work hard." Bocuse recalled Brazier taking the apprentices to the market to get the day's ingredients. In order to not waste any time, "Brazier would jump in the back of the little Citroën truck on the return to the restaurant and start shucking the peas" (Bocuse, interview by author, 2013). Bocuse claims that he largely learned his work ethic during his time with Brazier, "She led by example. She was the first one up and she was always working." Cooking was only one of the *commis'* duties: "We had to chop wood, we kept the pigs, we milked the cows, we even ironed the linens." Although she would regularly yell at the kitchen staff, Bocuse remembers her as having a heart of gold. "She was expectational." He recalled that the food was simple but perfectly executed.

After La Mère Brazier, Bocuse went on to Vienne to work with Fernand Point, one of the greats of modern French cuisine, at La Pyramide. Bocuse stayed with Point, with a brief interlude in Paris, until 1954, when his father asked him to come home to work in the family restaurant. In 1958, the restaurant at Collonges still had stainless steel cutlery and paper tablecloths, but Bocuse earned his first Michelin star, and a second star in 1960. In 1961, Paul Bocuse was anointed MOF. His star was rising quickly. Only a few years later, Bocuse became the youngest chef in the postwar period to earn three Michelin stars. He was thirty-nine.

One of Bocuse's major contributions to French cuisine was not only culinary: Bocuse changed the status of the chef from an unknown worker in the back of the house to a sexy celebrity in charge of his own business. Bocuse was a tastemaker shaping an important French cultural product: haute cuisine. Until late in life, Bocuse would often greet guests at the entrance of his restaurants and circulate in the dining room to make sure everything was perfect. Before Bocuse, the chef rarely breached the door separating the kitchen from the dining room. Chefs became visible figures of popular French culture; they started to appear on television and figure more prominently than before in print media. Monsieur Paul was the James Dean of French cuisine, appearing in photos straddling a Harley Davidson motorcycle and grinning at the camera as he displayed the *coq français* (the rooster that is a symbol of France) tattoo on his bicep. This iconic chef was a master of the classics but he was also an innovator. Often credited as one of the originators of nouvelle cuisine, Bocuse shifted the focus of French cooking to ingredients, which were prepared simply to showcase their quality (Rouèche 2018). Bocuse trained generations of chefs and instilled in them the importance of owning their own restaurants. His most lasting legacy is not his extensive restaurant empire but rather the knowledge he imparted in so many chefs who worked with him.

It is undoubtable that Paul Bocuse's name has become synonymous with French cuisine on an international level (Lane 2014, 132). Bocuse also helped maintain Lyon's claim to fame as the gastronomic capital of France. Between Bocuse's restaurants, the chefs he brought along, the culinary school he founded, and the Bocuse d'Or culinary competition (see chapter 4), Paul Bocuse has become the central figure dominating the narrative of cuisine lyonnaise. Even though Bocuse's story is intertwined with that of many women, his dominance of the field has obscured women's contributions to cuisine in Lyon. Particularly, when it comes to remembering Eugénie Brazier, it is Monsieur Paul's account that is most often cited.

Who Were the Mères Lyonnaises?

The interview started in much the way many others had: we were seated at a marble-topped table in the back of a cozy little restaurant, Marie leaned in toward me as if she was going to tell me some great secret. In her low husky voice, she asked, "Do you know the story of the mères lyonnaises?" I feigned ignorance and encouraged her to tell me more, although I imagined that I was about to hear a story I had heard many times before.

> After the First World War, the economy was very bad. Many of the big bourgeois houses here in Lyon had to let their cooks go. These cooks were women who had come from the countryside around Lyon to find work in the city. These women had no other place to go and cooking was really all they knew how to do, so they started to look for work in restaurants. No one wanted to hire a woman to cook in a restaurant. A lot of these mères opened restaurants with their companions,

> husbands, or *Charles*.[1] These little restaurants gained a reputation for serving honest food—the kind of food that reminded many clients of the food they used to eat at home when they had cooks. They quickly gained a following. This was also the era in which the *Guide Michelin* started. The reviewers praised these women as the guardians of Lyonnais culinary traditions. They cooked with local products, such as *poulet de Bresse* and fish like perch from the Saône River. The most famous of all these women was la mère Brazier. She had two restaurants with three Michelin stars. She was a sturdy woman who spoke tersely to her kitchen staff, but her clients loved her like a mother. She is perhaps the most important woman in French culinary history. Her *poularde en demi deuil* (chicken in half mourning) and *fonds d'artichaut* with foie gras (artichoke hearts with goose liver) were legendary. When Édouard Herriot was the mayor of Lyon, he used to be a regular chez Brazier. There were other women too.

Marie went on to tell me about the women who were part of this golden age of the cuisine des mères between the two wars. She finished by placing herself in this matriarchy.

Marie's story of the mères lyonnaises was not dissimilar from other accounts that I heard while working in restaurants or while interviewing culinary professionals. Almost all of these narratives talked about the economic downturn that moved cooks from the domestic sphere, where they were paid cooks, into professional restaurant kitchens in Lyon. Most of my participants told me about the role of guidebooks as a contributor to these women's success. They talked about the mères' ability to transform local ingredients into delectable dishes. All of the interviewees placed Eugénie Brazier as a prominent figure in this legend—there was not one interview in which her name was not mentioned. She is always portrayed as both a larger-than-life, exceptional figure, and the epitome of the mère lyonnaise character—an excellent cook, stern but also motherly. What struck me was the way in which these elements were nearly always present in the recounting of the story of these women who were clearly a critical part of Lyonnais gastronomic history.

Through archival research, secondary sources, and oral histories, I was able to piece together a picture of these doyennes of cuisine lyonnaise. What emerged was how women claimed their place as culinary professionals in the interwar period; at this exceptional moment in French culinary history, women were celebrated as keepers of France's culinary knowledge not only in the home but also in restaurants. Although there were most certainly women in restaurant kitchens in Paris, Dijon, Marseille, and most French cities, a distinct style of women's cooking came to mark cuisine lyonnaise and played an important role in making this city the gastronomic capital of France. This was food that had deep roots in the cooking style and expensive ingredients of cuisine bourgeoise; foie gras, truffles and the famous poultry from Bresse are common ingredients. This cuisine reflected Lyon's geographic position at the confluence of two major rivers (the Rhône and the Saône) that were transportation arteries. The city is historically a major crossroads for travelers coming and going from Switzerland and Italy. The Foire de Lyon, an annual fair first held in 1420, attests to Lyon's importance as a commercial center (Gutton 2000). Rich farmlands surrounded Lyon. It is a place where excellent ingredients abound.

By the end of the nineteenth century, the city of Lyon had a concentration of women working as professional cooks who were employed in middle-class homes due to thriving textile and banking industries, which caused an expansion of an economically prosperous middle class.[2] Many Lyonnais families had made their fortunes in the silk industry in the nineteenth century, but by the end of that century, artisanal silk production was waning due to greater foreign competition, silkworm diseases, and the mechanization of weaving.[3] In response to the decline of silk production, the Lyonnais developed a synthetic textiles industry and an associated chemical industry. Manufacturing and industry more generally also continued to grow. By the end of the nineteenth century, there was a substantial concentration of capital in Lyon, and the city became an important modern center for insurance and banking (Gutton 2000). The growth of the middle class that accompanied this economic expansion meant that there were a large number of households in Lyon that required domestic laborers to maintain or attain a bourgeois lifestyle, which often included family meals and the entertaining of guests at home (P. White 1989). In addition to work in middle-class homes, women also found jobs cooking in the small dining establishments that fed the growing ranks of single working-class men and women who were drawn to the city for work but who lived in rooming houses without kitchen access. The pull of domestic jobs drew female migrants to Lyon at the end of the nineteenth century (Winchester 1986, 64).

The French economy experienced a downturn at the end of the nineteenth century and following World War I. Fewer bourgeois households could afford their domestic staff; many cooks were let go and had to find work elsewhere (Piketty, Postel-Vinay, and Rosenthal 2006). Some women took jobs in restaurants, others found it difficult to get work in male-dominated kitchens, and a few set up shop on their own. Due to the restrictions governing women's public lives, many of these cooks started businesses with men—husbands or other male family members—to make the administration of their businesses easier (Schweitzer 2002, 49).[4]

This model of the family business was typical in many small eateries, ateliers, and artisanal activities. The notion of family may also be a source for the title of "mère." *Compagnonnage* (an itinerary that took apprentices all over France to learn from various masters), the *tours de France* that young apprentices in the trades would undertake as part of their training, provides another source for this nomenclature: the women, mothers, and aunts who would host young journeyman in their homes were frequently referred to as "mère" and "tante." Jean Butin notes that the mère des Compagnons was a formidable personage: she had a strong character and was capable of keeping people, young men in particular, in their place (1999, 96). This description of echoes how my interlocutors described the mères lyonnaises.

It is difficult to gauge exactly how many women were cooking in Lyonnais kitchens after World War I. Looking at business ownership and licensing records at the Chambre de Commerce de Lyon is somewhat misleading because on paper only men could own restaurants—women had limited legal property rights (Gollac 2017). Reviewing the *Annuaire Henri*, a listing of local businesses, there are a number of restaurants and cafés with names such as La Mère Guy, La Mère Brigousse, and La Mère Brazier. This gives some indication that women were at least the figureheads in these restaurants. The accounts of gastronomes who were early food writers give high praise to eateries run by women, recording this phenomenon in the 1920s and '30s (Varille 1928, Daudet

1927). What is clear is that these women were cooking food that diners enjoyed and admired, giving these cooks legitimacy. Adapon explains this culinary legitimacy as "the dependence on flavor, or a devotion to culinary works of art, gives women the legitimacy to expand their social and physical boundaries, forms of autonomy, morality and domestic power" (2008, 84).

The gendered division of labor in the small restaurants shows a clear separation of male and female duties and responsibilities that was common in other craft businesses. Susan Terrio's research on artisanal chocolate production in France clearly demonstrates the separate spheres of women and men in the chocolate maker's atelier, a male-dominated space, and the shop front, where women were the public face. Formal training and apprenticeship were all but closed off to women until the end of the twentieth century in many crafts and areas of skilled work (Terrio 2000). While there was a system of apprenticeship for restaurants, culinary school or formal training certificates were not necessary for employment in professional kitchens, making it possible for women to enter.

Many of the small family-run establishments in the early twentieth century in Lyon were bouchons (see chapter 2). There were also other small restaurants with female chefs that were a step up in décor and in their culinary offerings; these little restaurants came to define what is now known as the cuisine des mères. Although some of the restaurants of the mères lyonnaise rose up from what started as bouchons, the cuisine and clientele were quite distinct. The restaurants of the mères lyonnaises drew heavily on cuisine bourgeoise, a type of cooking that women had mastered in their prior employment in private bourgeois households.

Cuisine Bourgeoise

Cuisine bourgeoise is the cuisine of the French middle class. Friedrich Engels defines the bourgeoisie as "the class of modern Capitalists, owners of the means of social production and employers of wage laborers" (Engels in Tucker 1978, 473) After the French aristocracy was deposed during the French Revolution, the middle class came to take their place at the higher rungs of French society. It was no longer land but capital that held sway and allowed for entry into society—hard work, not a birthright, led to success and fortune. The expansion of industry and the accumulation of capital on the part of those at the head of banking, insurance, manufacturing and other industries built a new powerful bourgeois ruling class. Lyon, as a center of industry, had a large and wealthy middle class—it is no surprise that cuisine bourgeoise became a symbol of the city.

With a strong association with aristocratic cuisine, "cuisine bourgeoise in the *Ancien Régime* simplified, or, better yet, domesticated court or grand cuisine (*la Cuisine des Grands*). It is not an 'indigenous' style of cooking of the bourgeoisie in anywhere the same way that peasant culinary modes can be associated with subsistence cooking and local products" (Mintz 1996, 101). Cookbook authors, particularly in the late eighteenth century, sought to adapt aristocratic cuisine and make it available to a less affluent audience. However, as Priscilla Parkhurst Ferguson (2004, 40–41) notes, these households were still of great means and able to afford the ingredients and staff to cook the meals proposed in popular cookbooks like Menon's *La cuisinière bourgeoise* (1822). Menon suggests that a four-course meal for a table of ten start with two soups. This should be followed by four meat entrées, such as roast duck, mutton chops, and herb roasted chicken. For the third course, there should be two roasts, two smaller side dishes, and two salads. To end, a fruit course that might also include some light desserts like *gaufrette* (thin waffles) (5–6). The modern reader has to consider the aspirational nature of Menon's cookbook. The most affluent of the middle classes might have dined with this abundance as a way of demonstrating their wealth to guests, but most bourgeois families would have pared down these offerings for their daily meals. This is cooking that draws on haute cuisine, although many of the culinary techniques that require long cooking times, such as braising, roasting, and poaching, and are often associated with the domestic sphere and women's cooking (Trubek 2000, 27).

The French bourgeoisie claimed political and economic power in the nineteenth century, but they still held to values of hard work and generally abhorred the overindulgences of the aristocracy. These values are mirrored at the table: Ferguson notes that cuisine bourgeoise, with its emphasis on "economy, simplicity and health," can be seen in opposition to the "extravagance, excess and refinement" of aristocratic cuisine or haute cuisine (2004, 42). Although cuisine bourgeoise initially sought to emulate the fine cooking and dining of the aristocracy, it later came to embody bourgeois ideals about work, values, and health. Nineteenth-century cuisine bourgeoise placed an emphasis on quality, simplicity, and economy. Pot-au-feu (oxtail stew) exemplifies this logic: this dish is stewed slowly, the broth can be presented as a soup, the meat and vegetables are the main course, and any leftovers can be reconfigured into new dishes throughout the week. Maguelonne Toussaint-Samat (2001) points out that every region of France has its distinguishing canon of slowly simmered bourgeois dishes: for example, regional beef stews include daube Provençale (Provence's beef or bull stew marinated in wine and cooked in a cast-iron pot); *boeuf bourguignon* (Burgundy beef stew); Alsatian *baeckeoffe* with its slow-cooked mix of meats; cassoulet from the South, with its white beans that become a creamy condiment for the simmered meats. All of these recipes share a similar logic; the slow-cooking meat makes tougher, less desirable cuts tender and delicious, and leftovers can be transformed into new creations (Toussaint-Samat 2001, 23–24). These dishes are the epitome of domestic economy that mirrors the bourgeois logic of good fortune through hard work and saving. This type of cooking was "economical, full of ritual and comforting" (184).

Most bourgeois households employed domestic laborers, of whom one of the most important was the cook. Although men and women were employed in this position, women were well represented. In the early nineteenth century, most training to become a cook would have happened on the job. Later, women migrating from the countryside were trained in technical schools that taught them how to iron, sew, cook, and manage a household. By the end of the nineteenth century, the declining fortunes of the bourgeoisie shifted the labor onto wives and other women in bourgeoise homes. This is when we see a proliferation of bourgeois cookbooks that explain the finer details of home economics to women who had never had to do this work before. This is also when cuisine bourgeoise becomes more prominent in restaurants. This new setting maintained some of the rituals and traditions of the domestic table, but the preparations of the dishes became more elaborate and restaurant cooks began to use increasingly prestigious ingredients such as foie gras and truffles, which would have been reserved for more celebratory meals in the setting of the home.

Cuisine bourgeoise was a type of cuisine that was initially associated with the home but as the middle classes increasingly dined in restaurants, its popularity grew because of its quality and honesty in comparison to the overly elaborate dishes of *cuisine des grandes palaces* (fancy hotel restaurants), popular with international travelers. With the decline of households that could afford to employ cooks, the growth of tourism, and the rise of culinary guidebooks, cuisine bourgeoise came to define the local cuisine in Lyon and what is known as la cuisine des mères.

Gastronomic Literature and Guidebooks

In the early twentieth century, the burgeoning field of gastronomic literature sang the praises of women cooking in Lyonnais restaurants. In 1925, renowned gastronomes Curnonsky and Marcel E. Grancher published *Lyon, capitale mondiale de la gastronomie,* which lauded the achievement of food in Lyon: "Lyonnais cuisine participates in French Art, only that it never has an effect. It does not beg. It does not sacrifice to easy eloquence. Cuisine attains, naturally and without effort, this degree of supreme Art: Simplicity" (1935, 6). In praising Lyonnais cuisine, the authors go on to cite the contributions of numerous mères: Brigousse, Guy, Marateur, Garien, Rivier, Fillioux, Bigot, Pompon, Buisson, Rose, Trolliet, and Brazier. Mathieu Varille in *La cuisine lyonnaise* (1928) also gives the mères an important place in the hall of fame of Lyonnais cuisine of the day. Partly in reaction to an internationalized form of haute cuisine that they felt was not a good representation of French cuisine, many gastronomic writers praised women for the simplicity and fine execution of dishes in the canon of cuisine bourgeoise. Curnonsky and Grancher, in particular, were out to defend a French national cuisine that spoke of regionalism and values of the bourgeoisie, the dominant class in French society (Curnonsky and Grancher 1935). This type of gastronomic writing also served a hungry middle-class audience, eager to find a delicious meal as they increasingly traveled France for business and leisure. Gastronomic literature of the early twentieth century is a collection of commercial guidebooks packed with advertisements and self-indulgent treatises on dining out that could be compared to today's trend of posting food porn photos on social media. It was about consumption and taste making. Writers like Curnonsky, Grancher, and Varille were actively engaged in defining French cuisine and what they deemed to be good food.

The advent of the guidebook played an important role in making Lyon a tourist destination for fine dining. These guides originally developed in conjunction with the spread of train lines, then the extensive use of the automobile and the improvement of French roads (Harp 2001). Thanks to the growing market for cars and the consequent development of automobile-oriented tourism, the *Guide Michelin* quickly became one of the most prominent guidebooks.[5] Automobile tourism was a decidedly middle-class form of leisure—you had to be wealthy enough to own a car and be able to travel for pleasure. According to Lucien Karpik, the *Guide Michelin* encouraged the French to free themselves of the limits of train travel; it encouraged them to personalize their itineraries and trips (2000, 371–2). The *Guide Michelin* had an important impact on restaurants in Lyon.

This new tourism literature created a specific canon of notable restaurants and their signature dishes. At first, just the names of restaurants were listed in these books, but they soon started to give the specialties of specific restaurants. Jean-François Mesplède, former editor of the *Guide Michelin,* explained that the menus in restaurants like La Mère Fillioux and La Mère Brazier rarely changed because diners would arrive expecting to be able to order the specialty of the house, as listed in the guidebooks (Mesplède, interview by author, 2013). In 1933, the *Guide Michelin* included the following specialties: for La Mère Brazier, "*Quenelles financière, Volaille [poularde] demi-deuil Mère Brazier, Terrine Brazier,*" and for Fillioux, "*Volaille truffé, Quenelles au gratin beurre d'écrivisses, Fonds d'artichauts au foie gras truffé.*"[6] Both mères faithfully cooked their signature dishes, such as *poularde en demi-deuil,* each evening, for fear of otherwise disappointing clients who showed up with specific expectations of what they would find on the menu. In this way, tourists and gastronomic guidebooks began to codify regional cuisine: attaching specific dishes to individuals and places. Guidebooks helped middle-class consumers navigate the growing number of restaurants in cities like Lyon, and they also facilitated consumption and the display of cultural capital (Barabowski and Furlough 2001, 12). This played a critical role in defining la cuisine des mères lyonnaises for the growing number of middle-class consumers.

In *Lyon, capitale mondiale*, Curnonsky and Grancher are careful to point out that the quality of food is generally excellent in most dining establishments in Lyon, which was not the case in Paris. They claim that in Lyon it is hard to distinguish from large elegant restaurants (*les grands restaurants*) and the holes in the wall (*les petites boîtes*): "We are in Lyon, and in certain places with wood shavings on the floor, where we drink from heavy glasses, where the plates are substantial and rustic, these are reputable places, and they are frequented by people who would not dare go next door to dine, even if those places had beautiful mirrors and gilded interiors and shiny floors" (116). The focus is truly on the food and not the décor. It is the quality of food, not its price or presentation, that draws people from different social classes to humble establishments where they can rub elbows. In these writings there is a notion of "slumming it": bourgeois men fueled by copious amounts of wine are able to transgress class boundaries in search of good food. These gastronomic guides impart their very specific male bourgeois readership with insider knowledge, telling them where to find the real Lyonnais experience and food. In the process, these guides were tying women's cooking to notions of authenticity.

In the "Our Saintly Mothers" section in *Lyon, capitale mondiale*, the smiling faces of Madame Bigot, Madame Trolliet, la mère Filloux, and Madame Brazier grace the pages in a gallery format. There is high praise for female cooks, with the emphasis on "cook": "Madame Brazier is a very important cook—one of the most important there has ever been in our culinary tradition" (126).[7] Madame Bigot is also mentioned: "One of the most important Lyonnais cooks, the aforementioned is perhaps one of the best: I am talking about Madame Bigot, she is the excellent *cordon-bleu* in Chanvanne Street. [. . .] The dishes we were served were sublime; they were perfect from their description to their execution" (124).[8] Grancher and other gastronomic writers in the interwar period recognized and celebrated women's contributions to Lyonnais cuisine and cultural heritage. However, at the same time, they constructed separate categories for women through their use of the terms "cuisinière" (female cook) and "cordon bleu," both of which denote domestic labor and femininity and are never used to refer to professional cooks who are men.[9]

Early gastronomic writing played an important part in cementing the fame of the mères lyonnaises in French gastronomic history, but it is somewhat problematic because this was a group of men representing women. There were no female contributors to guidebooks at this time, and most women in lyonnais kitchens in the 1930s had little time to write. Putting pen to paper was not part of their work, and their knowledge was mainly passed along through oral tradition and apprenticeship. History's privileging of the written word has so often left out the working classes and people who did not leave a written record (E. Thompson 1991). In this case, men gave voice to women, but it was a specific voice: celebratory of the maternal, the comforting and authentic nature of women's cooking. In the historical record, the mères lyonnaises rarely speak for themselves; their voices are always appropriated for someone else's ends, in this case the construction of regional cuisines and the promotion of middle-class leisure. While it is exceptional that a group of women became central to a culinary history that was entirely male dominated, there is still a need to be critical of how this memory is constructed.

When I brushed off the dust of the archives and emerged into the light of the Lyonnais streets, I came back to thinking about how the narratives of the mères circulate and what meanings they hold for women cooking in Lyon today. As I talked to more women, I realized that they were taking back the memory of the mères lyonnaises, each in her own way.

Defending Tradition

As I walked into the small neighborhood restaurant in the Seventh Arrondissement of Lyon, I noted all the signs and symbols that told me that this was a bouchon: the tablecloths were red-and-white checked, a blackboard served as a menu, and there were only a few employees. Janine and Aishah, the owners of this restaurant, were having a bite to eat after a busy lunch service. They warmly invited me to join them at a table.

I started the interview by asking for basic details about their backgrounds; I wanted to understand how these two women had come to run their own restaurant and what drew them to this work. They explained that they both cook and serve in their restaurant. Aishah went to culinary school and passed her CAP diploma for cooking. Starting in the front of the house, Janine learned to cook at her previous restaurant jobs out of necessity—sometimes they just needed an extra hand in the kitchen. It did not take long for her to mention les mères lyonnaises. She began by differentiating the tradition of cuisine des mères and women's cooking from men and Michelin-starred cooking through the story of Paul Bocuse: "By accident, Paul Bocuse started out washing dishes for la mère Brazier. We are lucky to have this double culture in Lyon. We have the cuisine of starred chefs and la cuisine des mères." Aishah also shows the connection of starred chefs like Bocuse with the cuisine des mères, and she brings together the different levels and types of cooking happening in Lyon's restaurants, thereby validating and giving equal status to all forms of Lyonnais cuisine.

For Aishah, la cuisine des mères takes place in "little bistros where you have a woman at the *piano* and she makes food that she would make for her children." This is not the original definition of cuisine des mères, which had its roots in cuisine bourgeoise and was not everyday home cooking for the average family. What Aishah describes is more of the model of cuisine produced in bouchons, where men mainly dine on simple dishes that women often prepare (bouchons are explored further in the next chapter). What was clear to me as I talked to Aishah was that, for her, cooking is maternal and has a strong association with reproductive work.

The role of women is central in this bouchon, and Aishah and Janine reproduce the domesticity of food labor beyond the domestic sphere. They take dishes that are associated with home cooking, such as pot-au-feu, *poulet au vinaigre* (chicken cooked in vinegar) and *blanquette de veau* (veal stew in cream sauce), and bring them to the restaurant table for everyone to enjoy. These are not fancy dishes, and the way that Aishah and Janine serve them is simple. From the presentation to their flavor profiles, these dishes evoke the domestic kitchen—there is no extra working of sauces, no extraneous garnishes, no fancy flatware. If you close your eyes while you take a bite, you could be in your mother's kitchen. This sense of place is in the mouthfeel, the aroma, and the taste—the qualisigns of home cooking. The narrative of the cuisine des mères allows women like Aishah and Janine to place their style of cooking and professional food work in another frame of value that is validated by how they interpret the historic precedent of the mères lyonnaises. This interpretation counters the tendency to devalue women's culinary labor, domestic and professional (Cairns and Johnston 2015).

Keeping their establishment small scale, cooking from scratch, and using recipes in the tradition of the bouchon lyonnais were also critical elements for Aishah and Janine in their efforts to defend tradition. These two women explained to me that there really cannot be more than two people in the kitchen, and the restaurant should have a maximum capacity of thirty to be able to maintain the traditional menu and ambiance. They emphasized that was a lot of food to serve in such a small establishment. Aishah and Janine told me that they set out to create a restaurant in the spirit of the cuisine des mères because they feared that this tradition was being lost. Throughout the interview these two women referred to the culinary styles of the various mères of Lyon's culinary history—Vitton, Léa, and Brazier—and to a style of cooking that they defined as "food that nourishes, a generous cuisine with dishes that are often simmered." Other women I interviewed often used the word "generous" about the cuisine des mères, referring both to portions and the heartfelt nature of the cooking and its presentation. The food is not supposed to be fussy, with elaborate presentation and complicated sauces; much like home cooking, it is meant to feed and take care of hungry people. At the same time, the historic narrative legitimates this type of cuisine in a restaurant setting.

The narrative of cuisine des mères is not entirely liberated from attempts to devalue or exclude women's traditions from the restaurant. Aisha and Janine noted that cooking "true cuisine des mères" they frequently found themselves at odds with modern standards of hygiene: "In fact, a dish that is simmered a long time should be thrown out after four to five hours . . . so that Knorr can sell its dehydrated stock bases. Homemade sauces, mayo, whipped cream, pies set us apart." Janine and Aishah's commitment to uphold the culinary tenets of home cooking, namely scratch cooking, places them in opposition with industrial food safety standards that represent modernity. Aishah and Janine see these strict standards as an encroachment of industrial food on local culinary traditions. Most of these rules are geared to large-scale industrial outfits, not small-scale artisanal production (Black 2005). In her study of artisanal cheesemaking, Heather Paxson notes that the empirical methods that hygiene standards require, such as measuring temperatures using thermometers, are "often described as antithetical to women's customary ways of knowing" (Paxson 2012, 102). Through their cooking, Aishah and Janine were resisting the pressures of the food industry to use prepared products that were seen as time and money saving, in order to preserve traditional practices and tastes. While these two women believe in food safety and would never want to see their clients become sick from their cooking, they are pushing back against the homogeneity of taste that industrial food creates and the hegemonic control that this type of food and cooking has over the ways of doing in the kitchen.

The leisurely pace of the service, the cooking times, and the reproduction of women's culinary knowledge at Aishah and Janine's bouchon make it pretty much the opposite of fast food, what many French people see as the erosion of cultural traditions and values. The slow diner at the Lyonnais bouchon is the contemporary version of Baudelaire's flaneur (Smart 2014), from her table watching the world rush by as she slowly eats a sumptuous meal that took hours to simmer before it reached the table. As Wendy Parkins and Geoffrey Craig note in their book *Slow Living* (2006), the slow eater is conscious that she has situated her body in the context of a convivial setting, and has "an awareness of the nexus between the bodies that produce and consume food, in specific times and places" (87). It is this awareness that both acknowledges female culinary traditions and resists the disconnected nature of fast-paced modern life. The slowness of the eater and of the cooks is an act of resistance against the dismal rush of everyday life in the city. The narrative of the mères lyonnaises legitimates this act of resistance, giving it continuity and grounding it in both the unique place of Lyon but also in the agriculture areas that are tied to the city through its food.

The legend of the mères lyonnaises places Aishah and Janine and their little restaurant in the framework of a local tradition of women who cook. While their training and backgrounds are different from the mères of the 1930s, they tap into the spirit of female entrepreneurs who blur the lines between the domestic and the professional through their food (Abarca 2007)—they cook simple food that nourishes and satisfies a clientele that is increasingly wary of the industrial food that is creeping into local kitchens. The food underlines the strong connections between the place, the cook, and the diner. In the space of the bouchon this embeddedness creates value (Granovetter 1985).

Recognizing that tradition is not a stable category and that "all cooks have their own particular ways of doing things learned from people who also had different ideas about tradition" (Wilk 2006, 122), I hear Aishah and Janine telling me they are trying to save a way of doing that is becoming increasingly rare in Lyon. At their restaurant I understand that Janine and Aishah are actively crafting the category of tradition, which is often placed in opposition to modernity.

For many Lyonnais, the bouchon, its ambiance and its food, are seen as an integral part of social life and culinary culture—a cultural heritage that is deemed important to preserve. This bouchon is a place where people from the neighborhood can get an honest meal at a reasonable price.[10] It is a place where customers can come and have long conversations while lingering over several pots de vin. These values of honesty and culinary tradition were exactly what made the mères lyonnaises of the 1930s famous. It was also these qualities that gastronomes like Curnonsky and Rouff sought as they guided culinary tourists to restaurants where they could eat regional food that was not sophisticated. In their gastronomic tour of France, Curnonsky and Rouff emphasized the homey virtues of the food of the farmer's wives who they saw as artists in the kitchen (Ferguson 2004, 146). Women's cooking in France has long been seen as central to the preservation of culinary traditions. Here the legend of the mères lyonnaises places Janine and Aishah within a long line of women cooking traditional Lyonnais food in bouchon-style restaurants. For these two women, the legend is a legitimating narrative that emphasizes the importance of women's knowledge and skill and their ability to blur the boundaries between reproductive and productive labor to maintain a tradition that is under attack from the pressures and fast pace of modern life.

The Emotional Labor of Mothers

Sabrina and Danielle are another duo who run a small restaurant at the top of the Croix-Rousse *pentes* (slopes), in Lyon's Fourth Arrondissement. As I approached their restaurant, I noticed the small café tables set up outside, welcoming passersby to stop for a moment and enjoy the ambiance of the quiet street. Through the large glass windows, I could see the open kitchen where three women were bustling about. Two large communal tables dominated the room, with stacks of cookbooks off to one side. Only a countertop separated the kitchen from the dining area. What struck me immediately was that the kitchen looked like something you would find in a regular home with domestic appliances, a normal cooktop, and a home blender, and no industrial equipment, such as a gas range or a freestanding double-door oven. Sabrina, Danielle, and another woman who helps with serving preside over this welcoming space. On this first visit, I interviewed Sabrina and Danielle after the lunch service. As Sabrina continued to cook and clean up in the kitchen, she interjected periodically. I picked up on the dynamic between these two women from the way they finished each other's sentences; I could tell that they had been working together for a long time.

As I explained my project and began to ask my first questions, Danielle did not waste any time setting the tone. She explained to me that she and Sabrina work very much in the tradition of the mères lyonnaises: "We see ourselves as nurturing mothers. We like to think our door is open to everyone. It may no longer be workers who come to us but it is people from the neighborhood who come here." Danielle is referring to the sharp demographic shift in the Croix-Rousse neighborhood. Once home to the rebellious canut silk workers (Plessy and Challet 1988), this south-facing hill that dominates the city of Lyon experienced a period of gentrification in the early 2000s. With its hip cafés and bobo families (Brooks 2000), the architecture is one of the last standing testaments to the area's past as a working-class neighborhood. The four- or five-story buildings have tall windows to capture the light that was essential for the detailed work of weaving silk. The apartments still have the proportions of the Jacquard looms that would have monopolized most of the shared living and working quarters of the canuts. Historically, bars and cafés in the Croix-Rousse played an important role in the social life of the local residents—providing them spaces of leisure and community (Barre 2001). Although the demographics have changed, I observed on two separate occasions that Danielle and Sabrina's restaurant served the functions of community center and extension of the home—not so different from the mostly vanished cafés of the past. I noted this historic continuity of the social functions of restaurants as I watched children, groups of friends, and businesspeople gathering at the restaurant throughout the afternoon.

Danielle and Sabrina told me that they wanted a restaurant that would be like a second home for their children and their customers. Both women are mothers. Danielle has four children whose needs and schedules shape the business and her work life. On a second visit to the restaurant, one of Danielle's sons came in, sat down at a corner of a big table, and began to do his homework. After a while, one of the neighborhood kids came by to see if he could come out to play. After seeking his mother's permission, he was off down the narrow street with his friend.

Danielle went on to tell me that she felt their cooking and that of the mères lyonnaises was in the same tradition: "This is a cooking that is passed down instinctively through family rather than knowledge that can be learned in a school or a book." Danielle is talking about the apprenticeship that takes place between mother and daughter, which is started in childhood. The act of cooking requires constant observation and engagement (Sutton 2014, 124–15). The dishes that I saw and ate during my visits to this restaurant were often stews and braises. Unlike Aishah and Janine's bouchon, Danielle and Sabrina's cooking moved beyond the canons of Lyonnais cuisine and that of the bouchon to include Middle Eastern, Spanish, and Italian influences. I noted Danielle and Sabrina's large collection of cookbooks stacked neatly on the floor; this partly explains the culinary explorations evident in their dishes. In particular, the addition of spices like cumin and cinnamon move their stews into territory outside of Lyonnais flavor idioms that rarely include such spices. Lyonnais cuisine is more herb driven (thyme, parsley, bay leaves, etc.), and spices beyond pepper in savory dishes are rather limited. However, the culinary methods of slow cooking, simple sauces, and generous dishes served family style speak to the tradition of the mères lyonnaises. Although the ingredients are different, there is a base of techniques, such as braising, creating pan sauces from meat drippings, and careful seasoning with salt, that comes from the cooking these two women learned from their mothers and grandmothers. The cookbooks are the inspiration, but the skill is part of an oral tradition and an intuitive style of cooking.

Sabrina explained: "for me, to be a mère lyonnaise that means to welcome people and to share with them." Like with the previous example, this small restaurant creates value through embeddedness—people come not only to eat but to feel connected to their neighbors, the cooks, and culinary traditions. Sabrina and Danielle are not only mothers to their children but also for a moment to the diners who come through their doors and sit down together. As with Aishah and Janine, the mother discourse brings meaning and a connectedness that is tied to the reproduction of the domestic sphere in a special place that is open to the public. The legend of the mères lyonnaises legitimates and makes sense of this blurring between public and private lives.

Being a mother is not only about nourishing the body of others: I noticed that Sabrina and Danielle did not directly address the emotional labor that they do in their jobs, in addition to the physical labor of cooking. Arlie Hochschild brings to light the exchange value of emotional labor that, in this case, is part of the service and the price of the meal (1983, 7). This does not mean that these performances of emotional labor undermine the authenticity of Sabrina and Danielle's restaurant. On the contrary, the emotional labor of these two chefs adds value to the dining experience. This happens in the small gestures and comments that are part of the dining experience. When Sabrina lovingly serves the stew she has made and pats the shoulder of a regular customer who she can tell is having a rough day, she is doing emotional labor. When Danielle cooks up a special dessert for a customer who mentions her memories of eating clafoutis (a fruit and custard tart) at her mother's table, and serves it to her with a smile, she is engaging in care work. Using the notion of emotional labor in Hochschild's sense of the term (1983) to indicate the management of feelings to produce a physical public display of care reveals another layer of mothering and labor that occurs in the commercial space of the restaurant. Danielle and Sabrina did not articulate this part of their work as a commercial transaction, but they were aware that this work of caring is what makes their restaurant different from others—it's part of why people come back. Danielle and Sabrina articulated the emotional labor of cooking and serving food, which they talked about as motherly instincts, as a critical element of how they saw themselves working in the tradition of the mères lyonnaises.

In the context of this restaurant, emotional labor is gendered—when the cook who is a woman appears before her clients, there is a certain expectation that she will demonstrate care and emotional engagement (DeVault 1991, 239–40). The same is not true of male cooks, whose performances in the dining room seem to center on expertise and professionalism.

Mother and chef are not incompatible identities in this story. This framing of the living memory of the mères lyonnaises casts maternal behavior and instincts in a positive light. What it means to be a mother is multifaceted in both the past and the present. Eugénie Brazier was known as a severe mother, and her own troubled relationship with her son, which at one point ended in them only speaking to each other by phone for several years, was proof of her hard-headed character (Mesplède 2001, 36–37). At the same time, Brazier acted as a nurturing mother figure to guests whom she served tableside. This idea of the chef or cook as mother is malleable, and the legend of the mères lyonnaises is told in such a way that it supports each woman's unique notion of motherhood and what it means to cook food and to feed others.

Sabrina and Danielle's small restaurant on a quiet street in the Croix-Rousse is a place where the traditions of women's cooking in Lyon are both constant and always changing. Like the earlier mères lyonnaises, the restaurant was an empowering space for Sabrina and Danielle as they actively engaged the legend of the mères lyonnaises in their everyday performances of care for their families and their customers.

Role Models

Many of the younger women I interviewed had grown up in culinary families. Several women's fathers were MOF or Michelin-starred chefs, and they clearly had strong male role models. Nonetheless, the legend of the mères lyonnaises shaped the way they understood being a woman in the kitchen. This was certainly the case for Julie, a twenty-three-year-old Lyonnais and the daughter of a well-known chef in Lyon. Julie graduated with a culinary degree from the Institut Paul Bocuse, and she has apprenticed in a number of well-respected restaurants in France. Her family connections have helped her to gain valuable experience in the world of fine dining.

When I asked Julie about the mères lyonnaises, she told me that the stories of the mères lyonaises are very important to her: "you have to understand that for those women it was already really hard to make a mark in that period, to have your own business, to be a woman. But they succeeded in making their place, to make their mark, to say I am here, I do this kind of cuisine, I am known for this specific dish, for my quenelles. [. . .] Today we take them as an example, if they could do it, why can't we. It's great. I am an admirer."

For Julie, having strong female role models is inspirational but also critical to her goal of pursuing a career in haute cuisine: "There are not many women working at the top of the field, but women like Anne-Sophie Pic and Hélène Darroze really show what women can achieve. I just wish there were stronger networks of women working in haute cuisine. It is still very much a boys' club." In professional fields such as engineering, medicine, and law, there have been concerted efforts to encourage women's participation. Part of this has been improving mentorship opportunities between women. A number of studies have found that strong female role models and mentors help women to succeed in fields where they are underrepresented (Wiest 2009; Denner et al. 2005; Foor and Walden 2009). With regards to the field of mathematics, Leah McCoy notes that, "because female students are not aware of female mathematicians and scientists, they may internalize a belief that mathematics is not appropriate for women" (2001: 125). The situation is much the same in the contemporary French culinary world. Julie explained to me that the only female instructor she had at culinary school was in her accounting class. Of the young women I interviewed who were pursuing careers in haute cuisine, all mentioned that there were few women in kitchens when they were doing their internships and when they started working in restaurants.

In culinary professions, there are few female role models; this is particularly true at the top of the profession. The extreme underrepresentation of women in the most prestigious French awards and honors for culinary arts underlines women's minority status. Although cooking at the top levels is not everyone's aspiration, it is haute cuisine that is the focus of media attention and it is this elite world that makes many young chefs dream of what a career in the culinary arts could mean. For a lot of the people I interviewed, the MOF competition (see chapter 4) and the awarding of Michelin stars were the two top achievements that indicated excellence—these are also accolades that are celebrated in the news media throughout France.

Women are glaringly underrepresented in the MOF concours. This is just one of the symbolic forms of professional recognition where women are largely excluded. Symbolic representation is important because of the way in which this title is revered in the culinary world and in popular French culture (Kanter 1977). While Julie and I chatted, she told me how she noticed the prominent place of MOF chefs in popular culture: "TV shows always have a MOF, smiling in his chef's whites, it's always a man and he is an authority on French cuisine. Women on TV talk about home cooking, but people don't seem interested in that anymore." With the media rarely showing women in the culinary profession's top roles, it can be hard for women to imagine themselves in those positions. With so few women wearing the revered tricolor collar, which only MOF are allowed to wear, women in the culinary arts have a hard time imagining themselves as part of this exclusive and important group.

Michelin stars are another important form of recognition of achievement in the culinary arts. As noted earlier, some of the early recipients of the *Guide Michelin*'s coveted three-star status were Eugénie Brazier in 1933 for both of her restaurants, la mère Bourgeois in 1933, and then Marguerite Bise in 1951 in the first guide issued after World War II. There was a flurry of Michelin stars for French women during the interwar years, but then no three-star, female-led restaurants until 1986, when Sophie Bise regained her family's third star. The 2018 *Guide Michelin* recognized only one restaurant with a woman working as chef de cuisine, Anne-Sophie Pic, with its top award of three stars. Of the fifty new stars awarded, only two went to women. This prompted filmmaker Vérane Frédiani to start the Twitter hashtag #MichelinToo in protest of the guide's continued underrepresentation of women (Labbas 2018). Michelin stars can make or break a restaurant, and criticism is growing over the guide's lack of diversity in its awarding of stars (Reynolds 2018).

In 2011, World's 50 Best Restaurants, a restaurant-ranking organization, created the World's Best Female Chefs award (World's 50

Best Restaurants, n.d.). Some have argued that gendered awards are important for helping to improve representation of women in kitchens (Judkis 2018a, 2018b). However, there has been a backlash from those in the world of restaurant criticism and haute cuisine who find the prize sexist and demeaning to women. Amanda Kludt, the editor in chief of *Eater*, called the award "absurd" and "insulting" and noted that a male-only category did not exist (2019). Giving women a separate category has the effect of sidelining them and making them seem exceptional, rather than an accepted and legitimate part of a professional field.

In France, the male stereotype of the chef de cuisine is pervasive. As French journalist Vanessa Postec explains, "the chef is a man, this is a fact that is not disputed. Who other than a man to take charge of a brigade? Eminently masculine, resolutely military, the vocabulary of the kitchen is at the root of the issue" (Postec 2012, 27). Historically male dominated, the brigade system reproduces a rigid hierarchy with the chef de cuisine on top. As figure 1.2 shows, the organization of the brigade system is modeled on French military organization, using similar categories and language. The organization is patriarchal and is concentrated in a few positions at the top: the chef de cuisine and sous-chef are at the top commanding, while most kitchen workers are foot soldiers doing the daily drudge work of cleaning, prep, and putting out meals. It is only the few top positions that have authority and any artistic input; the rank and file must obey and follow in order to ensure efficiency. Charlotte Druckman notes that, "as relative newcomers to the professional kitchen elite, women often find themselves in subservient positions. And, since their lack of ability or desire to compete is presumed from the start, they are often hazed harder than the boys" (Druckman 2010, 30).

Julie explains to me her tactic for navigating culinary school and the many fine dining restaurants in which she has worked: "hard work all of the time, just as much as anyone else in the kitchen, but if someone wants to lift a heavy crate for you, why not." Julie felt it was important to prove herself through what she could produce and how she could keep up with all the others in the kitchen. She admitted that there were moments when she was treated differently because she was a *fille* (girl) but that she did not pay it much attention. It was not important. However, at some point it does become an important difference. This

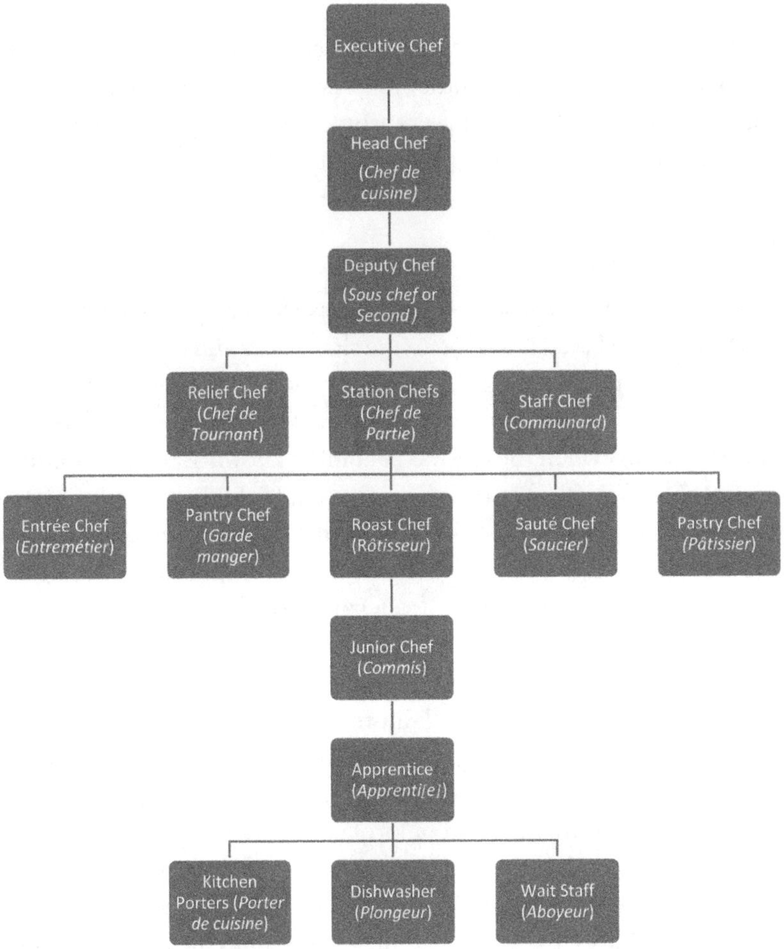

Figure 1.2: The brigade system.

is what I had set out to understand. Would there be a moment when Julie would progress no further with her career? Would she decide to drop out? For the moment, being a woman in the kitchen was not slowing Julie down.

Coming from a culinary family, Julie knew no other reality. As a Lyonnaise, Julie was also aware of what women had achieved in the culinary arts in her city. The mères lyonnaises show that it is possible for women to have a place at the top. This was echoed in the voices of women like Julie, who aspired to reach the heights of their profession.

Julie's case also shows that the legend of the mères lyonnaises can be channeled in many ways. You do not need to cook in the tradition of the bouchon or even be a mother to draw on this legend. It was enough for Julie to know that there were women who had come before her who had reached great heights. Why couldn't she do the same?

Conclusion

The more often I heard about the mères lyonnaises during my fieldwork, the more I paid attention to the similarities and differences in the ways in which people told this story. Many of the points were similar. In particular, the 1930s are presented as a magical moment in Lyonnais culinary history when the city was becoming known as the gastronomic capital of France. Women figured at the center of this important period as the guardians of "real" Lyonnais cuisine. Despite being a minority, these women demonstrated that they had an important place in the kitchens of Lyon. They are not relegated to the past. They are alive and well as part of an empowering legend.

Women cooking in Lyon activate the local history and legend of the mères lyonnaises in order to claim their place in the kitchen and in order to find ways of working that fit their objectives. For some women this means raising a family, for others it means producing food that is deeply tied to a long tradition of local cuisine, and for a younger generation of women it is about reaching the top of their profession. The legend of the mères lyonnaises brings value to the work of upholding culinary traditions, to care work, and it underlines the need to women to have role models in the kitchen. It helps women bring value to their productive and reproductive labor.

Nearly all the women I worked with during my time in Lyon situated themselves in relationship to the tradition of the cuisine des mères lyonnaises, placing themselves within a powerful female genealogy that celebrates women's contributions to the culinary arts in Lyon and France. Unlike in any other city in France, women have a unique status in Lyonnais restaurant kitchens due to the legacy of the mères.

2

DES FEMMES AVEC DU CARACTÈRE

Performing Gender and Authenticity in the *bouchon lyonnais*

As I walked into the Café du Jura, the autumn light streamed through the murky windows and made bright patterns on the sawdust-strewn floor. I looked up to see a serious-looking middle-aged man behind the bar wiping and putting away glasses. The interior of the restaurant seemed as if it had not changed since the 1960s. I told the man that I had called earlier and that I had an appointment with Madame Josserand. He grunted and indicated with his chin toward the back of the restaurant. My eyes followed this simple gesture, and there was Brigitte Josserand in her white apron drinking coffee and smoking a cigarette at a table near the entrance to the kitchen. I hesitantly started toward the back of the restaurant. Josserand's gravelly voice commanded me to sit down. I promptly obeyed. Many people in Lyon had told me about Brigitte Josserand: she is a known *femme avec du caractère* (a woman with character) in the tradition of the mères lyonnaises. This meant that she is a woman who is unafraid to raise her voice, take charge, and tell people what was on her mind. I was both intrigued and intimidated to be sitting across from this formidable woman whose nicotine-stained fingers tapped the table impatiently. Her eyes narrowed and fixed on me as she barked, "Et, alors?" (roughly, "So, what do you want?").

Figure 2.1: Brigitte Josserand relaxing after the service at her bouchon, Café du Jura.

As the interview began, I anxiously tried to think of how to ask Josserand what it means to be a femme avec du caractère. This felt like asking a bull how it feels to see red. I started off trying to warm up the conversation by asking some questions to learn how Josserand started cooking and the story behind this restaurant. The weathered woman sitting in front of me lit another cigarette and took charge of the story—the one *she* wanted to tell *me.* I straightened up and listened. What I quickly realized is that there are few questions you can ask in order to understand what it means to have character. You just have to experience it.

Some academics might call femmes avec du caractère a specific performance of gender (Butler 1999) or a way of doing gender (West and Zimmerman 1987). The performance of the femme avec du caractère allows women to shout, use rough language, and be direct in a way that has historically been unacceptable for women in polite society in France. These women who show their character are valued as productive cooks who are in control, making sure the work gets done well and that clients are well taken care of. How women create value around their labor is not simple. As I located women who cook and interviewed them in the places they work, I realized that the performance of femme avec du caractère takes places in a very specific setting that frames it and allows for transgressive behavior—the bouchon lyonnais.

As noted earlier, the bouchon is a historic Lyonnais eating establishment serving a rather codified repertoire of local dishes that are usually heavy on tripe and pork entrails. These restaurants have become a major tourist attraction for people looking for an authentic Lyonnais dining experience. Locals and tourists frequently contest this culinary authenticity. In this battle to protect and identify authenticity, a specific type of local cuisine is constructed. This chapter considers how women's cooking contributes to notions of culinary authenticity. It is through the dishes that women prepare and their performance of being a woman cooking in a bouchon that they legitimate their own labor and the authenticity of the bouchon. Many of these performances draw heavily on the traditions as the mères lyonnaises, who were women who prepared honest food that had strong connections to Lyon and its surrounding countryside.

The women that I bring together in this chapter represent Lyon and its traditions in different ways. Some attempt to carry on a tradition of hospitality that they see disappearing and a type of cuisine that is tied to a specific place. The space of the bouchon legitimates women as professional cooks. The bouchon also challenges stereotypes about who cooks in a restaurant. The presence of tourists allows women to define Lyonnais cuisine through their cooking and storytelling. In all of these narratives, food allows women to find value in their productive and reproductive labor.

The Bouchon as a Space of Authenticity

The rue Pizay is an unlikely street. It is just one road over from the magnificent Place des Terreaux, the site of the imposing town hall and an ornate nineteenth-century fountain depicting France as a woman reigning in four rearing horses that represent the four major French rivers. In contrast, rue Pizay is a narrow, dark street that still has cobblestones, which have twisted more than one high-heeled ankle. On the corner, there is a *tabac* (corner store selling cigarettes, postage stamps, and bus tickets). A music bookstore, a shoe shop, an administrative office for a bank, and a Tex-Mex restaurant are a few of the hodgepodge of businesses that occupy this throughway. Sandwiched between a theater company and a Latin nightclub is Chez Hugon. With its lace-curtained windows and door, this little restaurant is easy to overlook (fig. 2.2). It stands in stark contrast to the flashy burger joint across the street. The unsuspecting passerby does not realize that this a door to another time and space in Lyonnais history, but for people in the know, Chez Hugon is an institution—one of the last true bouchons lyonnais.

Figure 2.2: Exterior of Chez Hugon.

The first time I ate at Chez Hugon in the late 1990s, I realized that this was a special place as soon as I opened the door. I remember feeling surprised to find myself standing right in the middle of the dining room upon entry. I tried hard not to knock any of the diners with my coat or handbag. The place was packed, and people were sitting at their own small tables, but they were so close together that they might as well just be sitting all together. Laughter filled the room, and a red-faced server somehow navigated the tight space to deliver food to a table on the other side of the room from the kitchen. I noticed that there was no clear distinction between the kitchen and the dining room. From the small dining room with its checkered tablecloths, I could see Arlette Hugon at the *piano* (fig. 2.3) preparing poulet au vinaigre and *boudin aux pommes* (blood sausage with apples).[1] She was wearing a chef's coat and her blonde hair had been carefully blown out. Her cheeks were rosy from the heat of the kitchen; when she turned to me, her smile was warm and welcoming. It was clear to me that Arlette was all about hospitality. Her husband, Henri, was ensconced behind the bar, measuring out pots de vin. His nose was the deep red of someone who regularly enjoys wine, and his glasses were slightly fogged from the humidity of the tiny dining room that was packed with warm bodies and voices at full volume. Occasionally, Henri would toddle out from behind the bar to serve one of the heavy glass-bottomed bottles to a thirsty table and maybe take an order or two at the same time. It felt as if *maman* was cooking dinner and *papa* was entertaining the guests. Eating at Chez Hugon always made me feel like I belonged to Lyon. It is a space that brings together the locals and the foreigners, through food and wine binding everyone together to make them of the place.

Not all bouchons have women working in their kitchens, but those that do are often family-run establishments that reproduce the dynamics of the domestic sphere (Brunet 1997, 15). The layout of these bouchons re-creates the spatial structures and gender divisions of the home: the mother is in the kitchen, while the man of the house presides over the spaces in which the family eats and where guests are received. This is certainly the case at Chez Hugon.

Arlette Hugon explained to me that until the early 1990s there was really no separation between the kitchen and the dining room in her small restaurant—it was very *familiale* (homey). "Because of new hygiene regulations, we had to put up a wall between the kitchen and

Figure 2.3: Arlette Hugon at the *piano* in Chez Hugon. (Photo courtesy of Lucy Vanel)

the dining room." I observed that the wall is more of a partition: it does not reach the ceiling, and the *piano* is visible from the wide-open doorway. The smells and sounds of cooking permeate the restaurant. As the early twentieth-century gastronomic writer Rouff comments, these characteristics are particular of Lyonnais restaurants: "we can recognize them from the floors covered in wood shavings, that we are squeezed in eight to ten to a table, and finally most of all from the kitchen, which is in the middle of the place, always in plain sight" (Curnonsky and Rouff 1925, 26). He could have been describing Chez Hugon. Arlette's presence at the piano is an important part of the ambiance of this bouchon. Hugon lamented the ways in which "useless laws" had reordered her workplace—an encroachment of modernity on tradition in these historic spaces.

Until his death in 2013, Henri was in charge of the front of the house and the wine, a critical element in any bouchon. The bar acted as a sort of command station for Henri, where he would oversee the restaurant. He could often be found imbibing a glass of Beaujolais along with some of the regulars. Henri rarely crossed the threshold of the kitchen. Instead, Arlette would appear with scalding pots in hand, placing them down directly on the tables for customers to eat family style. As the lids were lifted, the diners would smile at the delicious promise of *poulet aux écrevisses* (chicken with a freshwater shrimp sauce) in its creamy pink sauce and generous pans full of fried sweetbreads. When I asked Arlette about this division of labor, she explains to me that this has always been the way in bouchons lyonnais: "The most famous mères lyonnaises like Brazier and before her la mère Fillioux served in this way, coming out of the kitchen to bring the food to the table in the pans and pots in which they had cooked it. This was the serving style in the great bourgeois households of Lyon. That's a thing of the past, but I want clients to feel at home."

For Hécate Vergopoulos (2014), when a person sits down at a table in a bouchons, "[we] pay to capture the uncapturable parts of a culture and its heritage. This 'we' is the tourist, who wants to experience, as if through a keyhole, [. . .] that which is invisible in a culture that which is no more or which is too much, too vast, too intense, too different" (148). The bouchon lyonnais is an intimate look into something deeply Lyonnais that barely still exists in Lyonnais homes, spaces to which few outsiders would have access. For tourists and Lyonnais alike, the bouchon is a place to experience Lyonnais culture and history. The consumable culture of the bouchons places value in the intimacy of the domestic—it is a place that valorizes the culinary talents and care work of women. According to Wilk, "Metaphorically, home cooking means a cuisine grounded in familiar shared history and in common knowledge of places and people. Home cooking is always concerned with quality, because people you care about will eat the meal" (2006, 202). The domestic framing of the bouchon within a coherent narrative of traditional gender divisions of labor that is legible to clients makes women's cooking a form of care work. Women are more than legitimate cooks in this context.

These small dining establishments initially catered to the silk workers who were the engine of the city's economy in the sixteenth and seventeenth century (Rouèche 2018, 37). The successor of the sixteenth-century cabaret, the bouchon was a place to buy wine to be consumed at the establishment or to take away. It was where workers could get a bite to eat at most hours of the day. These were important social centers in neighborhoods such as the Croix-Rousse, where male workers would congregate during breaks from work but also before and after for food and socializing (Mayol 1994, 38). The bouchon was also a place where merchants could go to do business and to eat when they were away from home. The mâchon, a light morning meal in which local wine features prominently, remains an emblematic nod to Lyon's past as a capital of textile manufacturing.

Today, the bouchon still acts as an important third space in their neighborhoods. The bar is a focal point for male socializing—men will come in for a glass of Beaujolais and a bit of sausage while they catch up on the latest neighborhood gossip with the *propriétaire* (the owner) or barkeep. There is almost always an eclectic, homey décor of family photos on the wall and knickknacks on any flat surface and small shelves along the walls. The tables are packed in tightly, and literally rubbing elbows with other diners is common.

Women's presence as cooks lends to the bouchons' credibility and authenticity. In this case, "authenticity" refers to a nostalgic notion of Lyonnais cuisine from a time before fast-food and chain restaurants, when women's home cooking was seen as the epitome of honest, tasty food. The presence of women signals to customers that the food is more likely to have been prepared in house from scratch and with some degree of care. There is a popular notion that women are guardians of culinary traditions in Lyon. This is not a new idea. In the 1930s, the burgeoning field of gastronomic literature helped to put the cuisine des mères on the map by juxtaposing women's cooking as the polar opposite of cuisine des grandes palaces, a rather homogeneous, sauce-driven cuisine that was ubiquitous in these restaurants throughout France.

Authenticity is a slippery and contested term when it comes to cuisine and bouchons. Authentic cuisine is somewhat a contradiction of terms because of the constantly changing nature of cuisines, which adapt to new technologies, social realities, and movements of people and goods (Sims 2009). From the setting of the scene with red-and-white checked tablecloths and presentation of classic dishes served by the cook at the table, most bouchons actively cultivate the signs and symbols of Lyonnais culinary traditions. The dining room is a space that creates an air of authenticity (MacCannell 1973) and where the mère and the père perform authenticity—this is the front stage where diners witness and experience the performance as they consume their food, the space, and the service (Goffman 1959).

In the bouchons where there is some separation between the dining room and the kitchen, few are privy to the backstage kitchen activities. When I did get a glimpse of some bouchon kitchens, I noticed some cooks were using frozen foods, pressure cookers, and other time-saving devices that can be seen as counter to the slow-cooked essence of bouchon cuisine. Just like their domestic counterparts, the professional mères find ways to ease the heavy burden of scratch cooking. There are different degrees of convenience and corner cutting, and the impact of these methods on the quality of the final product is debatable. What is challenged in questioning the authenticity of some bouchons is the backbreaking work of women in both the domestic and professional kitchen and what time-saving tools mean for the care work of mothering. What became clear to me was that the authenticity of a bouchon largely depends on how diners perceive the performance of authenticity and whether they accept or reject it.

A Battle over Authenticity

On the center of the front door of Chez Hugon there is a sticker with the well-known Lyonnais puppet Gnafron raising a glass (fig. 2.4)—this indicates that the restaurant has been certified as an "Authentique Bouchon Lyonnais."[2] The Association de défense des bouchons lyonnais was started in 1997 as culinary tourism began to increase in Lyon. Association founder Pierre Grison saw a need to guide tourists to authentic bouchons, serving quality food because restaurant critics, other journalists, and the chamber of commerce started to question the authenticity of some restaurants as more establishments began to call themselves bouchons ("Pierre Grison" 2012). Not all of these new offerings served quality food and wine. This protest against fraudulent copycats attest to the bouchon's centrality as an important cultural form representing Lyonnais identity and well worth defending.

Then, in 2012, the Association les bouchons lyonnais was created in conjunction with the local chamber of commerce and tourism office to safeguard the Lyonnais culinary tradition of the bouchon, both the

Figure 2.4: Plaques from the two competing bouchon certification programs. Robust culinary tourism in Lyon has made the authenticity of these establishments an important cultural and economic issue.

type of food served and the establishment. This association created a certification claiming "to guarantee the respect of Lyonnais culinary traditions, the quality and origins of local products, house-made cuisine that is made at the establishment, a warm welcome, and an ambiance that is typical of the historic setting" (L'Association les bouchons lyonnais n.d.).[3] This new certification created two camps, and a rift between establishments. The chamber of commerce wanted a more transparent process that had specific criteria to meet in order to be able to display the association's plaque. Many restaurant owners took issue with this new group because they charge 130 euros to join and 380 euros for the enameled plaque. Others worried that the founder of the group, Christophe Margin, was creating a club for his friends, not a certification that was protecting the authenticity of these historic dining establishments (Lamy 2012).

What is at stake with these certifications? Who gets to control and define authenticity and its recognition that will determine who profits financially? The bouchon lyonnais is central to the city's culinary identity. Unlike haute cuisine, bouchons are reasonably priced and accessible—a sort of anti–haute cuisine. They appeal to a wider audience, and many more tourists eat in bouchons than in Michelin-starred restaurants. The problem is that restaurants that do not respect the cuisine and ambiance of the historic bouchons use this title and undermine the work of those committed to upholding tradition. It is hard for the uninitiated to tell the difference between an authentic bouchon and a tourist trap. Arlette Hugon has been a vocal spokesperson for defending the bouchon, but she also does not think either the chamber of commerce or the tourism office should make a business of certifications.

As Lyon continues to assert itself as the gastronomic capital of France, tensions have arisen over what culinary culture should represent the city. SIRHA, the restaurant and hospitality trade show that takes place on the outskirts of Lyon each year, along with the Bocuse d'Or, an international culinary competition, play a critical role in tying Lyon's culinary culture to haute cuisine. The numerous Michelin-starred restaurants and the presence of Paul Bocuse's restaurant empire have also contributed to this high-end vision of food in Lyon. The homey bouchon stands both in stark contrast to fancy Lyonnais food and at the center of a strongly supported originating myth about local food. In this origin story, women like Arlette Hugon have long had an important place as upholders of tradition; they ground all Lyonnais cuisine in history and give it a strong local identity.

Mothers Who Yell

In the kitchen, Arlette Hugon is one of the more soft-spoken mères but there is more than one way to be a woman in a kitchen. *Les mères qui gueulent* (mothers who yell) are part of the local legends about women in Lyonnais kitchen. These were and are still today women who keep order over their charges in the sometime unruly space of the kitchen. The mère qui gueule is a Lyonnais archetype: she rails against her kitchen staff, keeping them in line, but when she comes through the dining room door she is calm and welcoming. Early on in my research, I was intrigued to understand all the different ways one could perform femininity in the kitchen.

At the start of our interview, I asked Brigitte Josserand if she considered herself a mère lyonnaise. She made it clear to me that this is not a title one assigns to oneself but is one that is bestowed. A number of local publications, restaurant critics, and her customers had declared Josserand a mère. I asked why she had been grouped into this category. She said that it probably had to do with the fact that she runs a bouchon and that she cooks all the Lyonnais classics from *tablier du sapeur* (fried tripe) to *cervelle de canut* (a fresh cheese mixed with cooked onions, named after its resemblance to a silk weaver's brains). Although the most famous mères of the past were known for their refined culinary techniques and rich cuisine bourgeoise, the term "mère" now seems to encapsulate more than just a specific style of cooking.

Brigitte explained that she had a certain character that was in keeping with how a mère is supposed to act in the kitchen and with her clients. When I probed further to understand what she meant by this remark, Josserand went on to explain that she likes to work alone because she does not get on well with other restaurant staff: "J'aime gueuler" (I like to yell). She told me that her yelling did not go over well with employees, and she just needed to focus on cooking. Josserand told me when it comes to the front of the house she is both welcoming and stern with her clients: "I treat them no differently than I would my son. Everyone knows who is the boss around here." Customers' expectations are set before they enter the restaurant. A sign on the door reads

> To my customers,
>
> Working with particular respect for ingredients, mealtime must remain a pleasure rather than a constraint.
>
> Also, I would like to invite customers who are in a hurry to chew on a sandwich or something they can eat on the go.
>
> My cooking is not made to fit in a microwave oven, which I don't have.
>
> Here, quality cooking has no idea what it means to be in a hurry.
>
> La Chef Brigitte Josserand
>
> (sign on the door at Café Jura, October 7, 2014)

Josserand makes it clear that customers need a certain frame of mind—one that puts food and the act of dining before other worldly concerns. This tone is certainly different from other restaurant settings where staff bend over backward to fulfill the customer's every whim. Josserand's approach is similar to that of Aishah and Janine, who also value slowness (see chapter 1).

Many of the original mères working at the turn of the twentieth century were women known for their authoritarian assertiveness in the kitchen and in the dining room. Paul Bocuse, when recalling his time as an apprenti in Eugénie Brazier's kitchen, called her "la mère qui gueulait." She was the queen of the mères qui gueulent: her kitchen staff reported that she yelled so vigorously at times that they needed to bring her a chair for fear she would pass out (Mesplède 2001, 36). She worked her cooks hard, demanding perfection, and yelling when this was not achieved. When Brazier presented dishes to her clients at the table, her demeanor was both motherly and stern. This change in her behavior corresponds with her movement from the working-class space of the kitchen to the bourgeois space of the dining room, which would have very different norms around gender behavior. Brazier and other women created a gender stereotype that both demands women in command in kitchens to assert themselves and also allows them to express their more feminine side, particularly in the dining room. These multifaceted gender performances are particularly common in the spaces of the bouchons lyonnais. From what I could see, Josserand was following the Brazier role model here.

In the long line of the mères qui gueulent in Lyonnais restaurant history, one who particularly stands out in this group is Léa Bidault, who was known as much for her cooking as for her strong character. Born in 1908 in Le Creusot in Saône-et-Loire, a village 160 kilometers from Lyon, Bidault learned to cook in a bourgeois household before working in a number of Lyonnais restaurants. In 1938, Léa opened her first restaurant in rue Tupin in the First Arrondissement. In 1943, she relocated to La Voûte, another small restaurant in the same neighborhood. She was noted for her "generous, rich, warm, simple but efficient cuisine" (Rouèche 2018, 238).

When doing her shopping in the market on the quai Saint-Antoine, Léa famously pulled a cart with a sign on it reading "Beware: weak woman with a strong mouth." Bidault made a public statement about her transgression of gender norms in the kitchen and at the market.

The social norm for women in the workplace was docility: "women were supposed to be silent" (Perrot 1978, 9). Acting out of character for a woman of her time was only one way in which Léa blazed a new trail: in 1978, she was the first woman to join the Toques blanches, a male-dominated network of prominent local chefs. She headed into territory that was largely uncharted by women in the postwar period.

Josserand, Bidault, and the mères lyonnaises, more generally, are women who "undo gender," which is something that happens when men or women do not fully follow traditional scripts (Deutsch 2007). There are other areas of work where women blur gender lines or play on masculine strengths as well as motherly stereotypes: in Barbara Pini's study of agricultural leaders, women both conceal their femininity through their dress and enacting some aspects of conventional masculinity (i.e., doing dirty work), but they also preserved their femininity by being "nurturing, communicative, and empathic" leaders (Pini 2005, 82). Similar to the ways in which the mères lyonnaises perform gender in the space of the bouchon, this undoing is not complete and categories are not entirely ruptured. We should care about these kinds of undoing of gender. They are the instances in which traditional and historic categories, which are often repressive and limiting, are negotiated. This makes room for new behaviors, positions of power, and a freedom of expression that is at times within and at other times beyond the accepted doing of gender. Women like Bidault and Josserand order people around, yell at their kitchen staff, and claim a central place in their restaurants and communities. Through these performances the undoing of gender in the historically male-dominated space of the professional kitchen becomes a place where women can express themselves, take up a powerful position, and be recognized for their skill. At the same time, these women are playing off the powerful trope of the stern mother and they are in no way accused of acting like men.[4]

Becoming a Mère

One does not necessarily start off as a mère—this can be something that a woman becomes. Early on in her adult life, Josserand decided to change careers. In France, there is a strong sense that you are born into a specific position and that is where you stay because class mobility is limited (Chauvel 2006). However, this is why it is important to hear personal narratives—individuals have agency, and some, like Josserand, choose to challenge class and gender norms. Brigitte, a native of Lyon, came from a working-class family and her first job was as an office clerk. At the age of eighteen, she married Henri Josserand. They loved eating out in bouchons, so after a year of marriage, they decided to buy a bouchon of their own.

Henri had a *coup de coeur* (fell head over heels in love) with the Café du Jura when he went to see it. This was a bouchon that dated back to 1867, where women had always run the kitchen. Only nineteen years old when she took over this historic kitchen on October 1, 1974, Josserand had no professional culinary experience. She learned to cook on the job from the previous owner's wife and with the help of her mother-in-law, who had cooked in the homes of some of Lyon's wealthiest families. During her summer vacations, Josserand would work at other restaurants to refine her culinary skills. She noted that, "at the time, there was no structured path to training. Women learned from other women."

When culinary training became professionalized at the end of the nineteenth century, there was an explicit belief that women were not worth training: "Our ideas from the past are still the same today, and we still think that it is impossible, even with the best training, for women to obtain perfection [in the culinary arts]" (Drouard 2004, 102). Until the 1980s, it was unusual to find women in culinary classes or training programs (Marie 2014, 175). While some might assume that women learned to cook through oral tradition and informal intergenerational apprenticeship, historian Yvonne Verdier (1979) argues that in traditional rural culture in France there was little culinary apprenticeship between mother and daughter: feeding the family was the exclusive work of the mother, work that was only taken on when a woman became a mother herself and had to nourish her family: "Cooking is an art that should be discovered alone just like with sex; the two are both improvised at the same time" (58). Verdier continues on to say that rural culture does not really consider a woman to be mature, sexually and culinarily, until after the birth of her first child. If she lives with her mother-in-law, she must finally be left alone to assume her role as the nurturer, the provider of food. In this way food and women's power were connected to reproduction (Ginsburg and Rapp 1991). Most of the original mères lyonnaises were farm laborers from the countryside surrounding Lyon, and they came from rural cultures similar to the one that Vidier describes. It is likely they had come to the city without much prior culinary knowledge. So how did these women learn to cook?

Claude Fischler (1990) argues that urbanization changed family structures, led to the salaried work of women, and transformed the way in which culinary knowledge was handed down (146). Urban jobs in bourgeois homes took cooking out of the context of reproduction; there is still the element of feeding a family, but the personal and reproductive connection is severed. In this context of domestic labor that removes women from their immediate families, they function within the logics of craft apprenticeship, a topic explored in the next chapter. As women moved from their homes to paid domestic labor and then to restaurant work, they began to create a professional role—they started to pass along their knowledge to those who worked with them. The women Josserand learned from were passing on culinary knowledge from one generation to the next, but not necessarily within their own homes or kin groups. However, through oral and embodied apprenticeship, they were keeping bourgeois cuisine alive as it moved from private households to the semipublic space of the restaurant. This move from paid domestic labor in private households to restaurant work was not without its trials.

It was the generation before Josserand who shifted from domestic kitchens to the back of the house in restaurants. As they tried to blaze a trail toward women's professional roles in kitchens, it was evident that the path was still not clear. Josserand explained that for women to succeed they needed to have a strong character: "you had to be able to assert yourself [*s'imposer*]," because there was so much prejudice in the kitchen at the time. Josserand attributed women's underrepresentation in restaurant kitchens to the "bande de macho" (bunch of machos) who dominated: "forty or fifty years ago, women had to pay their own way. To claim your spot, you had to get your elbows out to take your place amongst the men." In addition, when she started cooking, it was expected that women would continue to look after the children and the household even if they worked outside the home: "Men are always waiting for women to trip up. They have this idea that we are weaker than them; when, in fact, we have more endurance. We have to maintain our family life and our work life. We have two jobs that we do every day. The whole problem is there."

As Lyonnais women moved into paid labor cooking in restaurants, they brought with them the constructed social image of the woman as caregiver and the notion that women are the unpaid labor that feeds the family. Even though women had been paid for their culinary work in bourgeois households, there was still a domestic aura to the work that caused women to be paid less than men in restaurants. The kitchens of establishments like the bouchon complicated the relationships between the socially acceptable roles for women in the home and the workplace. The bouchon, with its unclear boundaries between domestic and professional spaces, afforded women opportunities to do work that would not be possible in other establishments.

Motherhood

The double expectation that a woman should be a mother and also be a central figure in the family business was one of Josserand's bigger challenges; reconciling family life and being the restaurant's only cook was not always easy. When I conducted this interview, I was seven months pregnant. I believe this is one of the reasons that Brigitte Josserand opened up to share her own experience of balancing pregnancy, work, and maternity: "I worked up until the day I gave birth. My water broke during the lunch service. I remember clearly that I was in front of the *piano* cooking. I finished the service and then went directly the to hospital to give birth. I was back in front of the *piano* a few days later. I had to be. Who else was going to cook? How else was my family going to make ends meet?" Brigitte told me that work was difficult when her son, Benoît, was young, and this was the reason why she and her husband decided not to have any other children.

This story of balancing the labor of maternity with the labor of the kitchen is one of the major hurdles that many women in culinary professions face. The lack of social support to allow women to take time off at moments when their health and that of their child is most vulnerable is glaringly obvious in this account, and these issues were a common theme in the experiences of other women who participated in my research. Women like Brigitte chose to be self-employed or employed in family businesses so that they would be able to define the way in which they worked in the kitchen and, in some cases, so they could set their own hours in order to have the flexibility to raise children. The same self-employment that offered them some freedom also created gender-specific difficulties. In small family-run restaurants, there is rarely another chef to cover during a sixteen-week maternity leave, and few establishments of this type could afford to pay for maternity leave and the additional labor of a substitute chef.[5]

These stories hit home with me. At the time I was conducting the majority of the fieldwork for this project, I was pregnant and then had an infant to care for. I had been in the second half of my pregnancy during my short stint in culinary school and while apprenticing in restaurants, and my own embodied experience helped me to understand what it was like to do hard physical labor in long shifts while pregnant. My feet and back still ache when I think back to my time in those hot, stuffy kitchens. Once my son was born, I longed to get back into a kitchen, but I could not fathom managing the needs of my infant, my bodily functions such as lactation, and back-breaking work. I had the good fortune of a three-month paid maternity leave from my research position, but the women I interviewed would never have been able to step away from their kitchens for this long without bankrupting their businesses. This precarity was one reason why some women I talked to made a conscious choice not to have children or to leave restaurant work when they did. I came to have a deep respect for both choices and realized that every woman has her own path to professional success and personal fulfillment.

Regardless of whether women have children or not, motherhood is a performance that female cooks in bouchons are expected to enact through their food and presence in the kitchen and dining room. Brigitte Josserand told me that clients come to her restaurant looking for their mothers' and their grandmothers' food. There is nostalgia for this food that people have stopped making in their homes: "People don't cook or eat as much at home anymore, but women used to cook a lot." Josserand noted that this nostalgia brings customers to her restaurant and also brings many people to the kitchen: "If you talk to any big chef and ask them why they are in the kitchen, they will say something about the memory of their mother or grandmother's cooking."[6] These comments started me wondering about how the desire for a glorified past was keeping the bouchon afloat with an aura of authenticity, and at the same time how nostalgia ossified what it means to be a woman in a restaurant kitchen. Could women only be motherly? Was this nostalgia driving the kind of food women are expected to cook? Did the myth of cuisine des mères lyonnaises relegate women to producing comfort food with strong connections to the domestic sphere?

Melissa Caldwell (2006) describes nostalgia cuisine as tied to place but also to a distant and recent past: "[it is] a form of time travel" (98). The temporal nature of culinary nostalgia is important for the ways in which the Lyonnais construct cuisine des mères and women's continued role in the production of this food that is emblematic of the golden era in Lyonnais culinary history. Even if most diners who now seek out the cuisine des mères did not experience the original popularity of this food in the 1930s, this is a past, as an unattainable place, experienced or imagined. According to Holtzman, "viewing nostalgia as a re-experiencing of emotional pasts it may also be seen as a longing for times and places that one has never experienced" (2006, 367). Slow-cooked meals made by professional mères satisfies diners' longing for their childhoods, or for the flavors they had hoped their childhoods would have held, and idea of a time in the past when friends and family still gathered to spend important moments together at the table, keeping alive disappearing traditions. Historian Yves Rouèche reflects that "the Mère Lyonnaise has become a rare creature who will soon only appear in the Lyonnais history books" (2018, 62).

As I explored the bouchons of Lyon and heard the stories of women from different generations, I began to wonder if the present notion of the motherly cook was a sort of longing for a past that continuously reproduces gender inequality. While nostalgia and longing for mothers remains a strong part of the discourse around la cuisine des mères, it is not the only force that shapes women's professional cooking in Lyon.

Playing the Part

When I went to speak with Florence Périer at her restaurant, she warmly welcomed me after the lunch service. Her little dog jumped up and curled into a ball on her lap as we settled into a cozy booth near the kitchen. Florence Périer presides over the Café du Peintre, a bouchon in the Sixth Arrondissement. Like the Café du Jura, the Café du Peintre reproduces the gendered division of labor of the home: Florence minds the kitchen and her son runs the front of the house. She will often come out to serve dishes and socialize with customers, many of whom are regulars. Périer explains to me that she considers them an extension of her family. Early on in our conversation, Florence began to tell me how she works in the tradition of the mères lyonnaises, from the dishes she serves to the type of establishment she runs. I probed further to understand what she meant when she called her restaurant a bouchon and nominated herself as a mère, something Josserand had been hesitant to do.

Périer told me that she still serves the mâchon. This was originally a meal for the canuts who had started their work day at five in the morning and stopped at nine for a meal in a bouchon. Later this became a meal for not only the canuts but also for businessmen, bankers, notaries, and other workers (Roueche 2018, 42). The mâchon is one of the marks of authenticity for a true bouchon. It transforms the bouchon into a third place: a place that is neither home nor work. The bouchon was an informal meeting place that is critical in this case to working-class men's social lives and the social fabric of the neighborhood (Oldenburg 1989).

Périer keeps her restaurant running smoothly, but she does so without raising her voice. She is direct but warm and motherly to her customers, apprentices, and the front-of-the-house staff. Périer is a kind and patient mother. Listening to Florence talk about her philosophy of running a restaurant, I came back to thinking about how no two mothers were entirely alike. There was room to personalize the construct of the mère lyonnaise.

"I do not have time for fancy cuisine. That is not what people come here for." It seemed to me that Périer was defining herself as a cook very much in opposition to the tendencies of haute cuisine, with its polished dishes and service, and museum-like atmosphere. Instead, the Café du Peintre had the feeling of home—from the food to the ambiance. However, Périer represents a number of contradictions, with one foot in haute cuisine, in her previous restaurant experience working in the front of the house of her family's restaurant, and the other in the most traditional form of Lyonnais cuisine. Her participation in the Association des toques blanches lyonnaises is one example of the way Florence straddles two worlds.

Started in 1936 as a fellowship of chefs who "as custodians of the culinary traditions of Lyon, [. . .] keep our traditions alive across the gastronomy scene from the mâchon, to the mères (women chefs), bouchons, the Halles de Lyon, and the Michelin-starred master chefs—all members are committed to great food, and promoting our city's cuisine and regional produce" (Toques blanches n.d.). Men working in fine dining establishments dominate this association, which only admitted its first woman in 1978. It currently has four female members out of a total membership of more than 110 chefs. Of the four women, three—Brigitte Josserand, Florence Périer and Catherine Roux—represent la cuisine des mères lyonnaises in bouchon-style restaurants. At the association's website, a special section recites the history of the organization, and the importance of the mères lyonnaises in the local cuisine is mentioned here: "The influence of the 'Mères' (women chefs nicknamed 'Mothers') on the history of gastronomy in Lyon was such that their legacy still lives on in our restaurants today," and these women are a continuing source of inspiration for Toques blanches chefs (Toques blanches n.d.). The selection of Josserand, Périer, and Roux is extremely arbitrary and somewhat political because these women all represent a very specific type of Lyonnais cuisine associated with tradition and the past. The choice of these three women represents a continuation of men's control of this historic narrative about women in professional kitchens and who should be celebrated as the keepers of tradition. The Toques blanches frame the contributions of the mères lyonnaises and their cooking as a nostalgic reference or relic, rather than an innovative source of the evolution of Lyonnais cuisine; women's participation in Lyonnais cuisine is valid only if it remains with a solid foot in the past. While the participation of women in networks like the Toques blanches is important for their recognition, the selection of only a certain culinary style is limiting and relegates women to a specific and inaccurate stereotype. This may be why women have also sought to create their own associations.

After she was refused admission to La Société mutualiste des cuisiniers de Paris in 1975, Parisian chef Annie Desvignes started her own women's group, the Association des restauratrices-cuisinières. Women's exclusion from professional groups continued on until the early 2000s, when the Association des maîtres cuisiniers de France refused membership to chef Anne-Sophie Pic (Chevallier 2018, 119). Professional culinary women have formed a number of their own associations, but none of them have had the explicit scope of promoting female chefs and their work. Les Nouvelles mères cuisinières, founded in 2001 by Hélène Darroze, Ariane Daguin, Elena Arzak, Christine Ferber, Caroline Ferber, Caroline Rostang, Judith Baumann, and Léa Linster is an all-star lineup of already well-known female chefs. Darroze declared that "we are not suffragettes, just a bunch of girlfriends who like to get together in the four corners of the world to simmer some good women's cooking between some good women" (Gaudry 2004). Clearly not out to incite a feminist revolution in the kitchen, Darroze and her girlfriends refuse to engage the politics of women's exclusion in the culinary world. This is the privilege of women who are already well-known, who have Michelin stars, and many of whom come from restaurant dynasties.

Figure 2.5: Florence Périer at the Café du Peintre.

Florence Périer's participation in a group like the Toques blanches is important because women need to have a place at these powerful tables. Discussions that will change gender bias, exclusion, and discrimination need to happen when men and women are part of the same forum. It will be interesting to see if the Toques blanches open up membership to more women who represent other types of Lyonnais cuisine.

At the end of the interview, when I asked Périer if I could take her photo, she quickly put on a fresh white chef's coat that was emblazoned with the Toques blanches logo (fig. 2.5). Her belonging to this elite group as well as the command of her own kitchen are important for this chef who defends Lyonnais culinary traditions with each dish of tripe she serves.

Representing Lyonnais Cuisine

Lucy Vanel is American, but Lyon has been her home since 2000. This is part of the story that Vanel tells to a group of tourists as she leads them up the pentes of the Croix-Rousse on their way to the bustling market along the boulevard at the top of the hill.

> When I moved here, along with a healthy obsession for la Cuisine Lyonnaise that was originally just a hobby, I had no idea that I was going to be working in the field I am in now. I struggled for six years in various office jobs where my experience and diplomas did not translate, which left me wanting more control over my professional advancement. My decision to take the CAP came from a business plan once the decision was made to open my own business, where the idea at the beginning was to legally be able to sell American-style pastry to local restaurants in addition to teaching cooking lessons. I abandoned the American pastry idea once I learned the French repertoire, however.

The CAP is a diploma that is required for practitioners and teachers in skilled trades in France. Lucy studied on her own, rigorously working her way through the curriculum, and seeking help from friends working in the industry. She is extremely proud of having passed the exam as an outside candidate, which she feels demonstrates her strong fundamental knowledge of basic techniques in French pastry—"cooking or pastry, at the level of the CAP, is a craft. A CAP is an entry-level

Figure 2.6: Lucy Vanel at Plum Lyon cooking school. (Photo courtesy of Lucy Vanel)

certification, where candidates are expected to grasp basic technique. It is not all that artistic or creative, because you have to have basic technique."

Plum Lyon is Lucy's cooking school, standing halfway up the Croix-Rousse hill. She offers cooking classes that focus on classic French pastry and seasonal market fare. The majority of her clients are Americans and other English-speaking foreigners. Passionate about Lyonnais culinary history, Lucy has researched the topic in depth. She actively incorporates her historic knowledge into her cooking classes and tours. This adds another dimension to her classes, and her students clearly enjoy learning the local lore and insider details behind the dishes they are learning to prepare. When I sat in on a class, it was clear to me that Lucy's students view her as a local expert and respect her knowledge and skill.

When Vanel was just starting her business, she had a baby, which made it much more challenging. Lucy decided to start her own business because she had no other choice. She found that it was not possible to work through the establishment: her foreign education and work experience were not recognized in France. She also needed a way to make a living that would give her the flexibility to raise her child. Lucy confided that the real barriers to starting her own business were in her own mind. There were no real external obstacles or blatant forms of exclusion once she learned to navigate French business regulations.

Lucy has found her calling: she gives private and small-group cooking classes in the gastronomic capital of France to the many foreigners who come to the city to immerse themselves in the local culinary culture. Most of these foreigners have a limited command of French, so they are grateful to find an instructor who speaks fluent English. Indeed, few local cooking schools aimed at tourist students have instructors who speak proficient English; nor do they understand that their clients want to learn more than just how to prepare a dish. Plum Lyon's Trip Advisor reviews show how much Lucy's clients appreciate her focus on the history of Lyon and how it connects to its unique cuisine.[7]

Now with her business well-established, Vanel has started to work on creating bridges between the U.S. and French culinary worlds, with a focus on women's advancement. This was one of the main drivers for Vanel's engagement as a founding member of France's first chapter of Les Dames d'Escoffier. In the early 1970s, Carol Brock, then the Sunday food editor at the *New York Daily News*, set about creating the first U.S. organization for professional culinary women. She was inspired by Boston's Les Dames des Amis d'Escoffier, a dining and philanthropic society of women formed in 1959 in response to the all-male Les Amis d'Escoffier. Brock's main mission was to raise the image and presence of women working in male-dominated food and wine industries. As of 2018, Les Dames d'Escoffier had forty-two chapters in the United States, Canada, the United Kingdom, France, and Mexico, with over 2,400 members. It remains to be seen if Les Dames d'Escoffier will continue to be a U.S.-dominated organization or whether it will gain traction with French women working in the culinary arts. Vanel hopes it will provide "a support network between women leaders in gastronomy with a goal of promoting the advancement of women in culinary careers."

It may seem counterintuitive to see a transplant to Lyon as a representative of the local cuisine, but Lucy Vanel, an amateur historian and culinary professional, is a very legitimate spokesperson. She welcomes tourists, teaches them about the history of the local culinary traditions, and engages them in the current practices. At times, it takes a person on the outside to see a complex object as a whole. This is what Vanel does when she takes her foreign students to the Croix-Rousse market to choose their ingredients and when she brings them back to her teaching kitchen. Lucy tells the story of women cooking in Lyon, and she lives the reality of a woman cooking professionally. Her example shows people from all over the important role of women in Lyonnais cuisine.

Production, Reproduction, and the Performance of Authenticity

"Women have always worked!" the feminist historian Sylvie Schweitzer declared during one of our meetings. She was also restating the title of her acclaimed book on the history of women and labor in France: *Les femmes ont toujours travaillé: Une histoire du travail des femmes aux XIXe et XXe siècles* (2002). Schweitzer told me I just had to know where to find them. The women I was looking for were hidden in kitchens that resembled those of their homes and they were engaged in both productive and reproductive labor that few considered worthy of the written record. The women in this chapter show how women today continue on in traditions of the past by balancing motherhood, care work, and cooking. The performance of being a mother and a woman avec du caractère allows women into the space of the restaurant kitchen, which is often reserved for men. These women's emotional labor also adds value to the experience of dining in a cozy bouchon.

At first, I misread the mères' heavy-handed gender performances as women trying to act like men. As I became more familiar with the history of women's work in Lyonnais restaurants, I came to see this behavior as an enactment of specific type of femininity that allowed women to be seen as productive in the professional kitchen without having to become men, so to speak. While playing the part of the mères lyonnaises allows women to behave in ways that are often associated with masculine behavior, yelling, giving orders, and laying down the law, this role of mère also affords women the opportunity to legitimate their work in the space of the professional kitchen, a place where their presence is frequently challenged. The veil of domesticity is part of a performance of authenticity that is critical for many of the bouchons where women work—the familial atmosphere and intimacy of these dining establishments is what sets them apart. The modern-day mères that I have presented here are often lauded as the keepers of culinary traditions and authenticity, with all its problematic connotations.

These performances of la mère qui gueule and doting mother can be seen as an extension of the legend of the mères lyonnaises that was presented in chapter 1. While the legend gives all kinds of women important role models and often legitimates their place in the kitchen, there is a problematic dynamic in this attachment to the past. Women's work is not necessarily legitimate because of what women are doing now but because it fits into a narrative structure that was valid in the past, which can make it hard for women to move forward, to innovate and define what Lyonnais cuisine is in the present and what it will be in the future.

The next chapter investigates how young women in culinary training programs fit themselves into the legacy of women cooking in Lyon. Does the legend of the mères lyonnaises have any influence on the way they are learning to be women in a professional kitchen? Is the next generation going to be stuck in the past, or will there be a paradigm shift in what it means to be a woman who cooks?

3

APPRENTIE

Reproducing and Subverting Gender through Culinary Education

I went to Lyon in 1998, when I was in my twenties. I was working on a research project in French gastronomic history, so the gastronomic capital of France was the perfect place for it. This is when I got the culinary school bug. I was too old to go to a technical high school, where the majority of French cooks are trained, and too poor from being a college student to be able to pay tuition at a private institution like the Institut Paul Bocuse. That is when I decided to put my professional culinary dreams on hold and focus on my academic studies of food. However, I managed to spend three years in Lyon working and absorbing the culinary culture before starting in on a doctoral degree in anthropology. My lack of culinary training always felt like a missing piece of my education. Nearing forty, I still wanted to understand what it takes to cook professionally.

Over fifteen years later, in 2015, when I was getting deeper into my research on the cuisine des mères lyonnaises, culinary school felt like a necessary part of the project. Although I spoke French fluently, I wanted to be sure I was well versed in the technical language of the kitchen. Knowing the ins and outs of the professional French kitchen seemed critical for gaining an intimate understanding of the culture I was studying. I wanted to know firsthand what it was like to be a woman in a professional kitchen in France. This is why I started out my year of fieldwork at a small culinary school on the outskirts of Paris. The first months, I spent five days a week in hands-on classes becoming versed in classic French techniques. Not always the most organized cook, I learned to keep order in the kitchen and how to be efficient; mise en place became my new religion. I got used to taking criticism and swallowing back anger and tears when the chef instructor yelled at me for being too slow and for "cooking like a woman."

I tolerated remarks constantly about how women cook incorrectly in a professional setting. For instance, one afternoon during a pastry class, a female classmate and I began peeling pears using paring knives. The chef came by and gave us a tongue lashing for not using a peeler: "Only housewives peel fruit like that. Where do you think you are? At home in your kitchen?" I felt my cheeks redden as I fumbled through my knife kit looking for my peeler. I noticed that the men in the class were not chided for cooking like men or women. They were yelled at for being slow or sloppy, but so was everyone else. That said, during my time at culinary school, there was a constant favoritism of men in the way their work was praised, in their apprenticeship assignments at the most prestigious restaurants, and the ways in which their potential career trajectories were discussed. The daily division of labor was also biased along gender lines: men were to do the dirty jobs and the heavy lifting, while women were supposed to do the fine detail work and creative tasks such as plating and decorating. When I tried to mop the floor or take out the garbage at the end of the day, I was usually told to go sit down and take a load off. It became apparent to me in the early days of my course that culinary school was for young men.

Culinary training is not only about acquiring techniques, it is about learning to labor in a specific cultural environment. During my short time in culinary school, I participated in and witnessed the ways in which women both reproduce and subvert gender norms. Women's early success in culinary professions depends on their ability to negotiate gender identities. In this chapter, I explore my own ethnographic experience of culinary school to understand the gender biases that are inherent in this type of training. Examining the history of culinary training and its current state, it becomes apparent that French culinary training and apprenticeship is gendered in ways that discriminate against girls and women. The stories of young female culinary students and apprentices who have won the Eugénie Brazier scholarship, a fund that supports young women from low-income families who want to go to culinary school, show how young women face being a minority in this field. Talking to Geneviève, Hamia, Amira, and Chantelle, I learned about why these young women, aged seventeen to twenty-one, chose culinary careers, about their dreams, and the challenges that they have already faced.

I set out to understand how culinary training played a part in women's success or failure as professional chefs. My culinary school experience helped me to connect with the young women I interviewed because I could relate to the stories they told me. At the same time, I knew their experiences were different from mine because of their age and backgrounds. When I interviewed these young women, I wanted to know who inspired them. Were the mères lyonnaises people they knew about? Did they admire or feel inspired by these women who came before them? I had witnessed the gatekeeping of culinary instructors and the chefs with whom I apprenticed, and I wonder if people like them with power had aided or blocked the way for these young women. Getting at their stories was a little more challenging than I had imagined.

Formation: Culinary School in France

In French, training is called *formation*. Culinary school really is a type of training that forms not only a certain way of thinking but also the body. Endless repetition and relentless correction of inefficient movements shapes the body, producing techniques of the body that sediment into the muscles (Mauss 2002). At first, my body resisted: after years of daily cooking, my hands did not want to hold my chef's knife in what was considered to be the correct manner. My thirty-eight years of existence worked against me as I tried to embody the correct forms of using kitchen equipment and ways of sensing what was happening in the pan. My whisking lacked the instructor's vigorous rhythm. My mayonnaise was slower to emulsify. I was frequently frustrated at how long it took me to become proficient in certain techniques but, slowly and painfully, my body began to conform. I started to understand why people start their culinary training so early, sometimes as young as fifteen. I also realized that, with determination and rigor, I could also come to embody professional techniques. This was just the harder path to travel, but I was not the first to travel it. I often thought of Julia Child, who attended the Cordon Bleu program when she was thirty-eight.

Until the end of the nineteenth century, the occupation of cooking did not exist as a distinct professional group; most cooks were domestic workers in private homes or employees in restaurants and relatively unknown. As Amy Trubek shows in her book *Haute Cuisine* (2000), many people working within the culinary arts in France in the nineteenth century tried to make cooking a profession, but it failed to gain any sort of official status. Culinary training was not incorporated into emerging systems of higher education until the twentieth century. This was largely due to the nature of culinary knowledge: the ubiquity of cooking is part of the challenge of creating a distinction between women's unpaid domestic cooking and men's professionally trained cooking (Giard 1994, 220). It was also the mundane, everyday, and domestic nature of cooking that demoted its status (Mayol 1994, 89). The ephemeral final product, food that would ultimately not last long as it was destined for almost immediate consumption, limits recognition because it is a fleeting social display. Despite these challenges, chefs attempted to create training schools for their occupation, which had long depended on informal apprenticeships for the transmission of knowledge.

The first culinary school in Paris, École professionnelle de cuisine et sciences alimentaires, followed from the 1880 Écoles manuelles d'apprentissage law. This was the state-sanctioned development of schools to train workers in the manual trades, which reflected a general push toward government control of knowledge in the industrial arts (Auslander 1996). The creation of the first culinary school was an attempt to take cooking higher up the social hierarchy, where it would be considered more of an art and less like manual labor (Ray 2016, 131). At the time, associations and journals were also promoting chefs as artists and intellectuals, rather than laborers (Trubek 2000, 92). The changing social status of work was playing out in French kitchens. Part of cooking's failure to professionalize in late nineteenth-century France was the continued centrality of apprenticeship. Hotels and restaurants were ambivalent about culinary schools and professional training because they had long depended on the unpaid work of apprentices, which they were unwilling to lose (Drouard 2004, 62). The general trend in France was the dissolution of apprenticeship as unskilled labor was increasingly engaged in industrialized work (Terrio 2000; Lequin 1986, 458); interestingly, the culinary fields were bucking this trend. While culinary school did not become the norm until after World War II, apprenticeship continued to be an important component of a cook's training—both because it offered free labor and because there are skills that cannot be attained through formal schooling alone.

The professionalization of crafts and skilled labor in late nineteenth-century France put up yet another barrier to women's participation in the professional kitchen. Chefs such as Auguste Escoffier went to great lengths to separate men's professional work in kitchens from women's production of food for the family in the domestic sphere. Escoffier declared men's cooking to be an art form, whereas women are incapable of artistry: "It is simply that man is more thorough in his work, and thoroughness is at the root of all good, as of everything else. A man is more particular over the various little details which are necessary to make up a really perfect dish" (Escoffier in Trubek 2000, 125) At the start of the nineteenth century, cooking was mainly considered women's work—it was neither a "métier" nor a profession (Drouard 2004, 35). In order to become a profession, cooking had to be wrested away from women. As Krishnendu Ray declares, "The divergence between native cooking and expert training is what provincializes one and universalizes the other. Such difference is shaped by the very structure of the modern world along lines of race, gender and nation" (2016, 111). A concrete element in women's exclusion from professional cooking was the creation of schools and certifications that were only open to men. Culinary schools failed to become the gold standard in the métiers de bouche until much later. However, the early schools laid the groundwork for creating a profession that purported to be beyond women's capability and aptitude.

The École professionnelle de cuisine et sciences alimentaires certification program was open only to men, but courses were offered to women. The women's curriculum had the aim of training women to be *ménagères* (housewives) through "cooking and home economics classes" (Marie 2014, 142). From the beginning, culinary training programs made clear distinctions between men and women's cooking and the separate places of men and women's work in the public and private spheres. *Cours ménagères* (domestic training courses) first became more frequent with the influx of young women migrating to cities from the countryside. The École de la Martinière in Lyon, which opened its doors to girls in 1879, offered courses in cooking, sewing, and household management to young women (Thivend 2010). This home-economics training was meant to prepare rural women to work in urban bourgeois homes. Eventually, with the decline in domestic labor in bourgeois households, middle-class wives took on household duties themselves. Cours ménagères then began to prepare these uninitiated women for their new domestic duties.

Alongside the opening of professional programs for the culinary arts, a number of publications cropped up to support the professionalization of cooking. In 1895, Marthe Distel started the magazine *La Cuisinière Cordon Bleu* and held cooking classes as a way to fight the gendered division of the profession. Although these offerings were dedicated to la *cuisine ménagère* (domestic cookery), they made no distinctions among haute cuisine, cuisine bourgeoise, and ménagère (Drouard 2017, 265).

Only after World War II women were admitted to culinary school, but few attended until the end of the twentieth century. This was the case when Julia Child took a ten-month training program at the Cordon Bleu: Académie de cuisine de Paris in 1950. After two days in the "housewife" course, Child sat down with the school's director, Madame Élizabeth Brassart, to enquire about switching to a more rigorous culinary training program. After displaying her disregard for Child, Brassart grudgingly agreed to enroll her in a course for "professional restaurateurs":

> It turned out that the restaurateurs' class was made up of eleven former GIs who were studying cooking under the auspices of the GI Bill of Rights. I never knew if Madame Brassart had placed me with them as a form of hazing or merely because she was trying to squeeze out a few more dollars, but when I walked into the classroom the GIs made me feel as if I had invaded their boys' club. Luckily, I had spent most

of the war in male-dominated environments and wasn't fazed by them in the least. (Child and Prud'Homme 2006, 59)

Julia Child's status as a foreigner may have helped her case as an exception because it took another several decades before French women regularly enrolled in culinary training. In Marie's interviews with chef-instructors, few recalled seeing any women in professional culinary training programs before the 1980s (2014, 174–75). Marie argues that schools were hesitant to enroll women because they knew they would have a hard time finding employment. Women who went to culinary school in this period recall that their families discouraged them from this line of work because it was considered inappropriate for women (175).

The tides have slowly turned, and at present there are numerous opportunities for French boys and girls to gain culinary training. Students as young as fourteen years old can take a BEP (Brevet d'études professionnelles) in their last year of *collège* (middle school/early high school). The BEP encompasses both training in culinary and hotel management (the full title of the degree is BEP des métiers de la restauration et de l'hôtellerie), giving students general training in both areas. In the first year, students spend equal time studying the two areas and then they specialize in one or the other. Marie estimates that only about a third of the young women in these training programs choose the culinary option (2014, 176). The most common avenue to a career in the culinary professions starts in high school with the CAP cuisine. This is a two-year training program that can be started after completing collège, in the first year of *lycée* (high school). Students are generally fifteen years old at this point in their education. The CAP can be taken at a professional high school, culinary school, hotel school, or CFA (Centre de formation des apprentis; Apprentice Training Center), and the CAP in cooking has either periods of practical instruction at a training center, punctuated by applied training in restaurants (*stage en alternance*) during the course, or a longer apprenticeship contract (*un contrat d'apprentissage*) after training at the school.

After the CAP, students can get further training in culinary through the BAC Pro Cuisine. BAC is the baccalaureate, which in France is the final exam upon leaving high school. Students can choose to specialize in a specific academic or technical area that will either prepare them for further study or to enter the work force in specific field. This is a three-year degree, or two after a CAP in culinary arts. After the CAP, it is possible to continue on to the BTS (Brevet de technicien supérieur), which can be obtained in two years, or some students complete an MC (*mention complémentaire*, a supplementary training course) in a specialized field like pastry. The goal of all of these degrees and certificates is to give students professional experience and prepare them to enter the workforce. The French education system in general is big on certifications; in most cases, it can be difficult to enter specific fields without the required certifications, even if a person has work experience. This is perhaps the biggest shift in modern culinary training, which used to be solely based on apprenticeship. Again, this is a move toward not only regulation on the part of the state but also an attempt in culinary sectors to further professionalize.

Looking at gender representation in the culinary arts, in 2017, the enrollment of young women in these programs continued to be strong (table 3.1). There were more young women (61 percent) than men in the BTS hôtellerie; the combined front-of-the house management training, which in general draws more women, and culinary might explain these numbers. In the CAP (41.5 percent) and the BAC Pro (35.4 percent), women maintained healthy minority enrollments. If we trace these statistics over a period of ten years, we see that the gender ratio has been largely holding steady. Despite a strong participation in training and certification programs, not many young women enter restaurant kitchens. One male chef-owner who I interviewed told me that "I would love to hire more women. Tell me where they are. For every twenty people who apply for jobs, there is one woman in the bunch."

This led me to wonder what kinds of careers these degree programs prepare students to enter. After the CAP or BTS, most culinary students start their career as a commis. This will likely be their first paid position—at the bottom of the kitchen hierarchy, just above apprentice (see fig. 1.2). Their culinary training will have given them basic skills and a vocabulary that allows them to complete the low-level tasks that will be asked of them. They will also understand the hierarchy and culture of the kitchen, but they will really learn to cook during their

Table 3.1. Females in CAP, BAC Pro, and BST degree programs in France.

2017	CAP	BAC Pro	BTS
Females	41.5%	35.4%	61%
Total enrollment	13,787	19,613	3,930

Source: Ministère de l'éducation nationale, *Repères et références statistiques*, 2018.

apprenticeships. Although the spotlight is generally on the chef de cuisine, one of the highest-ranking positions in the brigade system, culinary education prepares students to be cooks. Few will rise to the top. Sociologist Alain Drouard (2007) comments that there is too much focus in the academic and popular literature on chefs and not enough on cooks: most people working in professional kitchens are part of the rank and file. At the same time, it is still glaringly obvious that women are underrepresented not only in the lower echelons but particularly at the top.

While the French government has created a system for ensuring a baseline of professional skill through courses in a training facility, apprenticeship and practical experience are still the hallmark of culinary education (Dornenburg and Page 2003; Drouard 2004). It is not enough to read books, sit through lectures, and learn in a laboratory kitchen, which is essentially what people do in culinary school. Formal education is only one part of preparing students to enter into a community of practice—the professional kitchen in this case.[1] Students learn the vocabulary and start to understand the ways of doing, but they are not fully inculcated into the culture of the professional kitchen until they start doing *stages* and apprenticeships. Situated learning is at the heart of becoming a professional cook, which is why apprenticeship is still central to culinary education. I hoped that attending culinary school and getting some experience as an apprentie would give me a glimpse into the dynamics of the French culinary community of practice.

The Culinary School Experience

Professional culinary training is now generally a requisite for finding a job in a restaurant kitchen in France. There are a few opportunities to come to the profession later in life. The only ways are if you can

Figure 3.1: The author in culinary school.

convince someone to take you on and you can gain experience on the job, you can open your own restaurant, or you can take a course designed for people who want to change careers, *reconversion professionnelle.* This last option is what I chose to do.

I was not a typical culinary student: thirty-nine years old, a foreigner, and pregnant. After assessing all the culinary school offerings available to me, I realized that I was never going to be able to complete a multiyear course with a lengthy apprenticeship, so I settled for a program with a good reputation and a short apprenticeship component. I was three months pregnant when I started, so the clock was ticking. I needed to get all the training I could to better understand the current realities of professional kitchens in France and to understand the dynamics of culinary training.

Field notes—7/21/14

Today was the first day of class. I woke up at 5:30 a.m. out of excitement and fear. Would I catch the right train? What would my classmates be

> like? Would I fit into my chef's pants? From my little apartment in Pigalle, I nervously made my way out to Argenteuil on the outskirts of the city. I arrived without incident twenty minutes early. Slowly, everyone gathered around the orientation table. When it came time to introduce myself, I was breathless with anxiety, partly because of my rusty French. [. . .] Once suited up, we went to our kitchen. I couldn't help but feel we were like children learning to walk or maybe more like rehabilitation patients relearning. I was already questioning everything I thought I knew about cooking—second guessing myself and asking a lot of questions.
>
> Chopping mushrooms for a *bouillon aux legumes* [vegetable stock], my new chef's knife felt like an alien appendage—much bigger and sharper than my knife at home. Slowly, I began to let my insecurities fall away and my curiosity began to take over. [. . .] There was so much information to take in, and I knew that I needed to practice to let the knowledge sediment into my body—the body takes over from the mind in this kind of learning. A nice change.
>
> During the afternoon, we cleaned a lot of chicken carcasses for the *fond blanc* [white stock]. What fiddly work! I can't imagine doing this all day but I now have more appreciation for all of these little tasks that need to get done. [. . .]
>
> Our group is learning to be a brigade. I can already feel something starting to gel, especially when we did our clean up. Everyone worked really hard and helped each other.
>
> After my first day, my mind is spinning, my feet hurt, and I can't wait to go back for more. Is it OK to be in bed at 9:30 p.m.?

Even from my first day in culinary school, I was learning about the embodied nature of the knowledge I was trying to acquire. I was awkward and felt out of place, but I was excited to have access to a space and a culture I had long wanted to be a part of. I still felt like an impostor, but I was eager to become fluent in this new language of stocks, sauces, equipment, movements, tastes, and ways of working with others.

As days at culinary school passed, I realized that this type of "formation" was transforming me from the home cook that I had been to a professional cook. I learned to read recipes in a new way. In professional recipes, not everything is written out. There is an assumption that you have basic skills and that you will just know how to interpret the recipe and use the correct technique. This was certainly not the case at the start, and I stood corrected on a number of occasions. I was also learning the little *astuces* (tricks) that professional cooks just know, like leaving meat on a wire rack in the fridge the night before cooking so it dries. This helps with caramelization. When making emulsions, don't add too much oil all at once, use a spatula to make smoother emulsions, place your hand on the pan as you make hollandaise or zabaglione and remove the pan from the heat when your hand can't stand it—so much of this is about embodying knowledge and techniques. For many recipes, we used the same techniques over and over. It took me a long time to feel like I did not need to consult the recipe every two seconds to make sure I was doing it right. The chef instructor told us to cook with our senses, and I realized how much mine needed to be fine-tuned. I did not trust my body. In fact, at times it felt like my body was revolting against the sensory overload: one evening "after climbing the five floors to my apartment, my stomach started to churn a little. I think it was the large quantities of mayo and emulsions that I ate all day, tasting them, trying to get it right. I choked down a bowl of cereal for dinner" (field notes, July 26, 2014).

I always found Mondays hard. In part this was due to often having a new instructor for the week. Early on, I had one chef instructor who made Monday even harder by singling out the women in the class to criticize them more than the men. Throughout the day he chided us with comments such as "women should not lift pots of stock because they don't have the muscle," or "women take three hours to shop because they have to read the labels on everything." I did my best to bite my tongue, responding instead "Oui, Chef!" I was quickly learning that was the only answer any chef wanted to hear—no matter what the reality actually was.

Friday was also a difficult day: we had an exam, both written and applied, each week. I was anxious about both my culinary ability and my capacity to do everything in French. The written tests were challenging, and I preferred the practical exams. Cooking under the pressure of a time constraint made me more efficient and strategic about my mise en place. In the end, everyone seemed to be doing pretty well, but there was also some favoritism. The women would be yelled at if we touched an onion root to a chopping board, while the chef instructor would say nothing when some of the men would have chicken guts splattered all over their work area.

Culinary school taught me about all kinds of injustices:

> The violence of eating animals hit home today as I dropped a beautiful blue lobster into the pot. Its tail was tortuously trussed to keep it straight, so that it would be perfect for lobster thermidor. It was a lesson in participating in and accepting death, which is part of eating. We are frequently distanced from the violent acts that produce food, unable to acknowledge, accept or reject the murderous chain of events to which we are complicit. (Field notes, August 13, 2014)

Rarely have I had to kill animals myself as part of cooking. That lobster got me thinking about my place on the food chain and the potential violence of cooking and eating. While breaking down chicken after chicken and gutting fish after fish, my focus was on technique and the finished product. Throughout my time at culinary school, I challenged myself to also think about the environmental and social impacts of my actions. One thing that struck me each day was how much food was wasted while learning to cook. We were allowed to bring home what we cooked, but we threw out so much: delicious sauces that took hours to cook, expensive racks of lamb, and even delicate pastries that we had agonized over. There was no way I could eat everything I produced, and I had no friend network to pass the food on to. When I mentioned waste and sustainability to the chef instructors or administrators at the school, they just brushed off my concerns. When I started to work in restaurants, I quickly realized that waste is equivalent to throwing away money, and it should never happen. The wastefulness of culinary school further perplexed me: why were we not taught to be efficient, if that was one of the main requirements of our future work?

It was the beginning of a new week and a new topic. The thought of learning about pastry left me unmoved, while almost all the other students were most excited about this portion of the course. For the chef instructors, dessert lived in a vacuum and was its own thing—it did not have to have a relationship to the rest of the meal. The amount of sugar I consumed in this portion of the course left me jittery each afternoon, and it made the baby growing inside of me do somersaults. The chef instructor for pastry took it upon himself to exorcise the housewife and home cook from the female students. There were quips and sexist "corrections" that the women in the course endured each day, in the pastry and cooking classes.

I resisted pastry each day but, in the end, I may have learned the most in this portion of the course. Pastry made me a better cook. I became more precise. I learned to have a softer touch and how to be more artistic in my presentation of dishes. When making macarons, I had to measure the ingredients carefully, uniformly dose out the almond mixture on the baking mat, and learn to open the oven to let out the steam to dry the egg whites. I did not like the fiddly nature of baking, but I was pleased when my attention to detail and instructions yielded beautiful and tasty results. Was pastry bringing out my more feminine side? Was this part of a process that trapped women in this role? I started to think more about the gendered nature of apprenticeship and training.

In *The Body Impolitic: Artisans and Artifice in the Global Hierarchy of Value*, Michael Herzfeld talks about how apprentices "are fashioning selves—or, more precisely, modeling—relations among selves" (2004, 37). In the cobbler's workshop that Herzfeld observes, this process occurs among boys and their master. In the kitchen, this can be a mixed brigade of women and men. What happens when girls and women are put into this mix? Do women upend or throw off this social order? Herzfeld goes on to discuss how apprentices' bodies are trained: it is through processes of systematic inculcation that engrain the structures of power and social hierarchy in people's bodily habits. In my own culinary experience, I came to wonder how structures of power had come to sediment into my own bodily practices. Why did I hold and use a knife in the way I did? David Sutton's study of Greek home cooking shows the ways in which environment and social structures influence embodied practices. The women in Sutton's ethnography cut ingredients in their hands rather than on a cutting board on the counter because counters are either scarce or too high and uncomfortable. Also, cooking is social, and working on a counter would require the cook to turn her back to the people in the room (Sutton 2014, 51–54).

When the chef scolded me for using a paring knife instead of a peeler, I was learning a new grammar of kitchen tools. I had to develop new relationships with knives in general. When we started the course, all the students were given a knife roll with a set of knives that had our last names engraved on them. I remember feeling as if I had gained entry to some new club when I first gazed at these glinting beauties with my name on them. However, when I started to cook with my new chef's knife, I confirmed my status as a novice outsider. My new 10-inch knife felt like an unwieldy sword: it was far bigger than anything I had ever used in my kitchen. This was a knife made for a man's anatomy. The handle and hilt bit into my hands and made blisters as I learned to hold this new tool correctly. I felt awkward and slow, despite the hours I had spent cooking and using knives before I arrived at culinary school. Throwing off my housewife habits in the kitchen was an attempt to use techniques that my instructors saw as more masculine and more professional. It was not only techniques that felt gendered, it was also the kitchen equipment, from my knife to the weight of cast-iron pots, that reminded me that my body was not the typical male subject that was supposed to inhabit this kitchen. In his analysis of culinary training at the Culinary Institute of America, one of Ray's interviewees talks about how the kitchen itself and the equipment there make her feel out of place (Ray 2016, 140–41). The relationships of power in the kitchen are certainly in titles and positions, but they are also in ways of doing and the materiality of the work environment.

I recall that we were asked to cook ratatouille but given no instructions beyond the ingredients. This is a dish I knew well and had cooked many times. I had always slow-simmered the tomatoes, onions, eggplant, zucchini, and herbs together until the flavors melded to form a delicious unified jam-like substance that could be spread on bread. This is what I lovingly produced and I was thoroughly mocked when I presented it to that week's chef instructor: "What's that? It's a mess. We do not cook like that in a professional kitchen. Each ingredient should be cooked separately so that it is cooked to perfection and can be recognized. Ratatouille should respect and showcase each ingredient. You have made something any housewife could make at home." Cooking like a woman was deemed the opposite of cooking professionally.

When women are placed in the male kitchen, the notion of community of practice needs to be examined further because this is not necessarily a community where everyone belongs. Notions of masculinity are tied up in nearly all the ways of being and doing in the professional kitchen. At the same time, as Jacquetta Hill and David Plath point out, "novices are obliged to be responsive for organizing how they learn, for anticipating what they need to learn next, and for seizing it when it surfaces in the routine flow of work. To learn is to practice, and vice versa" (1998, 222). During my time at culinary school, I had to learn to move beyond the teacher-learner dyad model (Hutchins 1993) to understand how culinary training in school and through apprenticeship demand that I find my own agency. I had to decide what I was going to learn not only from the chefs who barked at me but from all of the people in the kitchen. As I worked alongside others, I learned to have confidence in my own ability to adapt to different situations, to acquire skills, and to open up to all the lessons that could be learned each shift. Even if the kitchen, its equipment, and my instructors were not made to educate my female body and ways of doing, I could still learn here by adapting to the setting.

I had a personal experience of strong gender bias in both culinary school and during apprenticeship, and I knew I was not the only woman to run this gauntlet. From an academic perspective, little is written about such gender bias. Most of the historical literature looks at men and boys and their apprenticeship experiences because those were the dominant groups engaged in this form of education. We have not paid attention to what happens when girls and women enter systems of learning built around men and boys' bodies and cultural assumptions about masculinity. My own culinary school experience taught me about the discrimination that women experience in this type of training and how different ways of doing become gendered through a derogatory, prescriptive discourse. I knew that my own experience was just one of many and I was eager to hear other perspectives. The recipients of the Eugénie Brazier scholarship seemed like an ideal group of young women to interview to learn more about what culinary school and apprenticeship were like for young French women today.

The Eugénie Brazier Scholarship

When I first started my research, Jacotte Brazier invited me to attend the ceremony for the Eugénie Brazier scholarship winners. When the day arrived, I made my way to the *hôtel de ville* (city hall) on the Place des Terreaux in Lyon. The monumental nature of this ornate nineteenth-century building made an impression on me as I showed my invitation and walked through the guarded entrance. Making my way to the imposing staircase leading up to the room where the ceremony was to take place, I could feel how important the choice was to hold the event here. The walls were sheathed in luxurious red fabric and gold, and crystal chandeliers twinkled festively. I could only imagine how the young women receiving these awards must feel as they entered the room and took their place in the front row of seats—nervous, excited, honored, small, recognized? After several introductions, including one from the mayor of Lyon, Jacotte took to the podium to announce this year's winners of the scholarships that she had created in order to honor her grandmother's memory. Jacotte's silvery hair gleamed in the spotlight, and her smile expressed a genuine pleasure in giving out these awards. I could see Eugénie's sturdy farmwoman build in her granddaughter, but Jacotte is refined and presents herself with all the bourgeois trappings, elegant clothes, jewelry, and carefully coiffed hair. Like her grandmother, Jacotte never married or tied herself to

Figure 3.2: Jacotte Brazier and the author at the Prix Eugénie Brazier award ceremony at the Lyon city hall.

a man. Rumors whirl about the various affairs of her youth, but now she is the respected aunt figure that everyone seems to love. Into this gilded room, Jacotte had come to honor her grandmother. She hoped that this next generation of women would follow in Eugénie's footsteps.

As Jacotte announced each young woman's name, I was struck by their youth—they were high school aged or slightly older. They beamed proudly in their chef's coats, all of them had their hair pulled back neatly, and they had an air of professionalism and hopefulness. Most of these young women came from low-income families, and this award was likely the first public recognition they had ever received. I was only beginning to understand the potential Jacotte's work had to change these young women's futures.

"I don't know how to cook," exclaimed Jacotte in one of our earliest conversations. This remark came as a shock, and I thought maybe she was joking. Jacotte Brazier is the granddaughter of Eugénie Brazier: her father, Gaston, was Brazier's son. Although Jacotte spent a lot of time in her grandmother's restaurant from early childhood, Eugénie never allowed her into the kitchen and certainly not near the *piano*. Jacotte says she had a little white apron, she was given a cloth, and she was told to polish glasses. Her grandmother was stern and not particularly affectionate with Jacotte. She had a vision of what the young girl's education should be, and it did not include learning to cook—Eugénie refused to teach Jacotte. Nonetheless, Jacotte went to one of the finest hotel schools, but this prepared her to work in the front of the house, not in the kitchen. A few people told me that Jacotte jokes that she started her foundation to help young women learn to cook professionally as revenge on her grandmother.

Jacotte explained to me that, while she was still running her family's restaurant, La Mère Brazier, friends encouraged her to start an association in her grandmother's name to help young women in culinary school. She told everyone she was too busy. A few years later in 2004, when she sold the restaurant and began to work for the Fondation Paul Bocuse, she thought about this idea some more. Jacotte first had to learn the ins and outs of forming an association. She found support among her friends and colleagues. She decided that the awards would be given to young women working toward the CAP cuisine.

The Association les amis d'Eugénie Brazier gave its first scholarships in 2007 to two young women. Jacotte told me: "It was a bit of a disaster. We gave 1,000 euros to these two young women. One was fine and has gone on to have a great career. The other one bought a bunch of equipment, spent all the money, and a few months later told me she did not want to continue a career in the kitchen. We have changed the way we give out the awards." Now there are five to six recipients for the culinary scholarship and another five or six awards for young women studying to work in the front of the house. The young women are now allocated 500 euros, and the association approves how the funds are spent. The money mainly goes to buying equipment, such as knives and uniforms. Scholarship winners can ask for additional funds for special training courses and travel related to school exchange programs. The French state covers the cost of professional programs offered at public schools.

Scholarships are given to young women from technical high schools in the greater Lyon area: Lycée François Rabelais, Lycée Hélène Boucher, Lycée Belle-Rive Robin, and Lycée Aiguerande. A few awards have also gone to students at the private Institut Paul Bocuse. After the first year, Jacotte decided to make the award to young women entering their second year of training, because they were more likely to continue. The teachers and the school principal sit down together to identify young women entering the second year of their BAC who seem promising and who need financial assistance. Jacotte then reviews the dossiers and makes the final selection.

It was not easy raising money to fund the scholarships; Jacotte explained that people in Lyon are not very supportive of charitable causes. This did not stop her. She asked her former clients, colleagues, and friends for donations. Jacotte continues to call in personal favors to support the association and its activities. However, she is now concerned with the sustainability of the association and how it will evolve in the future.

After the first few years that the association awarded scholarships, local cuisinière and journalist Sonia Ezgulian suggested to Jacotte that the association should add a literary prize to its activities. "Sonia thought this would be more media friendly and draw attention to all of the association's work, and she was right," explained Jacotte. According to the association website, these awards are meant to promote the transmission of culinary heritage and the activities of the association that support women's culinary work. Each year, the Prix Eugénie Brazier is given to a cookbook written by a woman or to a book that focuses on women's cooking (le Grand Prix), another prize goes to an illustrator or photographer of a cookbook (Prix de l'iconographie), another to a novel or an essay about food (Prix du roman ou de l'essai gourmand), and a last award to a cookbook in the Francophonie (French-speaking areas of the world) and elsewhere category. A jury of active members and supporters of the association, generally important figures in the French culinary and literary world, selects the winners.

Since 2007, the association has given scholarships to twenty-four young women, and Jacotte hopes to expand the number of awards in the future. She would also like to offer more support for professional development. After talking to Jacotte Brazier about the association's plans, I was curious to know how the young women who received scholarships lived this experience. Was this prize making a difference in their lives? What challenges did they still face? What were their dreams for the future? I wanted to understand if these scholarships were transmitting the legend of Eugénie Brazier to the next generation of women in professional kitchens, and if so, did it shape their experiences of being a woman in a professional kitchen?

Les Boursières

It was not easy tracking down the *boursières* (scholarship recipients): they were busy young women. There were classes and trying to catch them while they were actually at school. They were often doing *stages* at restaurants in Lyon and the surrounding areas, all with split shifts that broke up the day in uneven ways. They were young people trying to have social lives on top of their schooling and training, making them even more difficult to reach. Eventually I resorted to conducting phone interviews once I was back in the United States. This interview technique is not ideal, and in retrospect, these young women might have been more comfortable if I asked them questions via text message, which is how many young people interact these days. Indeed, for better or worse, our phone interviews had a formal and official air about them.

The first person I reached was seventeen-year-old Geneviève. She was completing her second year of the BAC Pro Cuisine at a technical high school on the outskirts of Lyon. Geneviève had already completed numerous *stages* in Lyonnais restaurants, from small bistros to fine-dining establishments. She explained to me that culinary training was not her first choice; she had initially wanted to be a photographer but realized that there are not many jobs. Geneviève told me that she finds a creative outlet in cooking and she particularly enjoys dressage d'assiette. She was one of four young women in a class of twelve. While Geneviève never felt discriminated against in her *stages* in various restaurants, she confided in me that there were times when her instructors at culinary school favored the boys in her class. For example, when it came time to assign *stages*, the boys were given the best positions in the more prestigious restaurants. Although I had seen this happen in my own training, only when Geneviève described this favoritism did I fully realize that this is one of the early ways in which young women are held at the bottom: without access to the top chefs and opportunities, it is harder to get ahead. Not only are young women not developing the strongest skills by learning from the best, but they are not developing the networks that will benefit them later when they are looking for jobs. Social networks are one of the keys to success in professional cooking (Lane 2014, 107). Geneviève told me she felt her "real learning" happened during her *stage*, where she really began to understand the organization of work and the pressures of time.

When I asked Geneviève about her future plans, she told me she would like to travel abroad to learn about other types of cuisine and cultures. She dreams of opening her own restaurant in Peru. Geneviève's curiosity and open-mindedness impressed me. She seemed to be looking out from Lyon rather than looking inward toward tradition. This was apparent when I asked her if she was familiar with the cuisine des mères. She was not. My question confounded Geneviève a little, and I had to suppress my surprise that she did not know about the mères lyonnaises, especially given that she had received an award in the name of the best-known mère.

Although she did not fully grasp Eugénie Brazier's contributions to French cuisine, Geneviève was proud to be receiving a scholarship from the Les Amis d'Eugénie Brazier. Not only had the award helped her financially, she felt supported by a broader network of professionals who want to see her succeed. When I asked her what chef inspired her the most, she told me: "Paul Bocuse, of course. He is a legend." Having worked at a number of the restaurants in the Bocuse group, Geneviève was well imbued in the lore of this local hero. As I talked to more young women, I realized that few of them had many female role models and that not many gave this much thought. This was a contrast to the older female chefs discussed in chapter 1, who cited the legend of the mères as support for their own careers. Nonetheless, the role models for these young women were Lyonnais. Growing up in the gastronomic capital had left its mark.

Twenty-year-old Hamia attended the other popular technical high school in Lyon that specializes in culinary and hotel training. She had no idea what she wanted to study when she started. Someone suggested culinary, and she gave it a try. She really liked the practical, hands-on side of culinary training, and found herself feeling out of place in her more "academic courses." Of the eight students in her class, only two were young women. Hamia told me that "the girls are stronger than the boys in the kitchen. It really bothers them [the boys]." Her favorite *stages* so far have been in brasseries; she likes this style of cooking and service. When I asked her if there were many other women in the restaurants where she had apprenticed, she told me there were only ever a few. However, she did not find that being a woman was a disadvantage in the kitchen. There were only a few times when she was sent to work in pastry, "because it was assumed that was where girls want to work." The pastry kitchen is what some chefs call "the pink ghetto" (Harris and Giuffre 2015, 190).

Hamia explained that receiving the Brazier scholarship had given her more confidence. She also told me about her dream to open her own restaurant one day. Having one's own business was a dream for many of these young women—it meant autonomy and creative license. When I asked Hamia about her inspiration, like Geneviève she cited Bocuse: "Everyone is always talking about him. He is everywhere." Said two years after Bocuse's death, this gave me a sense of Monsieur Paul's legacy and ability to inspire, even from the grave.

From her name and the few details I had about her background, it was apparent to me that Hamia was of Algerian descent. When I asked her about discrimination, I phrased my question in broad terms. I wanted to see if young women of color or those with Arabic names had experienced discrimination not based only on gender but also on race. This is a hard question to ask in French because you can't come out and talk directly about race—there is not really an appropriate or current language for the discussion in France. As discussed in this book's introduction, issues of race still have strong connotations of World War II and genocide. These are awkward conversations where the language is sometimes wholly lacking. I asked Hamia if she had ever experience discrimination based on her family background. Hamia was born in France, but her name announces her North African origins. My question seemed to confuse her a little, but after a short reflexive pause she answered with a firm, "No!" Few of the young women of color whom I interviewed acknowledged that race was an issue that had negatively impacted them. However, it is known that there is widespread discrimination against people of Arab heritage. Although it is illegal in France to discriminate against a job candidate based on ethnicity, race, religion, or gender (Simon and Madoui 2011), studies have shown that putting an Arab name on a résumé can eliminate a person from a job search (Fassin 2002; Martens and Denolf 1993).

Seventeen-year-old Amira, who is also of Algerian descent, was in the second year of her BAC Pro Cuisine at a technical high school in Lyon. Watching *Top Chef France* and other cooking shows inspired her to go to culinary school, where half of her culinary class was female. When I asked her how many of her chef instructors were women, she had to think long and hard about it. Apparently, there was only one female instructor last year for one course. Amira told me that her male instructors had made small quips at the young women for "cooking like girls" and sometimes told them they did not belong in the kitchen. Amira explained that her strategy was to just keep working hard. This fits in with the "hard work is the only answer" ethic of the kitchen. In these conversations, I noticed how this way of thinking about hard work instills a false sense of equality, and makes it difficult for the hard worker to see the structural issues that create gender inequalities in the kitchen.

This young culinary student had already done *stages* at three restaurants. In most of these kitchens, women were a minority, but she did not feel that she was put at a disadvantage or discriminated against because of her gender. In one of the Bocuse brasseries where she apprenticed, Amira had been impressed to see three women working in stations such as garde-manger and pastry. Yet these are the stations where women are often placed and from which they do not gain access to more prestigious stations on the hot line.

In response to my question about whether the scholarship had helped her, Amira said that the award had made it possible for her to buy the equipment she needed to participate in her classes. Amira would like to work abroad in order to learn more about the world and other cuisines, and like Hamia, she too would like to open her own restaurant someday. In the near future, she intends to take an additional degree course, an MC in pastry. She thinks this will round out her skill set and give her more opportunities for employment.

Amira had a hard time naming any role models or chefs who inspired her. When I asked her if she knew anything about Eugénie Brazier's story and life, she told me she did not. I thought that the legend of the mères lyonnaises had continued to be an inspiration for young women in kitchens in Lyon, but I was largely wrong. Where would these young women have heard stories about la mère Brazier, the mère Léa, and the others? Except for a mural at an exclusive restaurant on the outskirts of town (see fig. 1.1), there were few visible traces of these women who had shaped the local cuisine. French culinary students are not taught about the mères lyonnaises in their classes. It seemed to me that the contributions of these women were fading. The recently deceased Paul Bocuse seemed to overshadow all other culinary histories of Lyon.

Just when I was starting to feel down about the place of women in French culinary history, I had a conversation with another boursière who seemed more grounded in local history. Chantelle, who at nineteen had just finished her BAC Pro Cuisine, knew a little bit about la cuisine des mères and the woman whom her scholarship honored.

"When I think about les mères lyonnaises, I remember that, not only can women cook, but that they can do it really well." Chantelle tells me that winning the Brazier scholarship gave her confidence, which she needed after a few tough experiences during apprenticeships. "I found that in a lot of restaurants women were criticized more than men. I was told I couldn't do this work because I am a girl. It was really hard, but I told myself to just keep working and to do my best." It was not easy, even when Chantelle did have female mentors. Having had a chance to work under female chefs during her *stages*, she told me that "women demand perfection more than men. These were not always the easiest *stages*, but I learned a lot."

Chantelle explained to me that she chose to pursue a career in the culinary arts because her mother is a chef de cuisine and at a young age she had a chance to get a sense of this work. She always liked the pace of the restaurant kitchen and found it a little hard to slow down for courses at school. In fact, only two weeks after completing her degree, Chantelle was already working in a fine-dining restaurant in the south of France for the summer season. After, she was hoping to travel to Australia to see some of the world and learn about other cultures and their cuisines. Her dream is to one day become a chef and perhaps open a restaurant with her sister. Chantelle was the only girl to tell me that a female chef inspired her: her role model is Anne-Sophie Pic. Chantelle told me that "when I am in the kitchen, I never look at the time. I just get so into the work. You have to have a real passion for this *métier* [profession]. It is hard work." I wonder how much being in a culinary family and having her mother as a professional role model had shaped Chantelle's world view. She seemed more aware of the challenges of being a woman in the kitchen, but she also looked up to women in her profession.

I was able to interview four of the six scholarship winners. It was interesting to see the ways in which the scholarship and the recognition that came with it encouraged these young professionals. Being acknowledged for their promise and achievements made these women want to work harder and achieve more. Given their ages, from seventeen to twenty, I don't know why I found it surprising that the young women had not reflected more on their career choices. They all seemed to fall into culinary, rather than having made a carefully thought-out decision.

Only Chantelle had followed a passion she had discovered at an early age. As they progressed in their learning, these young women became more interested in cooking and came to see their dreams and future plans wrapped up in culinary professions.

When I asked about gender discrimination and challenges, most of the young women had little to say or did not share their experiences in school or in *stages* until I shared my own. I wondered if this was again a lack of reflexivity related to youth or if there was a sense of shame or vulnerability in admitting you had experienced discrimination. Perhaps the young women did not recognize certain comments or behaviors as discrimination or unfair treatment until I framed it as such. I did not want to lead my participants, but I had a hard time moving the young women beyond superficial accounts of their experiences. I tried to imagine my younger self and the times that I experienced discrimination and harassment in my front of the house restaurant jobs. At seventeen and even nineteen, I was not mature enough to respond to those harassing me. I was not courageous enough to stand up, and sometimes I did not fully realize what was happening to me until much later, when I reflected on why I felt awkward, ashamed, or angry. How much discrimination is accepted because it is structural and normalized? As a more mature woman, I had a very different experience of culinary education. I knew how to advocate for myself in situations where these young women may have felt less empowered.

From what I heard about these young women's culinary educations, I could start to understand how professional training often worked against them and how people in positions of power sometimes tried to discourage them from continuing or pushed them into working in specific areas of the kitchen. The difficulties I had interviewing these young women might have also been related to their culinary education: they had been trained to fall into the order of the kitchen and not to stand out. They were supposed to work hard and not complain. Their interviews reflected this attitude. As Ray points out, in culinary school there is an infatuation with masculinity and the physical toughness associated with it. A system of values is taught that celebrates masculine idioms of work: strength, ability to endure humiliation, and ability to never complain about working conditions. This draws heavily on homosocial military models upon which the brigade system is built (Ray 2016, 143–45).

Formation still means the shaping of male bodies without much consideration for how the experience might be different for girls and women. There is little difference in what young women are able to do, but being told they are incompetent or ill-suited to the work shapes young women in different ways. It either discourages them out of the field or it makes them more resilient and determined—a lot depends on a girl's background and character. During his time in the kitchen at La Mère Brazier, Bill Buford worked with one female *stagiaire* (student worker). He watched as the men in the kitchen sexually harassed, humiliated, and brought her to tears each shift. Later, when he went back to see what has become of her career, he learned that she left the kitchen for a career in marketing (Buford 2020). This is not an unusual story. However, the small number of young women who are able to resist discrimination push back on the system, making new spaces for other young women to follow.

In order to bring about change, it is not enough to have only bottom-up resistance; there needs to be change from the top down, as well. French culinary schools are doing little to address systematic issues of discrimination and exclusion. There are few female culinary instructors, and they do little to change the way in which culinary education is delivered. If culinary schools would actively address gender bias and discrimination, this would be a big step toward creating equal opportunity between young men and women.

The Eugénie Brazier scholarship offers encouragement for young women and helps them to believe in themselves. In many cases, it gives young women a support network that is critical to their success in the profession. This program is unique to Lyon, but more female-focused scholarship and awards could help change the playing field in the future. As young women head into their apprenticeships and their first jobs as commis, how are they prepared for some of the harsh realities of the professional kitchen? What tools have they developed as they resist a male-dominated system? Even after months of culinary school, I know I felt underprepared for the culinary challenges and social situations I faced during my short apprenticeship.

Apprenticeship: A Woman in a Man's World

For my *stage*, there was an option of working in a well-known Parisian bistro that had been started by a woman in the 1930s, the era of female chefs that had first sparked my interest in this research. The current chef de cuisine and sous-chef were both women. I was pleased when the apprenticeships were announced and I had been assigned to this bistro in the heart of the Rive Gauche. I was eager to see if having female leadership would make this kitchen somehow different.

The day of my first shift, I arrived early and timidly poked my nose through the front door. I was surprised that it opened up directly onto the small open kitchen, which was deserted after the lunch service. Crossing the threshold, I stood in the entryway gawking at my surroundings as if I were visiting a museum or a historic site. A waiter who was cleaning up after the lunch service raised his eyebrows at me. I explained that I was there to begin an apprenticeship in the kitchen. He introduced me to Cécile, the sous-chef, who was sitting slumped at a table, her dark hair pulled back and her chef's whites looking a little crumpled. She hastily greeted me and asked me to follow her so I could get changed for my shift. It was clear that she had seen many apprentices before. We exited the back door of the kitchen into the building courtyard. She pushed aside her apron to fish a long skeleton key out of the pocket of her chef's pants and unlocked a rickety wooden door. Cécile led me down crumbling cement stairs, and a dank smell filled my nose. The tiny bare lightbulb barely lit our way as I held out a hand against the chalky wall to steady myself. My new boss explained that to the left there was dry storage and to the right was the staff changing area. Cécile pulled a balled-up white shirt and dirty old shoes out of the bottom of a locker and told me that I could use it for my things. As I looked around the dingy vaulted room, I realized that this was the changing area for everyone in the whole restaurant. Although it was not a large restaurant, I was still surprised that there were no separate areas for men and women. During my *stage*, there were many times when male and female servers and cooks all changed together in the same area. That did not bother me so much as when I had to change by myself or with just one other male employee late at night after my shift. This was a space of potential nightmares. No one ever said anything about it, and I later learned that there were far more frightening spaces in the restaurant.

Once I came upstairs, Cécile quickly showed me around the *salle* (dining room). The small bistro tables were draped with crisp linens that picked up the warmth of the afternoon light filtering through the frosted glass of the high windows. The timeworn silver cutlery waited next to carefully polished glassware for diners to arrive for the evening service. The dowdy burgundy floral wallpaper clashed against the bright red banquettes and gave an old-fashioned feel to the place. The many historic photos and prints also nodded to the past. As I gazed around this room, I could imagine the sound of silverware clattering against the red-rimmed white plates and the secret conversations of lovers that passed unheard under the laughter of friends sharing wine as another group oohed over the roast duck just presented to their table. This was a place where the food was said to be perfect, but I could tell that it was not the center of the dining experience. The room told me that this restaurant was about people being together. Food and wine were the connective tissue of these encounters.

I worked long hours at this woman-run bistro, honing skills that I had learned in culinary school and carefully observing the ways in which men and women worked together in the kitchen each day. I came to realize that culinary school was a bit like reading a textbook, but apprenticeship was where the real learning began. I thought that school had been a heavy imposition on my body that had tried to sever me from my former ways of doing in the kitchen, but I discovered that the hours I spent in the restaurant doing repetitive and menial tasks were truly shaping, and breaking down, my body. This is where I learned to work in sync with others. It was also in the tight spaces of that hot bistro kitchen that I became increasingly aware of my female body.

Central to my research was trying to understand women's realities in professional kitchens. Experiencing my own reality was important for how I would later work with and interview female chefs—it shaped not only my ways of doing but also my way of seeing. I was starting from the etic perspective, foreign to this hot and intense environment, and I tried to appreciate the objectivity this afforded me. However, I longed to be an insider, to fit in and to be able to contribute to production of food. There were many moments when I doubted I would ever have access to the emic knowledge of the kitchen. I was an inexperienced novice in the kitchen, which already made me awkward and out of place; to top it off, I was a pregnant woman taking up more space than I should have. The productive, able body is essential to kitchen work. There is much lifting, crouching, and shuffling quickly. As my body grew bigger each week, I became increasingly aware that the reproductive body is not seen as productive in the kitchen. My coworkers were afraid to let me lift heavy items, and I often felt sidelined because of my pregnant state. I had a hard time constantly crouching to take things out of the oven, and my shuffling became slower and slower. I had to take bathroom breaks at inconvenient moments. The cooks and other apprentices grunted or just shook their heads at me, but I was determined to keep pace and participate fully. What did professional chefs do when they got pregnant? This was a question I would later ask many of the participants in my research in Lyon. What I learned was that pregnancy and maternity were shouldered in the same way as a heavy stockpot or some other task that requires grit. I came to see my pregnancy as just part of the hard work—it should not be complained about.

As an apprentice, my pregnancy also distinguished my advanced age. I was going to be a mother, I was married, I was "madame." This did not mean that I received more respect than others. In fact, when the male executive chef for the restaurant group came to visit, he took it upon himself to ridicule and criticize me more than others. Chef Hervé hovered at the passthrough, slim and elegant in his chef's whites. His sky-high toque seemed to magnify his critical gaze as he looked down on each plate, scrutinizing the food and the people who had prepared it. It was as if each plate reflected the cook's inner soul and Chef Hervé's pronouncements were the last judgement. I think I can safely say that no one in our kitchen was going to heaven. As I prepared a mushroom salad and brought it to the passthrough, Hervé sneered, "Madame, is that how you cook at home for your family? Start again from the beginning. Look at how the mushrooms are cut! There is too much sauce. We cannot serve that!" I could feel the heat of shame rise to my cheeks, turning them red. I looked away from Hervé, pushed my emotions down somewhere deep inside, and started again. "It is just a salad, not your book manuscript," I told myself, trying to place this harsh criticism in perspective.

During Hervé's three-day reign of terror, I witnessed a commis and the sous-chef Cécile reduced to tears. No one was spared, but I observed that the critique of the female staff was particularly harsh and personal. During one dinner service, Hervé sat at his perch goading Cécile: "Could you be any slower? Look at this sloppy plating! I have no idea who put you in charge, but I am going to find out and tell them that I am not impressed. Hurry up with table 3's mains! I don't think you are cut out for this job. Let Christophe take over. He'll get the job done properly." The executive chef's visit was an assertion of the patriarchal order of the kitchen, despite the fact that the chef de cuisine was a woman. In fact, after Hervé's visit, Chef Marion seemed more macho: she threw more insults at everyone and worked harder than ever to show that she was faster and better than anyone else in the kitchen. It was as if Hervé had re-instilled the masculine norms of the kitchen to save it from any possible domestic female encroachment that might delegitimize the professional culinary activities that were happening in this kitchen (Trubek 2000, 126). Hervé had been policing professional boundaries (Ray 2016, 142–44).

In general, everyone in the kitchen lauded and respected stereotypical masculine behavior, such as yelling, sexist comments, and showing off, whether a man or a woman was performing it. During shifts when Stéphane was working, I felt this was particularly true. Stéphane was a commis, one step above an apprentice, and one of the most arrogant and mean people I had met in a kitchen. He liked to make snide remarks about my body as it got bigger each week, he laughed at me when he could see me falling behind, and he reluctantly helped me when I could not find something or did not know how a piece of kitchen equipment worked. He was equally terrible with other apprentices. On the flipside, he was perfectly subservient to any kitchen staff with a higher rank, at least to their faces. I did not like working with Stéphane. I was always watching my back because I felt he might throw me down the stairs for the fun of it. When I mentioned Stéphane's aggressive behavior to another apprentice whom he had reduced to tears the night before, she told me, "Oh, no, we love our Stéphane. He is such an excellent commis. He is going to be promoted to a better restaurant soon." I was very surprised at this response, but as I gained more experience, I learned that those who reinforce the hierarchy are rewarded and even admired—only the strong survive and advance. The problem here is the stereotype of strength is one that is masculine and self-serving.

By the end of my *stage*, I began to see my pregnant body as a form of resistance. While I was berated like other apprentices to be faster, cleaner, and all around better, my body demanded accommodation and resisted the actual space of the kitchen. As I learned to squeeze efficiently through the tight areas of the kitchen, as I got faster, and made consistently good food, my presence was a reminder that all kinds of bodies can be productive in more ways than one. It was not easy to keep up or work at the level that was demanded of me, but I wanted to prove that women shouldn't be excluded from work, no matter what their physical state might be. I had something to prove, but I was also falling into the "work hard and shut up" ethic that I later would come to associate with the imposition of masculine norms onto all bodies working in professional kitchens. At the time, I saw my new work ethic as a form of mastery over my own body and of the skills that allowed me to work more efficiently. Later I would come to see this work ethic as oppressive and misogynistic.

Learning a Craft

The life of the apprenti is far from the glamor of the kitchen one sees portrayed in magazines, films, and cooking shows. Initially, apprentices are not allowed to actually touch food.[2] They spend their time cleaning, running errands, and doing dirty work (cleaning up messes, eviscerating poultry, washing down the walk-in cooler, etc.) that no one higher up the brigade hierarchy wants to do. Young chefs I interviewed told me about how at this stage they felt they were learning by osmosis, taking in the sensory experience of the kitchen, observing when they could, and asking questions. Slowly, apprentices are given tasks preparing food. I often found myself chopping what felt like bales of parsley or peeling and mincing cases of onions with my eyes burning and tears streaming down my cheeks. Other kitchen staff noticed my sad state and consistently taunted me: "Don't cry! One day Chef will let you cook something." It would be a long time before I would be called to the *piano* to even observe.

From prep work and mise en place, the next progression of the kitchen apprentice is usually preparing cold food. This station is called garde-manger. A number of women told me that this is where they got stuck. One woman I interviewed, who attended the Institut Paul Bocuse and then apprenticed and worked at many fine-dining establishments, explained: "Women are seen as creative and precise. This is often why we are told to work garde-manger or pastry. At many restaurants, I had to really insist on working at a lot of different stations." Depending on the size of the kitchen, an apprentice would then move on from prep and cold food to other stations such as *saucier* (sautéing foods and creating sauces), *poissonnier* (the cooking of fish), or *grillardin* (grill or hotline). Not all kitchens have all of these stations, but there is generally a division of labor based on what type of ingredients (different meats or vegetables) and whether the dishes are hot or cold. The hierarchy, which is also gendered, tends to put hot meat dishes and men at the top, and cold, vegetable-based dishes and women at the bottom. These divisions also follow popular perceptions of gendered food preferences and eating: women eat salads and men prefer meat (Counihan 1999, 10). This gendered division of labor that begins in apprenticeship can limit the apprentice's skills and their ability to have upward mobility within the brigade system.

During this circuit of experiences through the different stations in the kitchen, the apprentice gains specialized knowledge. Some people choose to focus on a specific area, and others gain mastery at many stations. This second group is generally the people who go on to be sous-chef or chef de cuisine, overseeing the entire kitchen. It is through *stages* during culinary school, longer periods of apprenticeship during or just after school, and the first experiences of being commis that cooks really start to learn their craft.

As many of the boursières noted, the *stage* is when culinary students learn about the pace and demands of kitchen work. These are the first moments when the novice understands if they like and can handle this kind of work or not. The apprentice needs to have precision in the many techniques learned in school, and she needs to perform these skills at a speed that seems impossible at first. For me, it was only through being pushed each day that I was able to get faster and become more precise. I often went to sleep at night with Chef's voice ringing in my ears: "*Accélère!*" (Accelerate!) The goal of kitchen apprenticeship is to become precise, efficient, and fast. All of this should be done without complaining or getting flustered. As much as the body is being trained, there is also a professional behavior that is developed as the apprentice becomes integrated in to a community of practice.

Talking about the process of apprenticeship more generally, Michael Coy (1989) explains that "craftsmanship also refers to the code of normative behavior" (2). Codes must be followed to avoid divisive disputes and destructive competition. A key part of culinary apprenticeship is learning these codes and how to behave within a well-established hierarchy. In talking about legitimate peripheral participation, Jean Lave and Etienne Wenger (1991) describe how "learners inevitably participate in communities of practitioners and that the mastery of knowledge and skills requires newcomers to move toward full participation in the sociocultural practices of the community" (29). In culinary education this is why *stages* and apprenticeships are so important: initially, it is not even so much about honing one's skills as it is learning to participate in the culture of the kitchen. There are different kitchen cultures, but the brigade system tends to dominate and impose a patriarchal order in most restaurants in France, and the culture of the brigade is what young cooks learn in their early work experiences. It is this knowledge that will later make the cook feel at home in nearly any kitchen that follows the brigade system (Ray 2016).

Before training in schools became a norm in the culinary industries in France, apprenticeship was the main way to learn to cook professionally (Dornenburg and Page 2003, 94–95). The apprenticing tradition continued on even longer for women because they were initially excluded from professional programs. The gender segregation of schooling, apprenticeship, and the workplace are hierarchical: "Women's jobs are less 'attractive' than where men predominate; they offer fewer career opportunities and lower pay" (Daune-Richard 2000, 111). This gender segregation was apparent in culinary apprenticeships at the turn of the twentieth century, when women generally learned under other women in bourgeois homes and men apprenticed in restaurants in male-led brigades. These separate paths often codified different ways of doing. However, with the decline of bourgeois households in the twentieth century, there were fewer places for women to gain culinary experience, apart from courses designed for home cooks. This may partly explain the extreme underrepresentation of women in professional kitchens until the end of the twentieth century. The women who already had experience flooded the market for restaurant cooks and sometimes even set up shop on their own. After World War II, there were not enough of these women in charge to reproduce domestic female-dominated forms of apprenticeship of the Belle Époque.

Once women were formally admitted to culinary schools in France, little consideration was given to how these structures had been created for boys and men. Few educators or industry professionals were asking themselves how women would learn and succeed in these spaces. It seemed that culinary education and apprenticeship in France was a sort of litmus test for women who wanted to work in professional kitchens. In particular, apprenticeship tested a woman's resolve. Jack Haas (1989) has compared apprenticeship to an initiation rite: "The apprenticeship process is characterized by the inclusion of an initiation or trial by ordeal where newcomers are confronted by extreme situations which test their willingness to adapt by adopting the group's ways and accommodating the larger interests of the group" (87). For female apprentices, this generally means adapting to men's ways of doing and internalizing and suppressing female logics of work, which are often far more egalitarian and cooperative, as shown in chapter 5. Apprenticeship can be an unbearable experience for women who encounter discrimination. Many apprentices are told that how they were socialized their whole lives is unacceptable. Much in the same ways that organization of labor defaults to the male worker, the organization of education does the same.

From my own experience and from speaking with the boursières, I came to realize the importance of being placed in a good *stage* or internship. In my class, some of the more talented male culinary students were placed in Michelin-starred restaurants, while talented female students were put in bistros and smaller restaurants to work with less-prestigious chefs. The boursières reported similar treatment at their high schools—boys were generally given first pick. This is one of the most significant ways in which culinary education and the apprenticeship system create long-term inequality. Not getting the *stage* that you hoped for might not seem like a big deal, but it has a lasting impact on a young cook's culinary career. Without access to the best teachers, the more experienced cooks, and the chefs in top restaurants, the novice will not acquire the connections, the best techniques, or the standards of top restaurants. This is not always the case, but there is more at stake than just learning skills: a good position is also about having access to the deepest and best networks and is critical in order to have a successful career (Dornenburg and Page 2003, 97; Ray 2016, 114).

In France, building a strong résumé with many *belles adresses* (well-respected references) is essential to a successful career. Working with a well-known chef and having a reference from that person opens up new doors; culinary schools and instructors act as gatekeepers for these first points of entry. From my research, I have seen that these gatekeepers often have a strong gender bias, regardless of a student's talent and promise.

Conclusion

This chapter considers the ways in which the professionalization of work in professional kitchens and the creation of culinary schools in France excluded women from cooking beyond the domestic sphere. In the late nineteenth and early twentieth centuries, chefs advocating for professional recognition and explicitly separated women's domestic cooking from the male-dominated work in restaurant kitchens. Once women were permitted in these training programs in the second half of the twentieth century, they suffered harassment and discrimination that were both implicit and explicit. From nasty slights on the line to second choice in apprenticeship appointments, women are consistently placed at a disadvantage in a system that creates a boys' club. Much of the talk and treatment at school and in restaurant kitchens reinforces stereotypes about women not being strong enough to do the work or not being good enough because of their gender. The young women I interviewed reported that the insults stayed with them and caused them to doubt their place in the kitchen. Compounding the situation, few culinary instructors and chef de cuisine are women, leaving female novices largely without successful women as role models. As Drouard notes, "the female cooks' battle continues still today because prejudice and machismo are strong in kitchens" (2017, 259).

The boursières of the Eugénie Brazier scholarship were not always aware that they were working in a strong female tradition in Lyon. Their age and their greenness make them turn a blind eye to the challenges they will face moving forward. Most had experienced some form of discrimination, but they chose to soldier on in order to fulfill their dreams of working in an industry they love. They were learning to espouse the "work hard and shut up" modus operandi of the professional kitchen—a sort of structural violence that women learn to subsume. In order to prove their worth, these young women have to work harder and endure more harassment and hazing than male apprentices. Drawn by the creativity and the excitement of cooking, they are still being shaped through the experiences they have in every new kitchen where they apprentice or work as a commis.

My brief experiences of culinary school and apprenticeship led me to conclude that these institutions were complicit in laying the foundations for gender stereotypes and bias that produce inequality and discrimination in culinary industries. At the same time, there are women who are trying to shift these structures and create kitchens in which everyone can work together and flourish. Chapter 5 looks at these women and the work they are doing to re-create the kitchen in their own image and logic. It is perhaps their escape from these institutions that allows them to see culinary industries from a different perspective.

While life in the kitchen is not easy for most women, some are not deterred and aim for the top of their profession to show that women cook as well if not better than anyone else. The next chapter considers two women with their sights set high.

4

STARS IN THEIR EYES

Ambition and Bias in the Kitchen

As a way of explaining women's absence from culinary competitions, some male chefs and French food writers have declared that women are just not as competitive as men (Motoyama 2018). This sexist discourse impedes women's access to lucrative positions and publicity. Winning culinary competitions brings prestige that goes beyond the culinary professions—in France, these awards are a mark of cultural achievement. Winners of culinary awards reap the financial benefits through increased business in their restaurants, lucrative sponsorships, consulting work, and more media coverage that fuels the cycle of more business. Beyond monetary gain, if women are not in this spotlight at the top of the profession, it is difficult to encourage and build support networks for the next generation of young women coming up through the ranks. Women's glaring underrepresentation here says a lot about gender bias and discrimination that trickles down through the culinary industry, but it also rings true for other areas of high cultural production in France (music, fine arts, cinema, etc.) (Zancarini-Fournel 2005).

French and international media increasingly focus on women cooking at the highest levels, changing the way the French public views women in culinary professions. Television shows like *Top Chef France* have given women greater attention compared with traditional forms of food media such as magazines and guidebooks. This media focus has had a real impact on women's enrollment in culinary training and presence in the industry (Marie 2014; Frédiani 2017). New media representations of women who cook are changing popular images of culinary professions, and this means imagining chefs as female (Hansen 2008). Women are also starting to shape the media's construction of the culinary arts through blogs, television presence, traditional press, and restaurant reviews.

Of the women I interviewed, Tabata Mey, a *Top Chef* finalist and rising start of the Lyonnais culinary scene, and Audrey Jacquier, a candidate to lead the 2014 French team for the Bocuse d'Or and 2018 MOF contender, stood out as two of the most ambitious. They are both trying to crack the glass ceiling on the highest achievements in the French culinary world. Their successes and struggles demonstrate what women can do but also they also show that there are many obstacles that still need to be overcome.

Why the Top Matters

While I advocated in the previous chapter for paying particular attention to the rank and file in the kitchen, the top still matters. Laura Nader (1972) encouraged anthropologists to study the middle and upper ends of social structures, in addition to the lower levels, in order to understand power structures and how certain individuals maintain or come to power. For women at the top of the culinary profession, what did it take to get to this position? Women at the top in this field are scarce. Tracing the careers of Mey and Jacquier can tell us more about how pockets of power are created and maintained in the world of haute cuisine.

Haute cuisine suggests class, privilege and hierarchy (Mintz 1989, 187). This type of cooking requires many labor hours and often calls for expensive and hard to attain ingredients. Only the privileged few have access to the cultural experience of haute cuisine (Trubek 2000, 3–4). It is an art form that is a high representation of French culture as a whole, even if not many people in France eat this way (Ferguson 2004, 33; Naulin 2012). Cuisine gastronomique is a more accessible type of French cuisine that still maintains a high level of artistry. To further define cuisine gastronomique, I borrow from Éloire's definition: a cuisine prepared by a chef using artistry and skill, high-quality ingredients, and dishes that are presented in a formal dining situation (2011). Compared with haute cuisine establishments, the gastronomic restaurant is less exclusive and has become increasingly popular. Some of these restaurants may have a Michelin star, but the focus is not necessarily on the service or the décor in the dining room—the food is the center of attention here. In 2010, the "Gastronomic meal of the French" was inscribed in the UNESCO World Heritage List of the Intangible Cultural Heritage of Humanity. It shares many of the values of what I am defining as gastronomic cuisine: good food (preferably local), a fine table setting, the accompaniment of wine, and multiple courses (UNESCO n.d.). Both haute and gastronomic cuisines represent the upper echelons of French cooking.

The most practical reason to care about whether women are making it to the highest positions in culinary professions is money—working as a chef de cuisine, an executive chef or a culinary celebrity usually means higher earnings. Until women are economically independent and able to earn the same wage as men, there is no equity (Stotsky et al. 2016). Certainly, the issue of equal wages is important: women and men should earn the same wage for doing the same job; however, if women do not have access to the same jobs as men, that conversation cannot begin. Additionally, research shows that women's presence in leadership positions helps to undo gendered workplace hierarchy and segregation (Acker 2006; Huffman 2013; Stainback, Kleiner, and Skaggs 2016)

If there are few women at the top, it will be a challenge for young women to find female mentors who can teach them how to navigate this male-dominated profession.[1] Learning strategies for getting ahead and avoiding pitfalls are valuable particularly for young chefs who are put off by negative experiences early in their careers. Apprentices also have a chance to learn from more established female chefs that there are other ways of doing and ways of being outside of the male-dominated models. It is unlikely that there will be any cultural shift toward a more equitable workplace in the kitchen until there is a greater emphasis on female mentorship.

The women I apprenticed under were some of the toughest and most exacting chefs, but they were also hardest on other women. I asked them why, and one chef replied: "It's just the way it is. It was that way for me. Why should it be different for anyone else?" It was one of the ways in which I saw women continuing a legacy of toxic masculinity in the kitchen. Established women did not always want to bring along young women and help them to avoid the abuses of the kitchen that they themselves might have experienced. As a woman, I had to run the gauntlet just like they had and prove that I was capable of doing top-notch work. If I could not do the work the way the chef wanted it done, I was told: "Maybe the kitchen is not the place for you." This made me want to try harder. Even now I am not sure if this was their intended outcome or if they actually wanted me to leave. What I understood was that women at the top weren't always paving an easier way for their sisters. These should not be sugar-coated stories.

Tabata Mey: *Créatrice*

I had been trying to interview Tabata Mey for nearly six years, with no success, so I was almost trembling when I finally approached her to introduce myself. Tabata was perched like a small bird, her long black hair tied back and her thin legs dangling daintily from the tall chair. She was sitting at the bar of her jewel-box restaurant in Lyon's chic Sixth Arrondissement, tapping away intently at her computer. I knew I was interrupting but I did not want to miss this opportunity, so I said hello and quickly introduced myself. Tabata swiveled toward me, holding herself with the perfect posture of a chef or a ballerina, and smiled warmly. I briefly explained who I was and the project I was working on. "Perhaps Connie mentioned that I was trying to contact you to arrange an interview?" I asked hopefully. No, she had never heard of me, although one of our mutual friends had tried to put us in contact several times over the years. My timing never seemed to be right, but I was feeling hopeful as Tabata nodded and handed me her card: "I am off to Paris and very busy, but let's get together for coffee after the 15th." I took the card and told her I would be in touch. As I sat back down at my table, I looked down at the simple card. It read: "Tabata Mey—créatrice."

Originally from Rio de Janeiro, Brazil, Tabata was studying medicine when she realized her real passion lay with food. In order to make sure this was her calling, she did a stage at a restaurant in Rio and liked it so much that she stayed on for two years. Tabata realized that she needed to deepen her base of culinary knowledge, so at the age of twenty-five she moved to Lyon in 2003 to start her formal education in French cuisine at the Institut Paul Bocuse.

As a culinary student, Tabata had the opportunity to do stages in some of Lyon's best restaurants: at Nicolas Le Bec's two-starred Le Bec, and at the restaurant of Christian Têtedoie, a MOF and Michelin-starred chef. She had always hoped to work with legendary Lyonnais chef Paul Bocuse, but she was told that he did not take female stagiaires because his restaurant did not have a women's locker room.

After Tabata completed her diploma in 2004, she began working for Nicholas Le Bec, one of the city's rising culinary stars at the time. She returned to Brazil for a year to work with Alex Atala, one of Brazil's most notable chefs. Upon her return to Lyon, Tabata was promoted to Le Bec's seconde at his flagship restaurant. She was influential in helping the restaurant earn its second Michelin star, and she largely ran the show at one of the city's most important restaurants while Le Bec was busy developing new concepts and opening restaurants. This earned the young chef great admiration in the Lyon culinary community. Before Le Bec's fall from grace, Tabata left his restaurant to start an upscale Asian-inspired fast-food restaurant in the heart of Lyon.[2] In 2010, she was also preparing for the MOF competition. Tabata trained at Paul Bocuse's restaurant in Collonges-au-Mont-d'Or. This gave her the opportunity to get to know Paul Bocuse, one of her idols, who would later give a boost to her career. Tabata made it to the MOF finals, which is still a major accomplishment in the French culinary world.

In 2012, Tabata was a contestant in the third season of *Top Chef France.* This catapulted her into the media spotlight, where she thrived. Tabata knew how to charm the camera, and the viewers were intrigued by what were seen as her exotic origins. Despite her success with the judges and the audience, she ended her time on the show in fourth place. Although she did not win this televised culinary competition, Tabata was becoming more of a household name in France.

Top Chef France is modeled after the U.S. *Top Chef* show. First aired in 2009, *Top Chef France* is now in its tenth season. The French version has fewer commercials, and therefore the chef contestants are seen cooking for longer. Alice Béja (2014, 214) notes that *Top Chef France* brings together two of France's obsessions: *concours* (exams) and cuisine. In contrast to *Master Chef*, which features amateur cooks, *Top Chef France* contenders are all professionals. The candidates are chosen for their skill but also for their personal stories, and Tabata was neither the first nor last foreigner to compete on the show. The judges are all well-known French chefs, some of them MOF and Michelin starred. As of 2020 there has been only one female judge.

Top Chef France is not about teaching people to cook food they could make at home—it showcases the food of fantasy that can only be produced by professionals (Ray 2007). The culinary competition show is about spectacle and showmanship: it puts a new set of actors on the stage. This is a growing segment in prime-time food TV, which has moved from an instructional format to a focus on professionalization and competition (Oren 2013, 25). Hugh Curnutt (2016) explains that the rise of the reality TV format has made it possible for cooks who do not have any particular acting talent to participate in TV shows: most cooks and chefs are largely invisible (144), or they were invisible until their public exposure through reality TV.

The general public has been increasingly interested in the world of professional chefs since the early 2000s. Anthony Bourdain's *Kitchen Confidential: Adventures in the Culinary Underbelly* (2000) and Marco Pierre White's *The Devil in the Kitchen: Sex, Pain, Madness, and the Making of a Great Chef* (2007) were some of the first works to bring this testosterone-filled world of the back of the house to a broader audience in all of its sweaty glory. Chefs became rock stars but men have largely dominated this genre and shaped the Western imagination about the kitchen as a workplace. There are women who have also entered this literary space, notably Gabrielle Hamilton with *Blood, Bones, and Butter: The Inadvertent Education of a Reluctant Chef* (2011), Illiana Regan with *Burn the Place: A Memoir* (2019), and Lisa Donovan with *Our Lady of Perpetual Hunger: A Memoir* (2020). However, these accounts have yet to overturn the celebrated machismo of the kitchen. Similarly, women's presence on *Top Chef France* has not undone the masculine ways of doing in the professional kitchen, but it has shown that it is possible for women to survive, and even flourish, in this space.

The television cooking competition is another way to bring professional culinary culture, something that largely happens behind closed doors, into a public forum. Oren points out that "Here, cooking is far from a means of pleasure or social sharing, but a strictly regimented, highly individuated, labour-hierarchy within an economic circuit" (Oren 2013, 30). The professional world of chefs becomes a spectacle for viewer consumption. While instructional cooking shows are generally feminized displays of domesticity that have aspirational qualities, often set in the home kitchen, shows like *Iron Chef* are set in a sports arena setting that trades on the same sorts of macho rhetoric and competitive vibe as sporting events (Holden 2005). These shows mainly further stereotypes of the masculine nature of professional cooking. The drama and tension of producing complicated food under time and other constraints makes for good entertainment but it also gives viewers access to the cultural capital of criticism (Oren 2013). Even if the audience cannot taste or smell the food, they become proxy judges of performance, evaluating the character of the chef contestants and the visual aesthetics of the food produced. Television cooking shows throughout the world have contributed to the celebrity chef phenomenon that has brought the culinary arts to a broader audience. This is particularly true in the United States, where Americans had not necessarily seen gastronomy as an important cultural form (Ray 2007, 56). In France, however, professional culinary competition shows have brought an elite world of cooking and dining to a popular audience, where it can be further celebrated as a national treasure and important cultural product.

Before televised culinary competitions were popular, Paul Bocuse and his hypermasculine media presence helped make chefs more visible and less anonymous in French culture. It could be said that Bocuse was France's first superstar chef (Fantasia 2018, 176). With his name emblazoned above the entrance of his three-star Michelin restaurant, Monsieur Paul was ever present at the door to greet guests. The French media adored Bocuse's machismo, photographing him alongside the beautiful starlets who paid him homage at his restaurant. With numerous cookbooks and a memoir to his name, Bocuse's public image was carefully crafted to build a sense of culinary mastery and dominance that is firmly rooted in virility.

Culinary shows have brought the role of the chef as a performance further into the spotlight of French pop culture. Each episode of *Top Chef France* is an assemblage of several days of cooking. It is set to music and carefully composed to draw out dramatic moments. As Béja notes, "the kitchens of *Top Chef* are presented as mythical places in which the candidates must earn their place" (2014, 215). In season 3, in which Tabata competed, there were some interesting trials such as cooking at a fishing port and making an entire fish-based meal, including dessert. In one episode, the contestants had to cook at a neighbor's house. The idea was to see if these professional chefs could adapt to using a domestic kitchen. Throughout *Top Chef* there is a constant opposition between domestic and professional cooking. When a dish is not well presented or is a little rough around the edges, the judges will make comments such as "c'est de la cuisine de ménagère, ça!" (that's housewife cooking) (218). This insult is directed at both female and male contestants. While contestants largely maintain their professional decorum, accepting biting criticism with the rote "Oui, chef!" response, there are constant activations of gender stereotypes and displays of hegemonic masculinity. The vocabulary of war, aggression, and physical violence is normalized in this competitive setting.

While *Top Chef* has put women on a popular media stage as chefs on par with men, it has certainly not been a remedy for the rampant stereotypes, such as commenting on women's lack of professional skill because of their association with domestic cooking or their inability to work in professional settings because of their physique, that undermine women's success as culinary professionals. Being allowed to participate is a partial step to greater equity that at least puts women on the playing field. There have been three female winners in ten seasons of *Top Chef France*, but women are still a minority as contestants, winners, and judges.

Tabata claims she went on *Top Chef* for fun—she already had the next steps of her culinary career planned out. One day while she was training for the MOF competition at Bocuse's restaurant in Collonges, he approached her: "*Ma cocotte*, come have a coffee with me, I want to ask you something" (Riatto 2014). Monsieur Paul was opening a new restaurant to pay homage to the mères lyonnaises and he wanted Tabata to be the chef de cuisine. The restaurant was to be called Marguerite, after the wife of Lyonnais cinematographic inventor Auguste Lumière, and it would be in the renovated Villa Winkler in Lyon's Eighth Arrondissement. Tabata was the first woman to open and head up one of Bocuse's restaurants. Bocuse described the cuisine as a new, lighter version of Lyonnais classics, prepared with a feminine touch. When Marguerite opened in October 2013, Tabata was at the head of a brigade of seventeen talented young cooks.

I had planned to eat at Marguerite, but I did not make it in time to try Tabata's food. I arrived in Lyon to start my research fellowship in September 2014. Tabata left the restaurant shortly thereafter—only a little over a year from Marguerite's opening. I had been trying to contact Tabata to set up an interview. She had been on my radar from the very beginning of my research; I always felt that Tabata was one of the younger generation of women who was shaping the Lyonnais culinary scene. I grew increasingly frustrated when Tabata did not return my calls. Little did I know that this was a period of turmoil and upheaval for her.

Through the grapevine, I learned that Tabata was going through a divorce. Her first marriage was already on the rocks when she fell in love with her second, Ludovic Mey. In an interview with the French tabloid *Voici*, Tabata described the beginnings of her relationship with Ludovic as a "passionate gastronomic love story." She explained that "we fell in love in the kitchen. [. . .] After our shift, we would go to the Antiquaires, the cocktail bar, where we kept all of our cookbooks next to the whiskey. We would spend the rest of the evening leafing through cookbooks while drinking cocktails. Our thing is to have a bottle of wine at home and spread out on the carpet to get out the cookbooks" (Voici 2016). This kind of media coverage of Tabata's career, which focuses on her marital status, has been the norm. This is not the case when the loves of male chefs are chronicled—their partners remain in the background.

After leaving Marguerite, the couple took a year to travel the world looking for culinary inspiration. They spent time in Tabata's native Brazil and one of the world's gastronomic hot spots, Denmark. Tabata and Ludovic decided they would open a restaurant together in Lyon. However, before the restaurant opened they married, and Tabata was pregnant soon after. Tabata explained to L'Express (Gaudry 2016) that their "first baby is a restaurant." Mey does not talk about the challenges of being pregnant and opening a restaurant. This is in keeping with her attitude that the kitchen either breaks you or makes you stronger (à la Nietzsche). Like the apprentices in chapter 3, Mey embodies the "don't complain, just work hard" school of cooking that is often engrained in young cooks from the beginning of their training. She seems to take it a step further than most. In an interview with *Business O Féminin* (D'Oriola 2017), Tabata explains that "the younger generation doesn't understand that to arrive at the top [of the profession] you have to give blood. I experienced times in the kitchen when people would hit each other. Often, I would only sleep two hours a night. A chef even locked me in a kitchen once. But all of that shaped me." She also admits that cooking has softened from being so violent and abusive. This is a good thing: "The better we work, the more we enjoy it, and the more we want to work."

Les Apothicaires is Tabata and Ludovic Mey's lovechild project. The dining room of this tiny restaurant offers an intimate setting where friends gather over creative dishes and wines from some of the hippest French vintners. Tabata and Ludovic describe their food as "a culinary duet that is a reflection of who we are, inspired by our origins, travels and experiences [. . .] a melting pot" ("Restaurant Les Apothicaires" n.d.). A confit tandoori eggplant with masala served over a potato cream and garnished with capers brings together flavors and culinary techniques from all over the world to create a delectable dish that is something entirely new and difficult to categorize. Burrata cream with fermented chayote, kombu, and thyme also fuses culinary cultures through taste and techniques. At times the descriptions of dishes sound like impossible marriages, but tasting them is proof that there is an entire universe outside of regional culinary constructs. The dishes at the Les Apothicaires attest to Tabata and Ludovic's creativity and their ability to work together. Although this restaurant is a collaboration, Tabata has remained in the spotlight, and her husband's involvement has not eclipsed her contributions. This could be because of Tabata's initial celebrity, or it might also be that it is easier to accept female excellence when it is in league with that of men.

Since its opening in 2016, this joint venture has garnered a great deal of media attention with feature articles in the French newspaper

Figure 4.1: Tabata and Ludovic Mey. (Photo by Nicolas Villion)

La Libération and international papers such as the *Wall Street Journal* and the *Guardian*. In 2019, Les Apothicaires won the prestigious Gault and Millau Grand de Demain prize, which recognizes some of France's most talented up-and-coming chefs. The restaurant was also featured on the "50 Best Discovery" list that is put out by the World's 50 Best Restaurants organization. Most recently, the *Guide Michelin* awarded Les Apothicaires its first star in the 2020 guidebook.

Recently, Tabata and Ludovic took on a large project to reinvent the space of the well-known Tour Rose restaurant in Vieux-Lyon. The Tour Rose, once a Michelin-starred establishment, closed its doors in 2016. Tabata and Ludovic transformed the cavernous space into an upscale food court—the Food Traboule, named for the famous passageways that crisscross Vieux Lyon. The new all-day dining center is 800 square meters and spread out over four floors, with a number of chefs and concepts. The food is meant to be casual but high quality. This new establishment, located in one of the most touristic parts of town, opened in January 2020 to much acclaim.

In press releases and news articles, Tabata is the headliner. Journalists focus on her fame as a *Top Chef France* contender to legitimate her role in this project and mention Ludovic as "son mari" (her husband) and as a supporting actor. Writing about the recent opening of Food Traboule, *Le Point* wrote: "'I want to give meaning to the word "gastronomy,"' stated Tabata Mey who, with her husband Ludovic, was in charge of the food part of this project" (Agence France-Presse 2020). Stéphane Méjanés (2020) notes Tabata's *Top Chef* fame in the first sentence of his article about the opening of the Food Traboule: "Tabata could barely hide her fatigue behind a bright smile—the same one viewers discovered on *Top Chef* in 2012." This is a shift in the usual language describing female chefs and their legitimacy in the culinary world; Tabata has not been eclipsed by her husband, who does a good portion of the cooking and creating in their restaurant. When interviewed, she is careful to validate Ludovic's role as her partner in life and business.

Having followed Tabata's career, I have noticed how this talented chef has used her skill, media presence, and discipline to create a name for herself. Despite the strong hold of the old boys' club that dominates the Lyonnais culinary scene, Tabata Mey is certainly one of the people who is shaping the future of the city's culinary identity. Tabata's status as a foreigner has not been problematic as she takes on the role as a representative of Lyonnais cuisine. Tabata's situation has even been advantageous, allowing her to work outside of traditional scripts like that of the mères lyonnaises. Other foreigners have been accepted and naturalized into the Lyonnais culinary scene, but Tabata is one of the first women to do so. Perhaps it was her training at the Institut Paul Bocuse, her benediction by Monsieur Paul, and her grit and persistence as a top-notch professional that have helped her to succeed. What is certain is that Tabata used culinary competitions, both the MOF and *Top Chef France*, to prove herself and gain legitimacy in the rather closed world of gastronomic cooking in France. Tabata served as a judge on the panel that selected the French team for the 2020 Bocuse d'Or competition, showing her place in the elite world of French cuisine. Passing to the other side as a judge is both a sign that a person has arrived and a major coup because there have been so few female judges.

Audrey Jacquier: Homegrown Talent

It was a warm spring morning when I headed over to Le Vivarais in the Second Arrondissement. I was perspiring as I locked my bicycle just in front of the restaurant in the pretty little square near the banks of the Rhône. Audrey Jacquier had agreed to meet me before she got too busy prepping for the lunch service. Le Vivarais is Audrey's family's restaurant and a sort of second home for her. The chef de cuisine is her father, William, and she works as his seconde. William Jacquier earned the title of MOF in 1996, after training with some of Lyon's top talent—Orsi, Gervais, Bocuse, and Pignol. I was curious to hear more about what it was like to grow up in a prominent culinary family in Lyon and to decide to pursue cooking as a career.

As I walked through the front door, I saw that the tables were set with light-colored linens and the silverware gleamed in the morning sun—the room had a casual yet elegant feel. Before this interview, I had studied the menu at Le Vivarais. The food reflects the atmosphere: Lyonnais staples revisited with a fine touch and lightness. The menu included a house-made Richelieu *pâté en croûte* (pâté in a baked crust) and mères lyonnaises artichoke hearts with foie gras and toasted brioche for starters, and pike quenelle with Nantua sauce and fresh frogs from the Dombes cooked in parsley butter for mains.[3] These dishes are all direct references to Lyonnais classics but with modern twists: for example, the quenelle is served with risotto, where it would usually be served on its own or with white rice on the side. There was also a vegetarian option on the menu, which denoted an awareness of current trends and changing dining habits in France. Prix fixe menus varied in price from 18 euros at lunch to 39 euros for a three-course offering. Audrey later explained to me that they have a faithful clientele from the surrounding neighborhood, which is notoriously bourgeois, Catholic, and conservative. I imagined this is the food that people in the area wanted to eat.

When I met Audrey, I was struck by her youth. She was twenty-three years old at the time. Her long dark hair was pulled back tightly in a

Figure 4.2: Audrey Jacquier at her family's restaurant, Le Vivarais.

ponytail, and under her crisp white chef's coat she was wearing a black turtleneck, despite the heat of the day and the kitchen. This lanky young woman showed me to a table and offered me a coffee. I gladly accepted her offer, sat down, and took in the welcoming space. I started by asking about her career trajectory. I wanted to get straight to questions I had about her status as a child prodigy and her renowned chef father, but I knew I had to let her tell me her story on her own terms. I wanted to see how she constructed her own narrative to represent and make sense of who she is today and how her gender played into her story.

I began by asking Audrey how she got started with cooking. She told me it was a family affair and that she could not really remember a time when she wasn't in the kitchen: "I had a pretty atypical career path because I was in the kitchen straight away. My great-grandfather was in the kitchen, my father was in the kitchen, so it jumped a generation.

On my mother's side, it was the same thing, so it was into the kitchen. [. . .] So, I know from routine and experience when a dish is good or not." Audrey explained that there are some things you just have to start young in order to feel comfortable with: "For example, me, I feel more comfortable in the kitchen than in the dining room or doing computer work. Well . . . I am fully immersed in it [the kitchen]." Although she had been learning alongside her father, Audrey also started her formal training at Lycée Jehanne de France. She was not impressed with many of her classmates who did not really know what they wanted to do and who were just trying out cooking. She found learning about other trades at school interesting, but she always knew she wanted to cook.

Before coming to work full-time in her family's restaurant, Audrey did a number of stages and worked as a commis in restaurants throughout Lyon. Her family name helped her access a strong culinary network. Priscilla Parkhurst Ferguson and Sharon Zukin (1998: 99) describe the way in which this entry into the "mafia," a very closed circle of influential people that are often related through kinship ties, puts a young cook into a social network that will put them in good standing for a lifetime. After interviewing several daughters of prominent Lyonnais chefs, I noticed that gender was not a barrier to access this exclusive network, if you were born into it.

I asked Audrey how it felt to often be the only woman in the restaurant kitchen or the culinary competition. She shrugged her shoulders: "I am of the generation where there are all sorts in the kitchen and dining room. It's not the same as it used to be. It's more mixed now, and much nicer because there is a bit of everything, diversity." The voices of the boursières who won the Eugénie Brazier scholarship echo here: those young women also told me forthrightly that women have as much right to be in the kitchen as men.

At the same time, Audrey told me that it was not always easy to be a woman in the kitchen:

> It's not like you arrive in the kitchen as a woman and everyone is like "ah, oui! You know how to cook. There you go." No, no, you have to know how to assert yourself. Man or woman, you are going to say it to me like that because if I ask you to do something a certain way, it's because there is a reason. It's not just because I want it to be that way.

> There is a reason for it. If I tell you to put 100 grams of butter, you put in 100 grams of butter, not 102. You really have to be insistent with what you say, with what you do. That's kitchen management. You have to fully assert yourself, you have to do it and if you are not okay with it, we can talk about it. There is a lot of diplomacy and support, you have to have a fair workplace.

Audrey was also using the same language as Brigitte Josserand and an older generation of mère-lyonnaise-type chefs. There was that term again: "You have to know how to assert yourself [*s'imposer*]." This is true for anyone in a leadership role in a kitchen, but from my interviews, this was particularly true for women. In order to claim your place, you had to make your presence known and be sure of yourself. At the same time, the second half of Audrey's comment reveals a softer, more diplomatic side; her rule in the kitchen is not entirely totalitarian. There is room for talking and discussion. Audrey emphasizes creating a fair workplace.

This is not always an easy task. Audrey told me she had a particularly hard time when she hired young people and they did not like being told what to do by such a young woman. At twenty-three, Audrey is her father's seconde, which means that she is in charge of the kitchen when he is not there and is capable of running the kitchen on her own. She told me that at times, young apprentis and commis questioned her authority because they did not always accept that she was more experienced than them: "Yes, it happens quite often, mostly when we hire people, young people would say 'You are the same age as me and you are in charge.' And, I would say, 'Yes, but maybe I have more experience than you or I do things differently. It's because I am twenty-three and you are thirty that you are not going to take me seriously.'"

When I asked Audrey how she would describe her cooking, she told me that it was feminine:

> Girls are more delicate, we have a better sense for details. Men are sometimes brutes. They can be delicate but not in the same way. When we do a Lyonnais menu, we do a "semi-gastro" Lyonnais, which means we take more time, we work the products more, we make them better. I am all about having something simple that has lots of taste. You can have something that is really beautiful, a work of art, but it has no taste, dull, overworked—it's not great.

Audrey relates femininity to simplicity and a move away from aesthetic showiness to focus on taste. She also echoed what other chefs had said about women having a certain sensibility in the kitchen. Some common descriptors of women's cooking in professional kitchens include delicate, detailed-oriented, and creative. After talking to many chefs, I still can't help but think that this is a stereotype that drives behaviors, like a self-fulfilling prophecy—women are expected to work in these ways. What I noticed is that these are all traits and ways of working that are highly regarded in gastronomic cuisine.

Audrey Jacquier first caught my attention when I saw her photo in the Lyon newspaper. The article talked about her bid to claim a spot on the French team for the 2015 Bocuse d'Or culinary competition. She was making headlines not only because she was the only woman in the competition but because she was also the youngest (aged twenty-two at the time). What made Audrey want to compete in culinary competitions? When I asked her about her participation in culinary concours, she told me:

> Yes, not everyone likes them, it's special. In general, they are challenges, you have to give the best of yourself. I haven't always won, but I haven't often lost. It's constant work. I have done quite a few concours, and sometimes I even forget I have done them, but it helps me to stay on the circuit. Am I still any good? I do outside competitions to see what they will give me. Thanks to these events, I have been able to promote myself—people recognize me a little now. [. . .] I do competitions for a laugh, to question myself, to improve my cooking. It's also a showcase.

Jacquier participates in culinary competitions of her own volition and for her own reasons. It may be the case that having a MOF for a father is an influence, but she was adamant about wanting to compete to become a better chef and to make a name for herself. Audrey Jacquier has participated in both the MOF and the Bocuse d'Or, and merely participating in culinary competitions garners attention and raises the profile of individual chefs, as it did for Audrey.

Concours are part of a tradition of French republican meritocracy. The term "concours" directly translates as competition but it is most often used to refer to the competitive entrance exams in schools and the exams to enter into the public service. Jean-Michel Eymeri-Douzans

(2012) explains that concours were important after the French Revolution because they were a way to abolish the nobility's privileges. Instead of a birthright, candidates are judged on their ability, which is cultivated through education. This is not to say that concours do not propagate hierarchical structures in governance and education. Despite claims of equality, the middle class is overrepresented in the best educational opportunities. Concours were not a French invention, but they have come to define French society and its social-class stratification. The French obsession with concours partly explains the popularity of culinary competitions and how they have become both entertainment and a part of French culture more generally. These culinary competitions, like their administrative and educational counterparts, also play a part in stratifying power.

There are numerous culinary concours in France but the most prestigious are the MOF and the Bocuse d'Or, an international competition that takes place in Lyon. Paul Bocuse started the Bocuse d'Or international culinary competition in 1987. The competition website states that Bocuse was "replicating the codes of major sporting events, he imagined a true show placing the emphasis on cooking and on the chefs" (Bocuse d'Or n.d.). This competition takes place every two years during the Sirha culinary trade show in Lyon. An initial national selection process winnows down the applicants to twenty-four teams from all over the world, who have five hours and thirty-five minutes to prepare a series of complex dishes in front of a live audience. A jury of chefs then judges the dishes. The event was a rather ingenious invention on Bocuse's part because it not only celebrates his legacy as one of France's most prominent chefs but promotes Lyon's position as the gastronomic capital of the world. The competition also puts chefs in the spotlight, long before TV shows were doing so in France, and they become media celebrities and important brands. As already noted, the emphasis on sporting events and competition also plays to masculine attitudes about excellence and the public performance of culinary mastery. As with the Olympics, there is a nationalistic aspect to this competition. In the stands, spectators wave national flags to cheer on their country's team as they cook.

In the competition's thirty years, there has only ever been one woman who has led a national team to victory—Léa Linster of Luxembourg in 1989. Audrey noted that when she was competing for her spot to lead the French team in 2015, she was the only woman vying for this position. There were commis who were women but no other women in the central spotlight. In the end, Audrey felt that the judges had taken her seriously despite her young age and her gender: "They told me that the dishes I made were excellent—my work should have been selected, but they did not know me yet. I am still young and I can still do things. I have time." Although she did not win, Audrey's selection as a finalist in the competition to decide who would head up the French national team brought her national recognition in the gastronomic world. This would not be her last competition.

Following in her father's footsteps, Audrey made a bid for the title of MOF in 2018. Given that this is perhaps the most challenging and exclusive culinary competition in France, it is not all that surprising that she did not make the first cut. It is common for candidates to try several times before making it.

The origins of the MOF competition date back to 1913, when art critic and journalist Lucien Koltz made a call to revitalize manual trades in France, a society where trades and apprenticeship were in decline in the face of growing industrialization. In 1924 the French government authorized the First National Exhibition of Work at the Hôtel de Ville in Paris, where the first concours took place. The event was a success, and the competitions continue today. In 1929, MOF René Petit proposed to other recipients of this award that they establish an association to promote the MOF and its winners.

The central goal of the MOF is to recognize manual labor and intellectual work, raising the status of artisanal production (Mériot 2002, 178–79). Since 1952, the Ministère de l'éducation nationale has been coordinating the MOF competitions and the awards are recognized as the equivalent of a diploma at the level of the *baccalauréat plus deux* (BAC+2) (Mériot 2002). The MOF recognizes and organizes competitions for 220 crafts (*métiers*). Although the MOF is a called a competition, it is truly a concours in the French sense: candidates are completing a series of exams. The MOF also further contributes to the professionalization of culinary work, and it imposes a hierarchical order within the profession.

The MOF in *Cuisine et gastronomie* (cooking) falls under the broader umbrella of métier de bouche. Ferguson (2014, 244) notes that the MOF and other culinary competitions realized Carême's dream from the nineteenth century: he thought culinary competitions would be good for raising the standards and profile of French cuisine and for creating a system similar to that of guilds, the *corps de métiers* (professional group). Recognized and legitimated by their peers, the MOF chefs are an elite group that go through a highly selective process in order to receive their title and membership into this limited group. In France, the MOF plays an important part in regulating and reproducing a "gastronomic field" (Ferguson 2004; Harris and Giuffre 2015) that places haute cuisine and its practitioners at the pinnacle of culinary professions. Ferguson asserts that the MOF is a competition that is less about pitting individuals against each other "than against an idea of excellence upheld by acknowledged authorities" (2014).

Held every four years, the culinary competition begins with a pool of several hundred candidates, from which thirty or forty semifinalists are selected. The average age of candidates is thirty-five (Mériot 2002, 179). There are usually only four or five winners. Between 1924 and 2000, only 131 MOF titles were awarded in the cuisine category (Fantasia 2018, 65). Unlike Michelin stars, the MOF title cannot be taken away. It is a lasting mark of achievement and prestige that brings with it recognition and notoriety in France. MOF are allowed to wear the tricolor collar on their coats, and their restaurants can display the official MOF plaque. Wearing the collar without the diploma is a punishable crime.

Although the title is described as a national honor, there is the unspoken reality that the MOF also brings economic opportunities. MOF chefs find jobs at the best restaurants and they command top salaries. They serve on boards, promote products and events, and have an easier time finding financing (Mériot 2002, 66). This is an important point in the discussion of gender equality: if women do not have access or if they are not well-represented in prestigious competitions such as the MOF, they will never have the same earning power, they will not play a part in constructing the gastronomic field, and it will be difficult for them to be accepted as tastemakers.

As Rick Fantasia remarks in *French Gastronomy and the Magic of Americanism* (2014),

> it is not a matter of simple, unadulterated "experience" or the specific culinary skills that win such contests but the social production of an

> outlook and comportment that reflects a measure of confidence in the experience that one has gained. In this sense, being stamped an MOF finalist might just represent the confirmation of one's place in a select group of chefs, as much as representing a sure point of entry into it. (68)

In essence, chefs have to show up to the competition already a part of the elite inner circles of haute cuisine, or at least perform as if they are part of that rarefied world. This points back to the discussion in chapter 3 about the gender bias in culinary education and access to top apprenticeships. If women are unable to access this elite world of culinary experiences, it is unlikely they will be able to attain such titles as MOF and reap the benefits that are associated with it. Also, if the jury envisions the "outlook and comportment" of a MOF as male by default, this poses a serious barrier for entry for women. When journalist Sono Motoyama (2018) asked Chef Christophe Quantin, one of three vice presidents of the 2018 MOF competition, why there is not more diversity in the competition, he responded: "We can't influence that. We take the candidates that sign up voluntarily. Even if there are more and more women in the profession, they have to have a competitive spirit. It's not always in women's characters to compete. In addition, it's competing against men, which could be an additional impediment." Quantin's comments demonstrate the stereotypes about gender and performance that are embedded in the profession and French society more generally. They also show that the organization lacks the desire to improve diversity or even acknowledge its structural inequalities. The women who compete in these exclusive concours are pushing back on the boundaries that these stereotypes create. In 2018 MOF competition, two women made the MOF finals. Neither were awarded the title.

Stéphanie Le Quellec, a Michelin-starred chef and the winner of *Top Chef: France* 2011, was one of the two female finalists in the 2018 MOF competition. She also made a bid for the MOF title in 2014. Having worked with a number of MOF chefs, she was inspired by their skill and mastery in the kitchen. Le Quellec made many personal sacrifices while preparing for the MOF competition. She explains how she had to sacrifice her family life in order to ready herself for the challenges of the MOF: "There's a lot of work. I don't know if that's an investment that women are willing to put in. [For me] it means that during the week I don't see my children. I don't think the MOF committee can do much; it's the reality of the profession" (Motoyama 2018). Le Quellec echoes the shadowy voice in French society that tells women that they can compete with men but that they also have to maintain their duties of the good mother, wife, and daughter all at the same time. Again, the double bind constrains women as they reach for the top. Despite Le Quellec's sacrifices, she was ultimately unsuccessful in her second bid for the MOF title.

The absolute despair and pain of unsuccessful MOF candidates is heart-wrenchingly chronicled in the documentary film *Kings of Pastry* (2009), which follows Jacquy Pfeiffer's participation in the finals for the MOF in pastry. We see Jacquy's partner taking care of children and offering emotional support throughout the preparations leading up to the competition and during the multiday trials. The all-male field of finalists are completely focused on their work, while their spouses and partners (some of them accomplished chefs in their own right) pick up the slack at home while leading their own professional lives. The MOF competitions focus on the individuals, but it is really a team of people from distinguished mentors to family members that ensure candidates' success. It is unlikely that a mere lack of desire to compete is what is keeping female chefs from trying to attain the title of MOF. The real reasons are structural: in many cases, women are not competing on a level playing field because they do not usually have the same family and professional support as men. It is also expensive to prepare and compete in the MOF competition: competitors have to bring all of their own equipment to the competitions, they hire consultants to help them train, they spend hours preparing, and they need an employer who will grant them the time and also sometimes offset the costs. Candidates claim that it can cost up to 20,000 euros to compete in the MOF finals (Motoyama 2018).

Audrey Jacquier is young to be competing in the MOF competition, but this is also to her advantage: she does not yet have a family of her own or other obligations beyond the kitchen. She may choose not to have children, like Virginie Basselot, who is one of two women who holds the title of MOF. For now, Audrey has the support of her father and his restaurant. She will likely attempt the MOF again. From an early age, Jacquier's father has trained her to compete, to hold up to the pressure, and she has come to enjoy the thrill of competition. Jacquier and Le Quellec show that women do like to compete and that they have something to prove to themselves and the world—that they can produce food of great artistic and technical excellence that is worthy of recognition.

Changing Media Representations of Female Culinary Professionals

Television shows and culinary competitions are just two of the ways in which chefs gain visibility. Print and online journalism are also powerful forums that shape the status of chefs. Like with television and competitions, women have tended to be underrepresented in these forms of media. Not much has changed since the rise of gastronomic literature in the 1930s in France—most food critics and journalists writing about food tend to be White Frenchmen. After the waves caused by the #MeToo movement, there have been some changes in this ossified boys' club. Women are beginning to make their place as prominent critics and food writers in France, and many have the objective of raising the profile of women working as chefs.

In particular, Estérelle Payany has been a prominent voice leading the charge to make women in kitchens more visible. Payany, a Paris-based *critique gastronomique*, mainly writes for *Télérama*.[4] Her restaurant reviews feature many ethnically diverse restaurants, pieces that are commentaries on guidebooks (including the *Guide Michelin*), and other news in the culinary world. She has also authored a number of cookbooks. Peyany collaborated with filmmaker Vérane Frédiani to create a database of restaurants in France who have female chefs. The database and a corresponding map were published in *Télérama* in March 2018 and circulated widely in the French media. This is one important example of the ways in which journalists have tried to improve the visibility of women in restaurants. Vérane Frédiani and Estérelle Peyany argue that the media focuses less on women because "they are not as present in haute cuisine [. . .] women are not as well-known as chefs. Many chefs love citing their mothers' and grandmothers' savoir faire, it is now time to recognize and affirm the work of women in the arena of gastronomy" (Frédiani and Peyany 2018).

Women's writing about food in France has largely been relegated to women's publications or inconsequential columns that talk about recipes to serve at dinner parties and how to be a good hostess. Since the #MeToo movement began in 2015, a shift has begun in French journalism—women are writing about food in more serious publications and in forms that men have long dominated. Christel Brion's writing is one example: Brion writes articles about important culinary figures and food trends in France for *L'Obs.*[5] A longtime employee at this weekly newsmagazine, Brion began in 2012 to focus on food writing. She does not write exclusively for women or about women—Brion's coverage is inclusive and her presence as the main food writer at a national weekly is a major win for bettering women's representation in the French media.

Camille Labro, journalist, author, and documentary filmmaker, is another food writer who has broken into the world of mainstream French news media. She regularly pens food columns for *Le Monde*, *M le magazine du Monde*, and *Vogue*. Labro focuses on issues of sustainability and vegetarian cuisine, as well as major events in the French culinary world. Labro's writing in *Le Monde* is another big step for women having a voice and shaping discourse about food for a broad audience.

Payany's, Brion's, and Labro's work as critics, writers, and tastemakers has already proven to be much more inclusive than their male counterparts. These journalists are aware of women's underrepresentation in their professions and also in the culinary world. They seek to represent ethnic minorities and their culinary traditions, as well as the growing movement toward a more plant-based diet. They are choosing to focus on issues of representation, often calling out the lack of women in prestigious forums such as the *Guide Michelin*. These women also have male allies who are supporting this movement to address the gender bias in food media. Of particular note is Alexandre Cammas, the cofounder of *Le Fooding*, a restaurant and gastronomic events guide that was started in 2000 in hopes of modernizing food guides. Cammas (2012) has been highly critical of the *Guide Michelin*, questioning the guide's ethics and the role of influential chefs in the awarding of stars.

When I began my research, there was nearly no talk of women cooking in restaurants in France. One of the most interesting developments in the course of my fieldwork has been to see the spotlight move to focus more on women. At the start of this book, I took issue with the ways in which early food writers, gastronomes, gave voice to the lives and work of the mères lyonnaises. With this recent movement in food writing, we are finally seeing women taking back their story, and this time as central actors.

Conclusion

Tabata Mey and Audrey Jacquier have both made names for themselves in the local Lyon culinary scene as well as on the national stage. Their stories show that some women do have a competitive spirit and a strong desire to prove themselves on the same stage as men—they want to be the best at what they do. Recognition of talent and skill is important not only for the individual ego (and, yes, women have egos) but also from a financial perspective. Winning *Top Chef* or the title of MOF means having access to sponsorships, business opportunities, and increased clientele. Women can never have equality with men if they are not financially independent and stable.

Culinary competitions and awards were created to raise the profile and the bar for artisanal skill in the culinary arts. However, when many of these competitions were established, they were developed based on patriarchal networks and hierarchies that are the backbone of the professional culinary world. In order to be more inclusive of women and minorities, the institutions that promote culinary excellence need to find ways to encourage diverse participants. This might have to come from restructuring the way competitions are run, truly making them open to all forms of excellence. Television shows like *Top Chef* are the newcomers to this forum, but they perhaps have the most potential to change the structural issues associated with cooking and gender. This will only come from a concerted effort to move beyond clichés and stereotypes about women in general. Seeing women not only as nurturing home cooks or as set decorations, but rather as top-notch professionals in commercial kitchens is one way of changing how the public view French women as chefs and cooks. This means framing women's food work as labor that is as equally as productive as men's.

In the age of the superstar chef, recognition is critical. This chapter discusses a variety of platforms through which chefs can gain notoriety in the public eye and within the profession. It also considers the role of the media in shaping and changing the public's perception of women cooking professionally. Until women are a norm rather than an exception as competitors, as winners of prestigious awards, as representatives of culinary professions, and as legitimate leaders in the industry, bias against women's participation will continue. At the same time, this bias is indicative of the broader social norms about appropriate work for women.

The next chapter looks at women who operate outside the standard norms and hierarchies of the professional kitchen to give value and meaning to their professional food work. These are women who have pushed back against the gendered organization of work and the structures of the professional kitchen to show that there are other ways of doing that allow for cooperation and creativity.

5

CHEFFE DE CUISINE

Women Redefining the Kitchen and Labor

As Marion called out orders to the hotline, the cooks working at the *piano* and the oven called back, "Oui, chef!" This is fairly normal language in the kitchen, but I wondered if I would ever hear "Oui, cheffe!" The *f* would be slightly more pronounced to denote that the person in charge is a woman. Why do language and kitchen norms not recognize women as leaders in the professional kitchen? Marion was the fastest and toughest person cooking in the entire restaurant, but the fact she was a woman was only referred to if she slipped up or if she lost her temper, which like a lot of chefs she did fairly often. Marion tried to be as tough as the men. To some degree, she was one of the boys—Marion was the chef. However, this also meant she could never fully express herself as a woman in this kitchen because the people working under her would challenge her authority if she let up her domineering male performance—authority was deeply tied to masculinity.

In French, nouns are either feminine or masculine. However, it was not until 2019 that the Académie française, the official watchdog of the French language, accepted the feminization of professional titles such as chef/cheffe. Prior to this decision, there were long battles over the need to create female titles to undermine the gender hierarchies within so many professions in France (Van Compernolle 2007). The Académie française admitted that professions with the very rigid hierarchies resisted this shift the most (Académie française 2014). This is certainly the case with culinary professions, where chef is almost synonymous with man. The Académie had some debate over how to feminize the title of "chef," but they finally adopted the term "cheffe" because it was already in use. Before the official acceptance of this title, feminist journalists—such as Vérane Frédiani and Estérelle Payany, who published *Cheffes, 500 Femmes qui font la différence dans les cuisines de France* (2019)—used "cheffe" to bring attention to women who cook professionally. The term is still in its infancy, and men and women working in kitchens contest its use. However, the term "cheffe" does signal the possibility for more equal recognition of women within the profession. While the feminization of professional titles has fallen out of usage in the English language and is derogatory or sexist, the opposite is true in French (Conrick 2009). The Académie française made a strong statement against proposals to move the French language toward gender neutrality, stating that such changes would lead to a "disunited language, disparate in its expression, creating a confusion that borders on illegibility" (Timsit 2017). The issue here is not sexism or inequality but rather linguistic coherence—French is a language that already uses gendered articles for nouns, so making them neutral would be incoherent. The academy found the Sapir-Whorf hypothesis, that language shapes how we think, unconvincing.

The association of men with professional cooking is deeply imbedded in language, with the term "chef" in current use. This can be seen in almost every aspect of the professional kitchen, from the heavy equipment (Harris & Giuffre 2015, 101; Ray 2016, 140–41) to the patriarchal organization of work into the brigade system (see fig 1.2), in which the chef de cuisine is the kitchen equivalent of a general (Trubek 2000). This chain of subordination plays strongly on masculine constructs of strength, bodily discipline, and superiority of skill. In general, the male chef who rises to the top is the one who is fastest, most precise, and often the loudest—commanding others around him and not shying away from the use of sharp language and physical violence to get his point across.

These hierarchies are part of the culture of small groups that Fine (2009) calls "idiocultures," which are a shared systems of knowledge, beliefs, customs, and behaviors that determine the boundaries of a group, a recognition of shared experiences, and a way through which members of the group construct a shared social reality (116). In his studies of professional kitchen cultures, Fine does not explore to what extent gender norms and gendered experiences play a part in creating idioculture. The sexualized workplace of the male-dominated kitchen can actively exclude or deter women's participation (Harris and Giuffre 2015, 114). A woman's acceptance into the workplace can depend on how she deals with sexual joking and teasing. If gender inequality is so deeply structural in professional cooking, how can there be a space for women to participate and succeed? In my research, I found that there were women who are "undoing gender" (Deutsch 2007) and questioning the patriarchal organizational structures (Acker 1990) of the French restaurant kitchen.

Focusing on the careers of Paulette Castaing, Sonia Ezgulian, and Connie Zagora, this chapter shows that it is possible to cook, and run a kitchen, outside of masculine gender norms. Castaing, Ezgulian, and Zagora have created new professional models in the kitchen. Women's presence and impact in changing the gendered dynamics of work in fields such as medicine and engineering have been well documented (Baudelot 2000; Powell, Bagilhole, and Dainty 2009; Jefferson, Bloor, and Maynard 2015), but there has been little consideration for how women are changing culinary fields. While some women take on male roles and espouse masculine stereotypes in the kitchen (Swinbank 2002), there are those who have reimagined culinary work outside of specific gender norms and stereotypes by reordering the kitchen, breaking down hierarchies, and changing ways of learning and doing in the professional kitchen. This is reflected not only in the organization of labor and workspaces but also through the types of cuisine prepared. Harking back to the legendary mères lyonnaises, women have been shaping Lyon's cuisine through this imposition of female sensibilities about food and through their ways of doing. This chapter builds on this history to look at the innovative ways in which women reclaim kitchen spaces and how they shape the construction of local cuisine in Lyon.

Paulette Castaing: The Last Mère Moves beyond the Legend

I had heard about Paulette Castaing from a number of chefs—some people referred to Castaing as the last real mère. A newspaper article about her hundredth birthday celebration caught my attention;

Figure 5.1: Paulette Castaing in her kitchen. (Photo courtesy of Danièle Chambeyron)

Paulette Castaing is one of the reasons I started this research when I did—I wanted to meet her. The thought of Castaing as the last repository of some special knowledge and her advanced age gave my grant proposals an urgent tone. Later, I realized I was wrong to see Paulette Castaing as a living relic and to think that her knowledge and memories would be gone when she left this world behind.

When I finally got back to Lyon in 2012, it was already too late: Castaing was still alive, but her story was already partially lost to the fog of dementia. At first, I was disappointed not to have the opportunity to commune with this grande dame but soon discovered that Paulette's stories lived on in her legacy—her family and the chefs she had trained. Castaing's daughter, Danièle, was extremely generous in letting me spend a day at her home interviewing her and rifling through a copious family archive. I pieced together Madame Castaing's life and contributions to French cuisine from these memories and snippets of paper. When I sat down with Alain Alexanian, a renowned Lyonnais chef and an adoring former apprentice, he helped me to further flesh out the outlines of Castaing's work and life.

Paule Germaine Célina Penel was born in Nîmes in the Gard region on March 14, 1911, but she was raised in Alboussière in the Ardèche. I wonder what it was like to grow up around the yeasty, buttery smells of her parents' bakery. Did being exposed to the labor of this métier de bouche from early on make Paulette gravitate to the kitchen, or did she have ambitions beyond her working-class roots? Did her gender stem her dreams? Paulette had been an excellent student and her teachers encouraged her to continue her studies. However, her father did not agree. Danièle told me that like so many working-class girls of her age, her mother "had to go to work." In 1927, the year after she obtained her *brevet supérieur*, the diploma just before the baccalaureate, Paulette started a culinary apprenticeship with Madame Cheynet at the Hôtel de la Poste in Alboussière. Paulette was fifteen. Danièle remarked that, "Cheynet was a *fin cordon* [excellent cook]," distinguishing her mother's first culinary teacher from less skilled female cooks. In 1928, Chef Chazotte, a former student of Auguste Escoffier, took over from Cheynet. The hotel was then sold to Eugénie Castaing in 1929.

By 1930, Paulette had become the chef de cuisine, and her apprentice was the hotel owner's son, Raymond. Raymond had gone to hotel school in Nice, and his mother had bought this inn as a place for him to hone his skills. Raymond's mother's investment would turn out to shape more than her son's professional career. On May 17, 1933, Raymond and Paulette were married. From 1935 to 1939, the young couple would spend the winter season in Megève, where Paulette cooked at the Coq de Bruyère, and the summer season at Alboussière. This was not an uncommon rotation for chefs at the time, but there were not many women on this circuit. In 1939–42, during the war, Paulette was the chef de cuisine at Albert Alaize's restaurant in rue Royale, down the street from the Mère Brazier in Lyon. Paulette had a chance to get to know Eugénie Brazier. According to Danièle, "[Brazier] absolutely wanted my mother close to her, but my mother never went to work for Brazier. Maman told me, 'At work, she intimidated me. I was scared of her,'" hinting that from the start, Castaing's way of being in the kitchen was not at all like the classic mère qui gueule.

I asked Danièle what it had been like for her mother as a woman in professional kitchens. She told me that Paulette had enjoyed her first two years with Madame Cheynet. It was perhaps the influence of a woman at the start of her career that made her realize she had a place in the kitchen. Danièle went on to say that it was easier for Paulette because her father was by her mother's side in the kitchen. However, early on Raymond decided that he had enough of the hot kitchen, and for health reasons he could no longer cook. "My mother said: 'No problem. I'll take over.' My father dealt with the front of the house."

After the war, Paulette and Raymond were ready to set out on their own, with some help from Raymond's mother. Danièle told me that her parents had considered buying the Auberge de Collonges from the Bocuse family. Instead, they were enchanted by a little spot along the Rhône river in Condrieu. Apparently, the couple found the Saône River morose. Danièle thinks it must have been raining when they went to visit Collonges and, when they went to Condrieu, it was sunny and the terrace was divine. The surging Rhône spoke to this hopeful young couple, and in 1946 they came to be partners in the Hôtel-Restaurant le Beau Rivage. The Castaings set to work renovating the modest rooms of the rustic inn, transforming the Beau Rivage into a luxurious destination for travelers along the popular D386 before the days of the A7, or Autoroute du Soleil.

Danièle, the couple's only child, was born in 1950. Paulette and Raymond worked tirelessly and continued to develop their business. They benefited from the rising prosperity of the French middle class in the postwar period. In particular, Beau Rivage gained popularity with the growing numbers of French tourists who were exploring the French countryside by car (Harp 2001). In 1954, the Beau Rivage became part of the Relais Campagne, a group of restaurants and hotels created by the couple's friends Jean and Nelly Tilloy to promote tourism outside of cities. The restaurant also received its first Michelin star in 1956, which sealed its popularity with tourists and contributed to Castaing's growing reputation as a notable chef. As the success of the inn and restaurant grew, the Castaings continued to introduce improvements. In 1960, they renovated the dining room, kitchen, and rooms.

These investments, along with hard work, paid off with a second Michelin star in 1964, which the restaurant held for twenty-three years. In 1967, the *Gault et Millau* guide gave the restaurant its prestigious three-toques rating. Danièle says that her mother used to joke that Paul Bocuse called her to tell her she had received her first star but not for the second because at that point they were then competitors. In Danièle's account, Bocuse becomes a recurring antagonist in her mother's culinary history. Nonetheless, Bocuse would sometimes come to dine at the Beau Rivage. According to Danièle, he was a fan of her mother's *matelote d'anguille* (eel soup), a classic dish of the northern Rhône. Although they may have been in competition, Danièle wanted to show me how this bigwig of the French culinary scene respected her mother's culinary talent.

Cooking was Paulette's passion, and she seemed to have been torn at times between her role as a chef and her role as a mother. When Danièle was an adult, her mother told her that her one regret was not having spent enough time with her daughter. Danièle was a regular at summer camps, and she admits that she rarely saw her mother. While chuckling, Danièle tells me, "It did not stop me from also going to hotel school!" Her initiation into the family business actually started much earlier:

> I started working in the kitchen at nine, ten years old alongside my mother. I would help her on holidays. She never praised me. I remember that one of her chef friends came and told my mother how impressed he was that I was capable of skinning sole and making stuffed oysters. I was happy about the compliment but I wish it had been from *maman*.

Her parents wanted a different life for Danièle: "When I had my first child, my father said, 'Raise your children, and then we will see.' They wanted for me what they did not have—time to raise their child." The tension between women's productive and reproductive roles in French culture in the late twentieth century resonated strongly in this family.

I imagine Danièle perched on a stool in her mother's kitchen, her keen young eyes observing her mother's every move, hanging on her every word and interaction with her cooks:

> My mother could be severe, but she was always fair. She knew how to encourage people, and they admired her for her demeanor and her professionalism. She did not want to be like the mères. She rarely raised her voice, only occasionally. She was modest, discreet, and professional. She did not seek the spotlight of the media, even when she won awards.

Men and women came from all over France to apprentice and do *stages* with Paulette Castaing. Danièle told me that one woman, who already had her own restaurant, came from Belgium to learn from her mother:

"Mother was an inspiration to others, particularly women." Paulette was deeply dedicated to her trade and her restaurant. According to Danièle, she rarely took a vacation and when she had to go away she would call constantly to check in: "she did not trust what would happen in the kitchen when she was gone."

Cook and journalist Sonia Ezgulian had an opportunity to work with Paulette Castaing on a project in the early 2000s. She asked Paulette how she had run her kitchen. Sonia told Paulette that she had struggled in her apprenticeship because of the male-dominated space and the foreign ways of doing in the kitchen. Paulette responded that it was a question of the chef. In her kitchen, she did not accept that anyone put themselves above others. No one yelled. Sonia noted that women don't tend to yell from morning until night. Paulette explained that people had tasks in her kitchen. Sonia recounted Paulette telling her about kitchen work: "For example, just like in a home, when we peel vegetables, we gather around a table and do it. We talk calmly and it's almost like being with family." Paulette's kitchen demonstrated a collaborative way of running a professional kitchen that turned out beautifully executed haute cuisine. Much like the women in Liora Gvion and Netta Leedon's study on women working as chefs in Israel (2019), Castaing perceived her restaurant kitchen as an extension of her home where her legitimacy was maintained through ongoing mentorship and dialogue with her staff that was based on respect, empathy, and emotional support.

Paulette Castaing was known for her skill at cooking fish and making sauces. Unlike the mères lyonnaises, who nearly always offered their same signature dishes regardless of the season, Castaing changed her menu almost every week, following the seasons and the freshest products. She also had signature dishes that were regularly offered à la carte, where dishes could be ordered individually, versus a menu, where the chef predetermines each course. Castaing's cooking strongly reflected Condrieu and had a great sense of place. Danièle Castaing shared with me some of her mother's recipes. The pike in Côte Rôtie reflects the influence of the Rhône. This is a simple and rich dish: the main ingredients are pike from the river, wine from the surrounding vineyards, and rich cream from local cattle to bring the two together.

The simplicity of the dish requires perfect execution—the fish cannot be overcooked, the sauce has to have the right balance between fat and acidity, and all the ingredients need to be fresh and of the highest quality. Her recipe for sea bream with thyme flowers demonstrates the delicacy of the flavors of Castaing's cuisine. Her poulet de Bresse à la crème is in the tradition of cuisine bourgeoise with its superior local products and rich cream sauce. According to Danièle, her mother never wanted to write a cookbook and neglected to put her recipes in order when she retired from cooking. This is not unusual for most chefs of her generation, demonstrating the centrality of apprenticeship in passing along culinary knowledge from one generation to the next. Sonia Ezgulian was able to work with Paulette to feature a few of her recipes in a book on Lyonnais cuisine (Ezgulian 2013).

It was not all sunshine and fortune in Condrieu for the Castaings. In 1975, Raymond was in a car crash that left him with limited mobility. On top of her job as chef de cuisine, Paulette took over the running of the inn, and continued to maintain the high standards of the establishment. Raymond died in 1984, and after that Paulette realized it was going to be a difficult adventure to continue alone at her age. Paulette sold the Hôtel de Beau Rivage in 1987 and retired in 1988 after sixty years in kitchens. It was not until the end of her career that she was recognized for her achievements in the culinary arts. In 1986, she became a chevalier in the Ordre du Mérite Touristique. That same year, the Toques blanches lyonnaises bestowed on Castaing a Diplôme d'honneur.

After spending time with Danièle and learning about the intimate family details of her mother's life and career, I was eager to hear other people's perspectives on Paulette Castaing and her accomplishments. I knew that she had trained a number of cooks who would go on to become celebrated chefs. Most of them were men. The Lyonnais chef Alain Alexanian was the person who had remained most attached to his mentor. I decided to get in touch with Alain to hear about his experience in Castaing's kitchen.

Alain was waiting for me at Place Guichard. He was smoking a cigarette and chatting with a friend who had been passing by, and he seemed very much at home in his leather bomber jacket, sprawled out on a spindly bistro chair. I learned later that this square is pretty much Alain's backyard—just a stone's throw away from his old restaurant and around the corner from his apartment. I took a seat across from Alain and thanked him for taking the time to meet with me. We had met once before, but I doubted he remembered; it was fifteen years ago very early in the morning at the old *marché gare*, a wholesale market behind the Perrache train station. The market is no longer there, but I remember it as the early morning hotspot to meet chefs and peruse the freshest produce. I also vividly recall Alain because he was so friendly and animated. He showed a keen interest in my research at the time on Lyonnais markets, and he did not hesitate to share his insights on the topic. I was looking forward to having a chance to chat with Alain once again.

I wanted to talk to Alain about his apprenticeship with Madame Castaing at Beau Rivage in the 1970s. I described my current research topic on the cuisine des mères and women who cook professionally, which started him telling his story of the mères lyonnaises. It was clear straight away that Alain strongly believes in the contributions that women have made and are making to French cuisine: "Women will be the ones to lead the real comeback of French cuisine." He might have also been thinking of his own daughter, who is at the start of her professional culinary career. Despite this support for women in the kitchen, Alain's thoughts on why women tended to be relegated to peripheral areas of the kitchen were not much different from the other male voices I had heard:

> Desserts and cold dishes bring out women's artistry. There used to be so much heat and steam in the hot line and the equipment was very heavy. It was very masculine. If women wanted to look after their family, pastry allowed them to not work in the evenings. It was hard to be feminine on the line. That's why women opted out of the "dirty" side of the kitchen. Women chose the more "noble" side.

Although Alain reiterated many of the stereotypes about women in professional kitchens, he also claimed that women had been an important force in shaping his own culinary journey—women showed him that you did not have to be tough and loud in the kitchen. It was important to be calm, work together, and observe with great care.

Alain's parents emigrated from Armenia in the 1950s, and he was born in Lyon in 1958. He found his love for cooking in his grandmother's kitchen and garden:

> When I would get hungry, my grandmother would say to me "Go into the garden and you will find something there." I would grab a radish. [. . .] The botanical world is not a big secret to me, neither is seasonality. [. . .] I think all great chefs are born in the countryside, the mountains or by the sea. Great chefs never come from cities. I don't know of any.

After completing several initial *stages*, Alain had enough of the creamy taste of butter and animal fat in his mouth and was left wondering if there was more to French cuisine than these heavy dishes that were hard to digest. He had time to mull through his gastronomic reflections while fulfilling his military conscription—he was a cook for a general in Verdun. That was also when he began to read about nutrition and apply for apprenticeship positions in the Ain region near Lyon. He had the great fortune to be offered a spot at Castaing's Beau Rivage.

In 1978, Alain arrived in the northern Rhône and began a two-year apprenticeship that would be one of the most formative experiences of his life:

> At last I had almost found the umbilical cord to my grandmother because from this great, great house and this grande dame, because there are no other words, I probably learned a cuisine, which was not entirely military, but a type of cooking where you could be graceful . . . that had kindness. Where you could give orders and say something in a simple way, and it was done because the person in front of you, in this case a woman, would execute the task perfectly because she had a mastery of the craft, and all we had to do is follow her lead. It was this cuisine that illuminated all other cuisine for me.

Alain explained to me that his time in Condrieu shaped his culinary practices, but it also taught him that you did not have to be macho in the kitchen and that working together as equals was important. Alain explained that it was not just Madame Castaing's craft that he learned—she had a different way of being in the kitchen:

> She taught me all these things about cooking but it was the way that she taught: you don't have to be hard to try to teach people to cook.

> This is something I have tried to follow throughout my career: I learned that I have a feminine side. She helped me discover that. It was already there with the influence of my grandmother, but I never would have been able to learn had I ended up with someone like Paul Bocuse or with someone where there was really a military sense of discipline with everyone in their place. You are a commis, you are a little soldier. He learns, he obeys. After that, you are a sergeant. A sergeant starts to give orders, etc. But the orders given by these big chefs, in that day and age anyways, were completely contradictory to the orders given by this chef here who was a woman, who . . . probably because she was a woman and that, with her gentle eyes and a smile, she could get the same thing done, and probably better, because everyone is more at ease during the service, which is exactly the same service. She had a way of explaining things directly (because it is always a little tense at any time in all kitchens), but she explained like a woman . . . and you bring your stress level down a notch to try to speak to "your mother."

Although Madame Castaing was a maternal figure for Alain and he attributes the feminized culture of her kitchen, such as no yelling and taking care with those who are learning, to her performance of being a kind, patient mother, it struck me that Castaing had a very different approach to how a kitchen should be run. Whether a maternal instinct or intention shaped that approach or not, what is important is that Castaing was able to instill in others, like Alain, an alternative model of work that moved away from the patriarchal order of the brigade. Alain claims that Madame Castaing was of the second generation of mères who were able to choose another way of doing because the first mères, like Brazier and Filloux, had forcefully blazed the trail ahead of them.

Paulette Castaing is remembered for her mastery of her craft. Those in the know about cuisine in the Lyonnais region hold up Castaing as one of the most accomplished French chefs in the country's culinary history. During her lifetime, her achievements were recognized with two Michelin stars and numerous awards. However, Alain laments that Castaing was eclipsed by her three-star neighbor, Fernand Point in Vienne at La Pyramide. Her lack of recognition was not due to any lack of talent. Rather, it was because Castaing did not demand the same media attention as Point. Alain noted that "it is always the man with the loudest voice who pushes to the front and demands the attention of the press." Castaing quietly labored in her kitchen, training the next generation of male chefs who would go on to trumpet their success.

Sonia Ezgulian: Communicating Food and the Kitchen

The first time I met Sonia Ezgulian in 2013, our conversation immediately touched on Paulette Castaing's culinary prowess. Most importantly, Sonia explained to me that Paulette had paved a way for how to be a woman in the kitchen and validated women's presence in this professional space—a woman did not have to be a man in the kitchen. Clearly, this greatly relieved Ezgulian, who had no plans to "man up" in the kitchen.

> Paulette Castaing was very, very important for me. Because I did not know . . . I did not know my place amongst chefs. I did not feel very comfortable, actually it was not my world. The world of chefs was too technical, too competitive. I liked them well enough, but I did not feel like a "chef." Me, I have always felt like a cuisinière—that's why I have always been fond of that title. It was complicated. It was . . . I did not want people to call me "chef." I wanted them to say that I was a cook.

Figure 5.2: Sonia Ezgulian in her kitchen. (Photo courtesy of Emmanuel Auger)

> And, I felt very, very good when I met Paulette Castaing [sharp intake of breath]. My God, what a grande dame!

Hesitant to call herself a chef, Ezgulian explained how she had worked as a journalist at *Paris Match* for more than ten years until she could no longer contain her passion and curiosity for food. She and her husband, Emmanuel Auger, left Paris to return to Lyon, where she had been born. This was the start of a new chapter in their lives. In her memoir, *6m2 de cuisine: Chroniques extraordinaires d'un restaurant ordinaire* (2011), Ezgulian details the six months she spent apprenticing at the Michelin-starred restaurant of the Villa Florentine before opening the restaurant Oxalis with her husband. Her life as a cook is at the center of this account, which is punctuated by recipes. From 1999 to 2006, Sonia worked in the kitchen, while Emmanuel was in charge of the twenty-seat dining room.

The transition from journalism and home cooking to running a restaurant kitchen posed a number of challenges for Ezgulian: she had to define herself in a world where none of the labels seemed to fit. Along with not wanting to be called a chef, Sonia also did not see herself as a mère. When I asked her about this label, she explained to me how she thought about the mères lyonnaises:

> It's not a pejorative term [to be called a mère]. Sometimes a person cannot be a mère, it's not about that . . . the mères in any case were special characters. Well, euh . . . When we opened our restaurant, some people said, "Oh, great, wonderful, it's the revival of the mères Lyonnaises." They meant it in the kindest of ways. But, it bothered me because I had the feeling I was being critical, but I said: "No, I am not a mère." A mère, she is a matron, someone who has an iron fist, and me, I said to myself . . . I don't feel like I am at all part of that world. But I did not disavow it either. I think I was more of a cook than a mère Lyonnaise. So, they are two different things. You really have to be in the spirit of what it was. It is certain kind of cuisine bourgeoise, but a little bit . . . *terroir*. It's very specific, it's a mess, so, I think that my cooking wasn't at all mère Lyonnaise cuisine.

While trying to push back against these titles that didn't fit, Sonia as a woman in Lyon also told me that it is hard to escape the legacy of the mères Lyonnaises: "By default, when you are in Lyon, you are marked by these women." Just after opening her restaurant, Sonia and Emmanuel were asked to work on a book based on a rediscovered text of an anonymous female Lyonnais cook (Anonymous 2012) and then another book about mères lyonnaises (*Carnet des mères lyonnaises* [2013]). They did the work in the evenings, Sundays, and whenever they could. Sonia told me how these books were a wonderful opportunity to get in touch with some of the most important women in Lyon, such as Colette Sibilia (a Lyonnais charcuterie maven and institution), Jacotte Brazier, and Paulette Castaing. "It is important to meet women who have a lot of good sense, and a certain philosophy. Voilà. They all had amazing life journeys and, on top of it, they say things that are hard to hear, not sugar coated, but it's good. No, but it's true, it's important sometimes."

In addition to these female culinary icons, Sonia told me that Danièle Mazet-Delpeuch had also inspired her to be a cook, rather than a chef. This meant not adopting a professional culinary persona or practices that did not feel authentic. One of the first things Sonia did in our interview was locate her signed copy of Mazet-Delpeuch's memoir and insist that I take it home with me. *Carnets de cuisine: Du Périgord à l'Élysée* (2011) chronicles Mazet-Delpeuch's life from her struggle to raise four children in the Périgord countryside to her sudden ascendency to fame as the French president François Mitterand's personal cook. In particular, Mazet-Delpeuch is critical of the petty power struggles between the chefs cooking in the Élysée; they clearly felt threatened to have a woman in the kitchen and one who was so close to the president. *Haute Cuisine* (Vincent 2012) is the popular film that was adapted from the memoir. After reading the book, I understood why Mazet-Delpeuch was a role model for Sonia—she helped make sense of a woman's place in the kitchen.

Finding a place in the kitchen can be particularly hard when you are the woman in charge: men resist women's presence in this male-dominated space, and it is worse when a woman is in command (Padavic 1991; P. Cohen and Huffman 2007). Sonia told me about her difficulty in finding someone to work with her in the kitchen. She chalked it up to very different ways of doing and learning. When she had her restaurant, she did not write down her recipes—there was no *fiche technique* (technical sheet) or recipe as there usually is in brigade system kitchens. "I really thought I could just explain! Because for me, they had always just explained it to me." Some of Sonia's earliest apprenticeship was with her Armenian grandmother. Sonia gave an example of the embodied apprenticeship she practiced with her grandmother:

> For example, my grandmother taught me to cook. When we were preparing dough for making raviolis or lots of other things. Euh . . . I knew there had to be flour. For certain fillings, you needed eggs, for others, only water. But there were not quantities. It depended on one thing . . . you had to knead, and we would touch our earlobes and the dough had the same texture as the earlobe. Then it was right. Me, since forever, I have flour on my ears—why? When I make dough. Because, I don't know the quantity. I do it like that [. . .] and these young apprentices would come to me and ask, "Madame! Madame! It takes how long? It's how much of this or that?" And, I would tell them, "But it depends." [. . .] Not everything is learned by numbers and mathematical equations.

Sonia's comments and reflections bring to light the contrast, and sometimes conflict, between different forms of learning. Culinary school creates apprentices who need recipes and equations. Often these neophytes are reluctant to use their senses to cook: they have not been trained this way, they lack experience, and they don't trust their own bodies to collect critical information. Here we can see the tensions between what have become gendered styles of knowledge production and learning (Konkol 2013). In her research on the male-dominated field of molecular gastronomy in France, Sophia Roosth (2013) comments on how male chefs and practitioners of molecular gastronomy like Hervé held the view that women's embodied knowledge was backward or primitive and that it should be questioned. Molecular gastronomy stands in direct contrast to the kind of cooking that Ezgulian describes: scientific, rational, and broken down into formulas that potentially anyone can reproduce. These scientific and technical forms of knowledge transfer, which men have historically controlled, have gained supremacy over the oral and embodied tradition of women's culinary apprenticeships.

In *6m2 de cuisine*, Sonia writes about navigating the foreign world of the professional kitchen during her brief apprenticeship. She admits that there were times when she wanted to hand over her apron because she felt she was always the "*bonne femme* [the nice lady] in a resolutely macho world." Sonia found the environment of the professional kitchen unbearable: it was loud, the military order of the kitchen was oppressive, and the heavy equipment was difficult to handle. She noted that "once I arrived in my own restaurant, I quickly got rid of all of the big heavy equipment."

Ezgulian eventually found her place in the restaurant kitchen, but it did not keep her from feeling like an outsider even in her own restaurant. When interviewing cooks for positions at her restaurant, Ezgulian had one applicant who at the end of the interview asked to meet the chef. There were those who refused to work for a woman who didn't have a CAP cuisine. Sonia's way of running the kitchen was so unfamiliar to one cook that he quit, telling Sonia that she did not yell enough and that he could not work without that pressure (Ezgulian 2011, 17). Finally, Sonia decided that in order to find serenity in her work she had to go it alone. She did this by adapting her dishes so that the labor would be more manageable. For example, she chose dishes that required less last-minute plating or presentations that were less elaborate. Other women I interviewed, Brigitte Josserand, Clothilde Martin, and others, also arrived at this solution—their selection of dishes keep in mind that they will be the only one in the kitchen working prep and the final service. Sonia reflected on this tendency of women to work alone: "Perhaps it is this isolation that allows women to create." In this case, codified practices and knowledge do not stifle a woman's creative views and ways of doing.

Sonia had the opportunity to collaborate with a number of chefs who were formally trained and she found their creative process interesting but very different from her own:

> I think we create differently. I could see this. It was amusing. [. . .] I would see it when we would create a dish, when we would think of new dishes for a new menu, for example, we would talk about . . . you know . . . vegetable peelings, leftovers, ways to save money, things like that. . . . Sometimes, men don't consider that at all. Their way is very technical, too bad if there is lots of waste.

Sonia made the point that she is not at all stingy, but she really felt there was a better way to work and respect the high-quality products they were using: "In the end, it is not a question of money, it is a question of respect. Because we know how this product is produced, etc. I come from the land, so I know what this means. For example, vegetables, I know it is a ton of work. The same with raising animals, it is the same for fish. [. . .] It's a question of respect for the producer." She insisted it is part of her culture not to waste something good.

I wonder how this anti-waste culture is tied to women's domestic practices and why. Waste in a restaurant means lost income—throwing usable food away is like throwing away money. So why do so many restaurant kitchens tend to be wasteful? My own reflections start in culinary school, where I frequently wanted to cry when we would throw away not only trimmings but also the food we had prepared. The lame excuses about food safety never sat well with me. Does this culture of professional wastefulness start in culinary school, where it becomes a norm? In contrast, cooks like Sonia Ezgulian, who have most of their training in the domestic sphere, particularly with grandmothers and older women, perhaps become part of a culture of thrift and economy. It is unfortunate that there is not more dialogue between these two worlds and, as Sonia's accounts demonstrate, there is much resistance to such an exchange of ideas that would lead to better professional practices. She thinks that anti-waste cooking really comes from women's everyday practices of managing the household: "In general, women pay attention to these things. And, they think of recipes that are good in terms of not wasting too much." This is echoed in food scholarship that focuses on thrift when shopping and cooking as part of women's domestic duties (Capellini & Parsons 2012), particularly in historic contexts (L. Shapiro 2009). Sonia's *tarte serpentin* (fig. 5.3) is a wonderful example of this philosophy of thrift: it uses vegetable peelings to make its colorful filling. Thrift can be colorful, playful, and delicious; it doesn't have to be tired and dull.

In 2006, Sonia and Emmanuel decided to close their restaurant, Oxalis. Perhaps it closed because it was too successful. The couple had more demand than ever to consult and collaborate on cookbooks and food-related projects. Journalism and culinary communication were calling once more.

During my time in Lyon, it was difficult to spend as much time with Sonia as I wanted to because she was in high demand—dashing off

Figure 5.3: Sonia Ezgulian's *tarte serpentin.* (Photo courtesy of Emmanuel Auger)

to Paris for a day to work on a publication, or jumping on a train to Marseille to collaborate on a project with a writer there. However, I do remember one evening when I managed to invite Sonia and Emmanuel over for dinner. I was anxious, and I wasn't even the one doing the cooking. As a main dish, my husband, Doug, had decided to make an elaborate lasagna with braised guinea hen. When Sonia and Emmanuel arrived at the door, I welcomed them into our two-room apartment. Our two-month-old son was cradled in my arms as I showed our guests to the living room. While Doug was preoccupied with serving wine, I peeked into the kitchen to check on the status of dinner—the braise was nowhere near ready, and dinner was a long way off. I tried not to worry. The wine and conversation flowed, but the dinner prep progressed slowly. It was clear that Doug needed help, and with the baby demanding milk and my warm arms, I was pretty much useless. Without a word, Sonia stepped into the kitchen, washed her hands, and began working next to Doug. She asked him inquisitively about the recipe and they chatted while they picked the meat off the guinea hens. She deftly whipped up the béchamel for the lasagna and worked in harmony with Doug to get the dish in the oven in no time. Despite arriving on the table at quite a late hour, the dinner was a success.

Later, while cleaning up the kitchen after our guests had left and our baby was asleep in bed, we marveled at Sonia's skill, grace, and generosity in the kitchen. I had been a little embarrassed that we had not been better hosts, but Sonia kept telling us how much she enjoyed helping out. That evening, I came to really understand who Sonia is in the kitchen. She managed to make me feel more at home in my own home. We were eager to cook for Sonia and Emmanuel to thank them for the way they had welcomed us and helped me with my research. That evening we felt Sonia had taken care of us, yet again.

From her numerous books to her blog to her many media appearances and presence on prestigious panels of judges for culinary and literary competitions, Sonia's career attests to her presence as a force that continues to shape Lyonnais and French cuisine. Her work popularizes practices grounded in women's domestic common sense. Sonia is an example of a woman who presents and promotes herself in the media, but she accomplishes this without yelling or creating a spectacle. She offers another example of how women can be at the forefront of the culinary arts by doing things her own way. Sonia and Emmanuel continue to forge ahead with their successful consulting business while actively seeking to promote other talented chefs, in particular women in the local Lyon food scene.

Connie Zagora: An Inclusive Nouvelle Cuisine Lyonnaise

At the end of my first interview with Sonia, she told me about a new little restaurant in her neighborhood that I absolutely had to try: "Oh, and the chef is a woman. You should go talk to her." And this is how I met Connie.

The first time I went to the Kitchen Café, I had no idea what to expect. It was lunch, and the tiny little neighborhood restaurant was packed. The place did not look like much from the outside. The seventies facade had been scrubbed, and the large plate-glass windows revealed seven little tables, a miniscule bar, and an open kitchen. The decor was simple: wood tables with sewing machine bases, sturdy wooden chairs, and a mix of modern art from a local artist and black-and-white family photos. The place was humming. People were animatedly chatting and enjoying their food, wiping up the sauce with their bread.

I did not have a reservation, but it was late in the lunch rush and a table was coming available. I sat down with a friend at a small corner table and we were given menus. There were not too many choices on the menu, and there was a list with lots of interesting wines from small producers. My friend and I decided to order one of everything on the menu, which was not as absurd as it sounds because only two appetizers, two main dishes, and two desserts were listed. As we were contemplating what to order, a diner at the table next to us turned to us and said, "Don't forget to save room for dessert—they are amazing here."

When the starters arrived, they were artfully plated. The trout gravlax—later I discovered that this was a nod to the chef's Swedish roots—was as delicious as it was beautiful. Next up was the fish of the day: perch, a local freshwater fish, served with purple haze carrots, puffed rice, peanuts marinated in soy sauce, and a tamarind jus. This was not mama's cooking. The fish was perfectly cooked, the textures gave depth to the experience, and the sauce made me wish there were more of this dish. Classic French techniques laid the foundation for layers of Asian and Southeast Asian flavors. Was that also a hint of something bitter in an edible flower adorning the dish? It was a perfect counterpoint for the richness of the sauce. I wanted to have a long conversation about this food with the chef. How had she come up with this combination of ingredients? Where did she learn to cook fish like that? I was already falling in love. Then dessert arrived. I had never seen anything like it: a big chocolate mousse pouf just off the center of the plate powdered with cacao. As my spoon dug in, it hit another layer, something hard and crunchy that yielded with a crisp snap. The silky smoothness combined with the crunchy secret layer nearly made my head explode with pleasure. Who was the genius making the desserts? How was all of this possible for just 24 euros? I wanted to eat here every day.

At the end of the meal, I approached the open kitchen to introduce myself to Connie and thank her for the delicious meal. I mentioned that Sonia Ezgulian had sent me, explaining my project on women who cook professionally. I asked if she would be willing to talk to me about her experience. Connie graciously gave me her card and returned to her busy kitchen. I desperately wanted to hang out in the tiny workspace, observe, and do any menial tasks so I could get close enough to learn how to cook like this. It had been a long time since I felt this excited about food, and I could not wait to find time to sit down with Connie.

Not long after that meal, our first conversation took place in a little wine bar near the Kitchen Café. We began at the beginning. Connie told me that she was born in Sweden in 1981 to Polish parents. She lost her mother early in life, and her father raised her and her sister on his own in Stockholm. Connie spoke fondly of her father, whom she says has always been supportive of her. She still has close ties to her family in Poland, and Polish culture is an important part of her identity. Connie's professional focus was not initially on food: she thought that music would be her life, but as she discovered the world of professional musicians, she began to hesitate. She was still looking for the place where she felt she truly belonged.

Connie Zagora went on a vacation in France and fell in love with it—she decided that she wanted to live there. In 2003, she moved to Paris. She learned French and worked while she decided what she wanted to do. She met Laurent, her current partner, and decided to stay in France. "I worked a little in restaurants in the front of the house while I was studying French. After that, I decided that I wanted to study cooking. Cooking is more inspiring and creative than waiting on tables." Connie started her formal culinary training at Ferrandi in 2005. She chose this particular culinary school because it is one of the best schools in France, but it is not as expensive as schools like the Institut Bocuse. "[Ferrandi] also took people who were a little older, like me. I was twenty-four years old. The French start early. Therefore, I arrived ten years late." She first passed her CAP, "a degree most French people pass at fifteen or sixteen." Connie went on to complete a BTS. She found the CAP to be more technical: "Hygiene, knife skills and things like that." She told me that the BTS gave her the foundation for running her own business, which she is now doing.

When it came to apprenticeships, Connie explained: "I decided to start at the top so I could eventually work my way down to the bistro. I started with the most difficult in order to learn faster." She did not get a leg up from the school when it came time to find a position: she knocked on doors. "I got two offers straight away one from Georges V and the Ritz. I chose the Ritz because I had a good feeling about [Chef] Michel Roth." I asked her what it was like to start in a grande palace. Connie told me that she "was surprised that there was a really good ambiance in the kitchen at the Ritz." She had heard horror stories about these big restaurants. "There was a great deal of professionalism. People did not walk all over each other. They wanted to do their best. People worked well as a team."

Her goal at the Ritz was to work in every station. Roth encouraged his apprentices to do this but it was not something that all apprentices jumped at. There were not many women working in this kitchen, only one woman who was in charge of making fruit baskets and plates. "At times it was a little daunting to find myself with fifty men. I was always the only woman. Yes, it was intimidating." However, the work conditions were good: the pay was excellent, the hours were not terrible, and the work culture was good. Connie stayed on for two years at the Ritz, which, she explained, is a long time for most apprentices. Roth had asked Connie to continue, but she knew that she had to gain experience with other chefs. He understood and asked her where she wanted to go: "This was a true sign of his respect for me." Chefs pave the way for their apprentices' next positions, particularly if the chef is well-known and reputable.

Connie's next stop was Paris Vendôme to work with Jean-François Rouquette, where she went straight to being a *chef de partie* (a full-fledged member of the kitchen staff who reports to the sous-chef). "It was a difficult position because there were lots of rivalries in that kitchen. Everyone is always trying to show who is better and you have to prove yourself." In contrast with the Ritz, there were lots of women in this kitchen. Rouquette specifically looked to hire women: "He wanted to have a gender balance in the kitchen." Connie reflected on this experience of working with other women: "We have a different sort of contact and relationship between us. In the end, women are more exacting and demanding." Here Connie reflects on her own cooking style to draw out what is positive in what she sees as her feminine approach.

After gaining a variety of experiences in some of the best kitchens in Paris, Connie moved on. Laurent wanted to leave Paris, and they knew that staying in the capital made their dream of opening a restaurant more challenging. Even though he is from the Paris region, Laurent found life there too hectic. They chose Lyon for its just-right size and its quality of life, moving there in 2011. Laurent found work right away with Nicolas Le Bec. It took Connie longer to find her feet. Eventually, she took a position at the Sofitel, but she had to come down in rank from her last position in Paris. She was not too pleased to be starting as a commis, but within a week she was promoted to chef de partie. She stayed at the Sofitel for a year before she and Laurent started their own restaurant, which opened on January 15, 2014.

A small bistro in the Seventh Arrondissement not far from the universities, the Kitchen Café is a true neighborhood spot, on the corner of two side streets with more pedestrians and bikes whizzing by than cars. There are nineteen seats inside and, when the weather is nice, there are another fifteen on the sidewalk. The restaurant opens for breakfast at 8 o'clock, and it quickly became a daytime meeting place for people who live and work in the neighborhood. Sticky cinnamon buns (inspired by Connie's Swedish roots and perfected by Laurent), slices of lemon cake, house-made granola, and a savory Scandinavian-style platter are on offer for breakfast. Lunch is served from noon to 1:45 p.m. There is a prix fixe menu with two or three courses. Desserts, pastries, coffee, and tea are served until 6:30 p.m. The initial concept was for a dessert-focused restaurant, but they quickly shifted to give equal importance to the lunch service. Connie and Laurent decided that their restaurant would only be open during the daytime—they wanted balance in their lives. Connie remembers working split shifts in Paris and not having enough time to go home to rest. She told me that she bought a monthly movie pass so that in the darkened theater she could, if she wanted, sleep between shifts. She did not want to go back to that kind of life.

Connie Zagora is the chef de cuisine and Laurent Ozan the pastry chef (fig. 5.4). The gendered division of labor in culinary school and

Figure 5.4: Connie Zagora and Laurent Ozan at their restaurant, the Kitchen Café. (Photo courtesy of Emmanuel Auger)

many kitchens pushes women toward pastry while men cook most of the hot food. This is not the case at the Kitchen Café. Connie tells me that it is not always easy to work with her partner, but their skills are different enough that they tend to have their separate spheres in the kitchen. However, it irks Connie that some clients still come up to the open kitchen and thank Laurent for the meal—they can, after all see Connie cooking.

Connie laughed when she told me that Laurent is getting used to being the "mari de . . ." (the husband of . . .). With more press coverage about the work that both Connie and Laurent are doing at the Kitchen Café, it is clear that Connie is the culinary genius and Laurent is the man behind the delectable sweet creations. In 2018, the French premium television channel Canal+ aired an episode of *Planète Chef* featuring Connie. The series focuses on international talent as essential to contemporary French cuisine. This artful documentary focuses on Connie's culinary inspirations and process. Media coverage like this is helping Connie make a name for herself, and she is starting to get the recognition she deserves for her work. At the same time, she has not actively sought media attention. Rather, it seems to find her.

Fresh local produce drives the menu at Kitchen Café. Connie works closely with Gérard Essayan at Les Jardins de Vartan, an organic farm in Décines on the outskirts of Lyon. Rather than call up a wholesaler and have produce delivered, Connie frequently visits Gérard's farm to discuss the fruits and vegetables that are available. The menu at the Kitchen Café changes each week to reflect this seasonality. This approach to cooking means more work for the chef, and she has to tap into her creativity on a weekly basis—she needs to come up with new dishes or work out variations based on the available ingredients. This way of working and thinking about restaurant food breaks from what has become the norm of established menus that rarely change. It is exciting for diners and offers a constant creative outlet for the chef.

I began frequenting the Kitchen Café in the fall of 2014. At the start, I noticed it was mainly Connie and Laurent in the kitchen, maybe with one other person helping out with the dishes or a bit of prep. There was usually just one server and sometimes two if the patio was open. As the restaurant's popularity grew, it became more difficult to get a seat. When I asked Connie Zagora about this success, she told me that it had really helped that the *Guide Michelin* had given the restaurant a Bib Gourmand, a designation that means a restaurant has good quality and good-value cooking. In 2016, Connie and Laurent were also honored with the Prix Jeune Talent from the *Gault et Millau* guide. The role of guidebooks in launching and sustaining restaurants has not changed all that much in the past hundred years. As business picked up, Connie found that she needed an extra hand with the cooking. She and Laurent also rarely had any time off. Having another cook meant that she had a little more space to breathe.

When I returned to Lyon in 2017 for a brief visit, I noticed that there were more cooks in the kitchen. Connie seemed pleased that she could now take more than one day off a week. She told me this gave her time to recharge her batteries but also time to work through her creative process. I asked Connie about her hiring practices and whether she tried to hire other female cooks: "I do not hire based on gender. I look at a person's skills and their attitude." However, she told me about a time when she had too many male cooks in her kitchen: "Even the men complained about it. Dynamics are important in the kitchen." For Connie, gender can play a part in having a good kitchen culture.

As she learned in her apprenticeships, it is also the chef who creates the culture of the kitchen. This happens through hiring but also in setting an example of appropriate kitchen behavior and creating a bar for the quality of the work. This is particularly true in a small kitchen like the one Connie runs. She sets the tone: she works quietly, calmly, and consistently to produce excellent food. Seen in the kitchen, she seems tireless. This is the example that Connie sets, and she inspires other to work in a similarly exacting and professional manner.

Connie and other chefs I spoke with lamented the high turnover in kitchen staff. It was hard to keep good help. Part of this is because cooks are seeking to learn from as many people as they can, but in this line of work it is also hard to find people who are reliable and who fit into the culture of a kitchen. Connie's friend Julien, who is the chef owner at M Restaurant in Lyon, told me that he would hire more women but there just weren't as many women as men out there on the job market. He said it was hard to find qualified cooks at all.

While Connie is pleased that the business is now going well enough to be able to hire other cooks, she misses working with other chefs. She misses the opportunities to learn like she had when she was at the start of her career and gaining experience in many different kitchens. Nonetheless, Connie participates in culinary events throughout the year where she works with inspiring chefs. On a trip to Norway, sponsored by trout producers, Connie had a chance to get to know a group of Lyonnais chefs, including Julien, who is a member of the Toques blanches lyonnaises. "I would probably never have crossed paths with Julien because the Toques blanches are sort of in the other camp from the group of chefs I am friends with and with whom I collaborate. They are more the old guard, traditionalists, and we are the nouvelle cuisine lyonnaise." Connie explained that, as she got to know Julien, she began to appreciate his cuisine. In fact, when I asked Connie out for dinner while I was visiting Lyon, she chose Julien's restaurant. As we enjoyed our meal, Connie remarked on Julien's excellent technique and presentation. So what made Julien's cooking different from Connie's? Her comment about nouvelle cuisine lyonnaise intrigued me, so I asked her to tell me more about this term.

Connie explained that she is part of a group of young chefs cooking creative food that they call nouvelle cuisine lyonnaise. At the core of this group are Tabata and Ludovic Mey from Les Apothicaires, Hubert Vergoin from Substrat, and Arnaud Laverdin, Thomas Pezeril and Stephen Theibaut-Pellegrino from la Bijouterie. They hang out together, share ideas, and push one another's thinking about food and cooking. I have been fortunate enough to eat in these restaurants, and they all place locally sourced seasonal products at the center of their cooking. Their techniques range from classic French braising and poaching to Asian-inspired steaming and raw meat and fish preparations. The flavors are eclectic, with herbs such as thyme or tarragon that are familiar to French cuisine but also incorporating ingredients from farther afield, such as miso and jalapeños. The portions are dainty, and the presentation of the dishes is artistic but not overdone. There is an artistic touch to much of this cuisine, which is often associated with women's cooking. When you finish eating a meal, you feel good—it does not leave you feeling overfed or with your senses saturated. These restaurants have a relaxed atmosphere and they all eschew tablecloths as stuffy and not environmentally friendly.

In 2015, Hubert Vergoin, the chef from Substrat, Gaëtan Gentil, the chef at PRaiRial, the blogger Julien Le Forestier and communications expert Romain Bombail formed the association Bande de gourmands. Their motivation was to promote a new type of cuisine in Lyon: a cuisine that "sees the pertinence of culinary fusion that is open to the world, that defends local products, and provisions using a short supply chain" (Reynaud 2016). The central goal of the association was to bring together like-minded chefs, writers, and producers to push back against the dominating cuisine to show that another cuisine is representative of Lyon at this time. Although the association website is no longer active and their Twitter feed has slowed down, the spirit of this group is alive and well in a growing number of kitchens in Lyon.

This group of chefs includes foreigners and French people set on exploring the techniques and flavors of the world. They are pushing the boundaries of Lyonnais cuisine and claiming their place as the new trendsetters outside of the Michelin-starred sphere. This group is part of a broader bistronomie movement in France: restaurants that do not have linen tablecloths, where the menus tend to have a limited number of seasonal items, and the food is meticulously prepared using fresh local products. An article in *Forbes* defines "bistronomie" as "a combination of simplicity and the best traditions in French cooking" (Rodriguez 2017). Payany declares that the traditional upscale restaurant will disappear in 2020 (Payany 2019). Good news in her opinion. Although she couldn't know what was coming to change the restaurant landscape, the coronavirus pandemic might be the impetus that transforms fine dining.

Often when Parisians or French people from other regions think of Lyonnais cuisine, they claim it is classic French food, the traditional dishes with heavy sauces. The dishes that people associate with Lyon make up the canon of the cuisines des mères, la cuisine bourgeoise. This is still the sort of food that is served to tourists in the bouchons that line rue Mercière and the cobblestone pedestrian streets of Vieux Lyon. However, it is important to remember that Lyon was at the center of the first postwar food revolution of nouvelle cuisine. Lyonnais chef Paul Bocuse was one of the champions and front-runners of this new way of cooking, which avoided heavy sauces, placed an emphasis on the freshness of ingredients, and paid close attention to the artful presentation of the scaled-down portions.

With the new millennium, France is coming to recognize its colonial heritage and cultural diversity, but not without a great deal of resistance and xenophobia. At the same time, French cuisine has become less of a monoculture. At a popular level, the kebab is one of France's most ubiquitous forms of fast food. For some this has caused an identity crisis (Sage 2014). However, at the level of the bistro and fine dining, this new openness to cultural diversity has meant an opportunity to incorporate ingredients and techniques from around the world—cultural diversity has brought incredible innovation to the Lyonnais kitchen. The locals are gravitating toward lighter fare, and tourists are drawn to Lyon to indulge in the classics but also to experience the future of French cuisine.

The group of young chefs who identify with the nouvelle cuisine lyonnaise includes many foreigners and women. The numerous culinary schools, in particular the Institut Paul Bocuse, which attracts many non-French students, have been drivers in making Lyon one of the centers for this culinary development (Cheshes 2018). Graduates of the Institut Paul Bocuse Tabata Mey of Les Apothicaires and Ruijun Sun from the Table de Wei both demonstrate a grounding in classic French techniques with strong influences from their own cultures and an openness to experimentation. At the same time, their food respects and showcases the seasonality of local products. I would argue that this is what makes their food truly Lyonnais.

It is not only students of local culinary schools who have flocked to the city—there are aspiring chefs from the world over who come to apprentice with notable chefs. Often this young talent stays because it is less expensive to open a restaurant in Lyon than somewhere like Paris, and there tends to be an openness to novelty in Lyon. In particular, there are numerous Japanese chefs, such as the Michelin-starred Takao Takano and Tsuyoshi Arai, who cook French food with a strong Japanese influence. Connie's neighbor Katsumi Ishida at the restaurant En mets fais ce qu'il te plaît (lit., in the plate do what you like) has been an influence on her and one of her biggest supporters. There is a strong dialogue between many of these chefs and they are building a sense of a movement. In a 2018 *GQ* article, Tabata Mey talked about the Bande de gourmands: "We are really close. We share recipes, we share producers. There are no secrets, like there were in the old days" (B. Martin 2018). As Mey suggests, this is more of a collective movement, rather than a competition.

When Connie talks about finding her place in the kitchen, she explains that "it is a bit like being in love—there is a sense of well-being and creativity." In Lyon, Connie has become a respected chef in the local culinary scene. She has gained the admiration of diners and chefs through her delicious, artful food that represents values of quality, respect for ingredients and the people who produce them, and creativity that knows no boundaries. Being a woman and a foreigner have not put Connie at a disadvantage or made her an outsider. This is in many ways due to her participation in the growing wave of nouvelle cuisine lyonnaise, which has actively embraced diversity as one of its central tenets. Lyon is still on the map as the gastronomic capital of France, and this is largely due to the influx of new talent that has mixed with the homegrown base of culinary knowledge.

Many Ways to Be a Woman on the Line

While les mères lyonnaises helped cement Lyon's culinary reputation and they may have paved the way for women in professional kitchens, they represent one way to be a woman in the kitchen. Eugénie Brazier was the mother who yelled at her cooks, and Léa Bidault warned of her own loud mouth as she pulled her shopping basket through the market on Quai St. Antoine, but not all women raise their voices. Paulette Castaing, Sonia Ezgulian, and Connie Zagora show that there are other ways to be in the kitchen.

Paulette Castaing rose to great heights of her profession with a steady, exacting work ethic. She demonstrated that a kitchen did not need to be organized along the lines of the patriarchal brigade system. Paulette's kitchen included more egalitarian structures of work in which everyone collaborated and contributed equally. Castaing embodied a steady, supportive leadership that helped shape the culinary careers of many notable chefs. She instilled values of patience, collaboration, and work that valued intuition.

Sonia Ezgulian works in a similar fashion. She came to the kitchen as a mature woman who knew who she was and who had a strong sense of her culinary self. She had the openness to experience the brigade system, but this also taught her that she did not want to reproduce that in her own restaurant. Sonia demonstrates the courage to cook food that is outside the canon of Lyonnais classics but, like Paulette, she also shows how this could be done differently. In the end, she decided that she prefers to cook alone, something that other women in Lyon also do, but this does not mean she does so in creative isolation. Sonia takes part in a larger conversation about food that easily crosses borders. As a journalist and professional communicator, she shows that women do not labor silently in their kitchens. Ezgulian's numerous cookbook projects, newspaper articles, television appearances, and place on prestigious culinary juries are a testament to women taking their place as professionals in a public discourse on food that honors women's creativity and resourcefulness.

Connie Zagora is also changing the face of professional cooking in Lyon. While becoming a respected member of the local culinary scene, Connie has pushed the boundaries of what it means to be local and make local food. She and other talented young foreign chefs are riding the wave of nouvelle cuisine lyonnaise, a movement that embraces culinary diversity. Connie's success is also surely due to her work ethic, talent, and desire to explore and create delicious food. Zagora is another woman who shows that you don't have to act or cook like a man to be respected in the kitchen.

These three women, Castaing, Ezgulian, and Zagora, who come from different generations, show that gender stereotypes do not have to dominate the organization of work or shape the type of food that is produced. They all have different ways of doing that help to draw into question notions of professionalism in the culinary arts because the title of professional has often excluded women, foreigners, and minorities (Trubek 2000, 126; Ray 2016). Their stories show how women are reshaping the category of culinary professional. They set the economic and cultural value of women's productive labor. Connie and Sonia actively communicate their different ways of doing and they present an alternative that creates space for more people—not just White French men—in the kitchen.

CONCLUSION

During my last interview with Sonia Ezgulian in 2019, she told me about her experience of being a judge for one of France's most prestigious culinary competitions.

> It was four or five years ago, I was invited to be part of a panel of judges for the Bocuse d'Or, the French competition. It was the first time . . . there were ten judges and there were five women, yes, five women and five men cooks, chefs. Listen to me, I tell you that it really surprised me, it's not that you have to make an event out of it every time there are women, but no one did an interview, no one took a photo of those five women together. At a certain point, there were just the five of us in a corner with our chef's coats and I said, "Can we take a photo, because it is an event for the five of us to be here together?" And, we did the photo, but I looked around at the press and all the others, and if we hadn't taken the photo no one else would have.

It felt like everything had changed and nothing had changed. Women may be granted more of a prominent place in the culinary world but their achievements are not recognized or celebrated in the same way as men's successes. When I began this research in 2013, people were not talking about women in culinary professions. This is one of the reasons that I started with archival research and the mères lyonnaises.

My feeling in those early days was that women were minor players in the Lyonnais culinary scene. Spending a year in the city helped me to locate many of the women hidden away in kitchens. Getting to know these professionals, following their successes, and keeping track of the newcomers over six years has shown me the evolution of women's place in the kitchen. Lyon is now attracting culinary talent from all over the world, and women are part of a group of exceptional newcomers.

Women have always been in kitchens, domestic and professional. This book sheds light on why women's presence in and contributions to culinary fields has often been eclipsed and why women still remain

Figure 6.1: Women from the Bocuse d'Or panel of judges, circa 2015. Left to right: Amandine Chaignot, Sonia Ezgulian, Adeline Grattard, Stéphanie Le Quellec, and Flora Mikula. (Photo courtesy of Sonia Ezgulian)

a minority, particularly at the top. While the original mères lyonnaises may have paved the way for other women's acceptance and even success in the restaurant kitchens of Lyon, these women's stories have remained a footnote that prominent male chefs nod to in acknowledgment before turning the spotlight back on themselves. The mères lyonnaises set a precedent, but their accomplishments are rarely fully celebrated—they remain an anomalous blip in French culinary history. In doing archival research on the mères and listening to people talk about these women's place in local history, I wanted the mères' lives and stories to have a bigger impact on creating a place for women in kitchens. While I see how the legend of the mères lyonnaises is an important way for some women working in the culinary arts to legitimate their place in the kitchen, it is not enough. Just saying "well, there were these badass women who came before us, so why shouldn't we be here?" does not make the path to professional culinary success easier. Narratives are powerful, but they make up only part of the social reality that is responsible for creating gender norms and bias—men still set the dominant discourse for themselves. In this conclusion I don't want to limit or underestimate the impact the mères have had on women's culinary careers, but it seems necessary to shift the focus to women's marginalization in the culinary arts. At moments, it was tempting to write a power anthem to all the women cooking their hearts out and kicking butt at each *service*, but that would contribute to a lie. We should celebrate women's accomplishments, but I would be negligent if I did not conclude with a call to arms. It is not enough to celebrate the past and the few exceptions—we need to dismantle the structures that keep women and other underrepresented peoples down in the workplace and in society. This means understanding and valorizing women's productive and reproductive work not as separate spheres but as interconnected. We need to create economic and social structures where the domestic and public spheres are not working against each other. This means questioning and realigning the value of different forms of labor so we can see and appreciate the ways in which they contribute to a more equitable society. This book is not only about women and restaurant kitchens. My hope is that this case study will have implications for larger issues of inequality.

The Challenges of the Professional Kitchen

While the rise of the celebrity chef has given new value to culinary work (Ruhlman 2006), the fact remains that most people working in kitchens work long hours, doing manual labor, and are not paid much above the SMIC (*salaire minimum interprofessionnel de croissance*, minimum wage in France). Restaurant kitchen work is largely blue-collar labor. There has historically been resistance to women's presence in professional kitchens because women are a threat to men—they fear women will debase the professional work that men have tried to elevate. Irene Padavic (1991) notes that, particularly in blue-collar work, reproducing notions of masculinity as male dominance is important because of the low pay and struggles to uphold the notion that the man be a family breadwinner. This is increasingly challenging in the current neoliberal economy that has pushed down wages and encouraged women to enter the formal workforce. This new economic and social order has meant challenges to patriarchal order, particularly among low-income workers (M. Cooper 2017). It has been hard to overcome this bias since women's domestic labor continues to be exploited; although women work in the formal labor force, they still shoulder the majority of domestic labor (Cairns, Johnston, and Baumann 2010).

Rather than conform to male expectations of women in the workplace, some women working as cooks have decided to do the job on their own terms. When women are in positions of power, this can mean reorganizing the structure of work to be more egalitarian and collaborative, creating flexible working hours, and even making the decision to work alone. However, it is not always possible for women to make their own rules. The women in chapter 5 demonstrate ways of working that move outside of patriarchal structures and enable women to flourish. In the kitchens of Lyon, there has not been a revolution with women throwing off patriarchy—there has been a quiet movement grounded in professionalism at all costs.

Women often pay a heavy price to survive in the male-dominated professional kitchen. This can mean not advancing in the hierarchy due to a lack of access to strong networks and the best training. In some cases, the price can be dropping out. Despite the persistence of discrimination against and sometimes aggression toward women, activist movements like #BalanceTonPorc (the French version of #MeToo) have not gained much traction in addressing specific cases of abuse. This could be partly due to cultural differences in the use of social media and a culture where abuses of power related to sex do not generally make the news (Sarmiento-Mirwaldt, Allen, and Birch 2014). Journalist Karina Pisner notes that there is a sentiment in France that U.S. puritanism endangers the French sexual liberties and masculinity (2018). Few of the accusations against prominent men in media and politics have had legal repercussions.

When I returned to Lyon in 2019, I asked a number of the participants in my research if they felt that the #MeToo movement had an impact on the restaurant industry; most of them told me that there had been no spectacular cases. When I probed further, a few women pointed out the insular nature of the restaurant industry. One said, "Voices travel quickly if someone behaves badly. Reputations are important in such a closed world."

One positive outcome of the #BalanceTonPorc movement has been female journalists pushing back more persistently against women's underrepresentation in the culinary arts. Vérane Frédiani's film *À la récherché des femmes chefs* (2017) shows how French culture is starting to question male dominance and stereotypes in the culinary fields. Over the past five years, more female food writers have risen to prominence in mainstream French news media, providing more even coverage of men and women working in culinary fields. Chapter 4 shows how women have begun to change the ways in which mainstream print media and blogs portray women as culinary professionals. Food-focused columns in major media outlets such as *L'Obs* and *Le Monde* have raised the overall profile of women's food writing. Once relegated to discussing recipes and talking about food fads, more articles are critically assessing gender inequality in the kitchen, and writers are working to bring women's professional culinary labor into the spotlight. While print media has made some progress, television remains largely attached to superficial representations of women as desirable objects for consumption. Television cooking competitions offer women visibility, but the women chosen to compete on shows like *Top Chef* conform to popular standards of beauty—slim, White, with clear complexions and desirable features. Culinary shows in France and North America remain largely male dominated (É. Cohen 2015). Slowly, media images of "the chef" are changing, but this is not without its issues.

Feminist journalists have begun to view women in the culinary arts in new ways. These writers have made a broader public aware that women are present in kitchens and they are sometimes the chef de cuisine. While women who work as chefs have lagged in self-promotion, there is now more media coverage of women who cook. Slowly, this coverage is moving to a more realistic and less sexist representation of women's professional realities. This is helping young women to imagine themselves as chefs and to consider the culinary arts as a viable career path. This is one of the reasons why more women than ever are enrolling in culinary education programs (Marie 2014). At the same time, women still have higher rates of attrition early on in their culinary careers, and this is an issue that should be addressed early in culinary training. There need to be changes to culinary education to stop the proliferation of gender stereotypes and bias. First, the presence of more women as chef instructors in private and public institutions would help young men and women more readily accept women as authority figures. A strong presence of women as instructors would help to abate the sexism and bias that the young women in culinary school reported in interviews for this book. It is also possible that female instructors would demonstrate ways of doing that male instructors might not consider. For example, they might model forms of collaboration that are outside of the brigade hierarchy. Second, having women as role models and mentors would create support systems and networks for young women. This is symbolically important so that young women have role models they can relate to from their earliest moments in professional kitchens. Third, greater accountability of instructors through antibias training and reporting of gender discrimination would help create a more inclusive educational environment. The main qualification for most chef instructors is their experience in the field—this does not mean that they are particularly well prepared for teaching, and they may be more likely to reproduce the same unequal gender dynamics that they experienced in the workplace. These changes are unlikely to happen unless both male and female chef instructors receive antibias training and learn to address the pitfalls of their own education.

Initially, I had thought that formal networks of women in the culinary arts were part of the solution for helping women succeed in these fields. However, I began to see female-only networks as not the best answer for strengthening women's position in the industry. Female mentors are important, but expecting the few women at the top to support women coming up puts an unfair burden on them (O'Meara and Stromquisit 2015). Women also need access to the best mentors, no matter their gender. Groups like the Toques blanches are largely boys' clubs with a few women relegated to the margins, but they are an example of a group of highly skilled chefs, and women could use access to the expertise of these men. It is important for women to feel support from others who have shared their experiences but, without access to the most skilled practitioners, women have little chance of reaching the top of the profession if that is their goal. By the end of my research, I was convinced that women needed to fight to become central members of male-dominated culinary groups, from the Toques blanches to the MOF.

Representation in male-dominated professional associations is an important step toward women being able to succeed in the culinary world. However, another key element is access to financing. A number of women I interviewed told me that they suspected banks had denied them loans because they were women. One woman explained that she was unable to carry out renovations to her small restaurant in order to keep it competitive and to update her kitchen equipment because the bank would not give her a loan because she was a woman working on her own and a single parent—she did not have the security of a man backing her, and she felt the bank saw her as a high-risk case. She told me that being undercapitalized was having a negative impact on her business and she was frustrated because she could never seem to get ahead financially. Joan James's documentary, *A Fine Line* (2020), and chef Iliana Regan's memoir, *Burn the Place* (2019), also document the discriminatory practices of U.S. financial institutions. Finding investors and getting financing from banks is a problem that women all over the world face in running food businesses. This is perhaps one of the biggest setbacks for women and one of the reasons why we do not see more woman-owned restaurants and food businesses. The negative stereotype of women as incapable businesspeople needs to be dispelled.

These broader structural issues are harder to remedy since they lie deeply embedded in cultural norms and daily practices of French life. Stereotypes that reinforce a gendered division of labor are only one part of the structural barriers keeping women from achieving. For professional women in both blue- and white-collar work, there is still a double bind—women are expected to work on an even playing field with men, but they are generally expected to also bear children, raise them, and be responsible for running the household. This gendered division of labor that is prevalent in most European societies is often the root of gender-based power differences. Women's domestic labor is unremunerated and undervalued, and it detracts from women's ability to contribute to the formal economy (Saltzman Chafetz 1991, 75).

Although France's social welfare system ensures three months of maternity leave, this does not mean that women, if they choose to have children, have equality with men in professional kitchens. Women in my research reported being worried about taking leave, and others told me that after they took maternity leave they were relegated to menial tasks when they returned to work. Paternity leave was introduced in 2002, and a 2018 study showed that nearly 70 percent of men take this leave. However, the short duration of this leave draws into question the effectiveness of paternity leave in achieving a more equal balance in the amount of time both parents spend with their children (Pailhé, Solaz, and Tô 2018).[1] Some women told me that even with supportive partners they could not make restaurant hours fit with the realities of their young families. For example, the hours for public daycare did not correspond with the split shifts they were expected to work. Some women told me that they only worked the lunch shift as a way to meet the demands of their employer and their families. A few of these chefs explained that this choice meant that they were systematically overlooked for promotions.

Others I talked to decided to leave restaurant work to go into culinary education or catering, two areas with more flexible work schedules. These stories explained how women were supposed to adjust their work lives and career trajectories to fit the needs of their families. This was not the case for the male chefs I spoke with. They talked about working long hours and how it had been hard on their families, sometimes resulting in divorce, but there was no mention of reducing hours or only working certain shifts in order to share household tasks and childcare equally with their partners.

The women I interviewed who refused the reproductive role made a conscious choice to put their careers first. Not all women want to be mothers. Choosing to not have children is a complex decision informed by multiple factors. However, many female participants defined this choice as a form of resistance to patriarchal social norms so they could progress in their careers.

New Trends and the Future

While larger structural changes around parental leave and childcare are necessary, a number of reforms within the profession would encourage all women, not just those who choose not to have children, to stay in the field and would help them to advance. Would more flexible work hours make it possible for more women to stay in the profession? If the culture of work in restaurant kitchens were more collaborative and supportive, would all members of the team perform better, even at challenging moments in their lives? With more chefs de cuisine who listen and take into consideration the complexities of their workers' lives beyond the kitchen walls, these structural changes would be possible. Chefs have to start considering that their workers have lives outside the restaurant and that having a life beyond work does not represent a lack of professionalism. This requires a move away from the efficiencies that capitalism imposes on the workplace, to a view of labor that is connected to families, communities, and general well-being.[2]

If talented and hard-working women can find proper support at all stages of their culinary careers, they are more likely to succeed and rise through the ranks. Change is necessary within the industry to bring about better working conditions and to shift the culture of kitchens from male-dominated spaces of abuse and exclusion. To keep women in this field, there also needs to be more social support for women in the workplace in general, particularly for women who choose to become mothers—they need support during pregnancy and child rearing. I became acutely aware of this as I lived my first experiences of maternity during this research. Although I was not working in kitchens the entire time, I felt my professional role as an academic constantly challenged by the social pressures of motherhood. "Why are you trying to work? Why don't you just enjoy being a mother?" These were a few of the voices I heard frequently toward the end of my pregnancy and in the first year of my child's life. I felt as if French society expected me to stay home and be sidelined from my career. I can only imagine the additional pressure women in the culinary arts must feel as they juggle hard physical work and the unforgiving hours of the kitchen. Things do not get easier once a baby is born—there is sleep deprivation, possibly a sense of guilt for not being with one's baby all of the time, the cost of childcare, and in some cases the pressing realities of breast-feeding. I have yet to see a restaurant with a dedicated pumping room or any sort of appropriate space for this important food work.

Until women are no longer seen as default caregivers, it will be hard to keep mothers in professional kitchens. It is ironic that Lyon's most famous female culinary figures were known as mères, while the professional kitchen has proven inhospitable for mothers. Being a mother does not mean women can't be professionals, but in such a demanding field it is unlikely that most women can hold up the standard of maternal goddess in addition to ass-kicking cook, nor should they be obliged to be both or either.

Scholars in the Kitchen

All of these pressures are enough to drive a woman away from both cooking and reproduction. Feminists avoided the study of women cooking because of its ties to domesticity (Avakian 2005). In *The Feminine Mystique* (1963), feminist Betty Friedan viewed cooking as a way in which women continued to subordinate themselves to men; she saw home cooking as a task associated with low status, of little value, and with little demand for intellect (244–45; Giard 1994, 213–28). As Kate Cairns and Joseé Johnston (2015) note, Friedan and other feminists "offered women a language to critique domestic expectations" (8). This second-wave feminism encouraged privileged middle-class women to leave the home to pursue paid work. The low-wage labor of working-class and women of color filled the gap that then occurred in domestic food labor (Allen and Sachs 2012, 25). Second-wave feminism placed domestic work, cooking included, in opposition to feminism (Hollows

2007, 34). Although women's labor in the professional kitchen falls outside of the domestic sphere, it has been hard for this paid labor to shake the stigmas of domestic oppression that are attached to it.

Despite feminist calls for a new field of feminist food studies (Avakian and Haber 2005) and women's growing participation in nondomestic food labor, there has been little connection made between the material, sociocultural, and corporeal domains of women's food work (Allen and Sachs, 23). In the U.S. context, the focus is on the shifting of White middle-class women's domestic labor to working-class and women of color (Tronto 2002; Duffy 2005) and the racial hierarchies of women working in the material domain (Glenn 1992). This racial displacement of domestic labor has been less prominent in French society: it has been more of a class shift in which middle-class women displace their domestic labor to working-class men and women. Despite successful French state policies to bring women into the workforce, these same policies have not created a fairer gender division of unpaid domestic and care work (Windebank 2012). In the French context, scholars have paid little attention to understanding why women drop out of male-dominated occupations.

This book has contributed to considering why women leave specific fields but also how women's place is changing in sectors that take on new cultural values and meanings. As chapter 4 discusses, the rise of the star chef has brought kitchen work into a more public light. Through this publicity, a broader French public has come to appreciate the work that happens in professional kitchens. Representations of culinary work have focused on the role of the chef de cuisine, the person at the top of the kitchen ranks. This has caused a skewed perception of what happens in restaurant kitchens: not everyone gets to engage in the creative process of coming up with new dishes and most of the work entails repetitive tasks that require limited skills. The focus on a singular creative genius, particularly in haute cuisine, has given professional cooking new cultural value (Ingold and Hallam 2007). The idea of the chef as a creative force and skillful master has lifted up the overall image of professional culinary work.

At the same time, this focus on the singular person of the chef as the generator of innovation gives a misleading idea of how dishes are created in a kitchen. The chef does not work alone. As many have recognized in other fields (Ingold and Hallam 2007), creation takes place in a social, collaborative space. Cooks in the professional French kitchen possess a socially shared grammar that is constructed through apprenticeship (Greenfield 2004, 150). The circulation of knowledge in French kitchens comes from the many cooks who move from kitchen to kitchen. New ideas are born from this collective knowledge and sharing. Women are part of this shared knowledge base, and they are even prized for their creativity. However, the problem lies with authorship—women are less likely to lay claim to their creations or they are not in a position that allows them to do so. There are those who are happy to be part of a collective project and who do not see the point of ownership over ideas. For example, when I asked Sonia Ezgulian what she thought about the circulation and reproduction without attribution of her serpentine tarte, she replied, "it makes me happy to see people like the idea and they are cooking this tarte." The male-dominated hierarchies of the kitchen work to protect and consolidate the power of those who hold it. In this logic, creation cannot be communal—ownership is about exclusion and power. Chefs often obscure the collaborative nature of innovation in order to lay claim to the authorship of dishes.

So where do women fit into this creative vision of kitchen work? While women are often praised for their creativity and attention to detail in the kitchen, these skills are used to relegate them to garde-manger stations and pastry. Rarely do women reach the top ranks, where they would have the opportunity to control the creative process in the kitchen. Women like Anne-Sophie Pic demonstrate what women are capable of doing when given the outlet for creative expression. Pic's cuisine is like art on a plate—not only are the dishes visually pleasing, the taste and texture engages every sensory aspect of eating while creating a sense of harmony. Women's potential for this kind of production and leadership in kitchens is great, but the glass ceiling excludes them from positions that would give them the most creative license and potential.

While the position of the chef de cuisine is seen as celebrated cultural and creative work, the rest of the kitchen remains largely male-dominated, blue-collar workspace. Although the United States has seen a larger movement of middle-class teenagers going to culinary school (Ray 2016), in France the majority of culinary students come from low-income families. While the culinary arts are often seen as a valuable element of French culture, the work is still undervalued and society sees it as manual labor, rather than the skilled craft that it can be at the upper levels of the profession. For this reason, culinary education has remained somewhat stigmatized, and women and girls have been discouraged from entering this blue-collar field.

Two of the women I discuss at length, Tabata Mey (chapter 4) and Connie Zagora (chapter 5), both come from middle-class backgrounds and started their careers relatively late—in their twenties. While both women are exceedingly talented, it may also be that their foreign origins allowed them to overcome certain barriers to entry into the field. This is not to say that they did not put in their time doing the everyday grunt work in the kitchen before assuming more creative roles as chefs de cuisine. Additionally, Zagora and Mey are part of the nouvelle cuisine lyonnaise movement that elevates the creative process and does not always follow French traditions in the kitchen.

Nouvelle cuisine lyonnaise offers an example of a movement that is creating room for breaking with tradition, part of which is the maintenance of the patriarchal structures and hierarchies of the kitchen. Women in all sorts of kitchens find ways to push back against the limiting structures of their work: they put their heads down and try to work and talk like men to fit in; there are those who actively challenge the male-dominated order of the workplace by calling out bad behavior; there are those who choose to avoid men by surrounding themselves with women or by working alone. All women in professional kitchens have to find a strategy that works for them in order to survive and even thrive. Whatever the strategy, women's presence in professional kitchens has some impact on subverting male dominance enacted through work.

Candace West and Don Zimmerman (1987) argue that gender norms and expectations are reproduced through day-to-day interactions in the workplace where men and women "do gender." Barbara Risman (2009) asserts that this conception of doing gender is not critical enough of gender inequality and serves to maintain the male-female binary. For this reason, I have gravitated toward Francine Deutsch's (2007) concept of undoing gender, which looks to the ways in which gender norms are eroded when men and women do not follow traditional gendered scripts. While working in kitchens, I came to recognize how men and women enact different elements of gendered scripts depending on the context and their desired outcomes. Some women choose to "man up" while working male-dominated positions such as the hotline; this was a way to keep up with the boys but on their own terms. Other women choose to let men lift heavy boxes and equipment for them, conforming to the weak female script, while they focus on advancing their work in more precision areas such as recipe creation and artful plating. Rarely were strategies for navigating gender norms straightforward. There were many instances in which men and women undo gender as they try to work together in a tight space focused on the same immediate common goal to get tasty, beautiful food to customers in a timely manner.

Women who occupy positions of power at work have opportunities to challenge gendered ways of thinking and doing (Stainback, et al. 2016). When women are at the top of the brigade hierarchy as chef-owners of their own restaurants, I found that negative gender stereotypes toward women start to break down (Ely 1995). Women in positions of power can also dictate the ways in which others will work, and they have the last say on hiring practices, which can help to improve women's representation and appreciation in the workplace (Hultin and Szulkin 2003). While it is important to have women in central creative and leadership roles, it is also essential that male chefs de cuisine are allies in addressing gender bias in the kitchen. The answers to women's exclusion in the culinary professions lie not just with women.

What We Can All Learn from Studying Kitchens

Through studying gender bias in professional kitchens, we can learn more about this issue in other kinds of work that require a great deal of collaboration and that employ hierarchical structures to maintain order in a workflow segmented by task and skill. In male-dominated fields like finance, engineering, and law, which are highly stratified, there is the most gender segregation and discrimination. In the culinary arts, there is also an element of managing creative work. Who gets to be part of the creative process? How is it related to skill? How is creativity gendered so that men can maintain their hold on this valued process?

The chef de cuisine is now seen as an important cultural figure who is at the head of the creative process but is also the top manager of the operation. Chefs are generally in charge of thinking up new dishes, deciding on the workflow, and hiring and firing. If we consider the chef as a dynamic manager, we can learn more about the management of creative processes and production in general.

The kitchen can also teach us about the construction of value in specific forms of labor. How do values on skill and its transmission become gendered? What are the economic outcomes of these biased processes? As cooks rise through the ranks, they move from blue-collar workers to artisans, valued for their skill and creativity. How do women acquire the knowledge needed to climb the ladder when there are often barriers to apprenticeship, mentoring, and skill development? Women's strategies can teach us about resilience but they can also inform the creation of better processes for training workers and construction of inclusive work environments that allow everyone to achieve their full potential.

Professional kitchens are unique places to study gender because there are no other professional sectors where women's domestic labor is so closely related to professional, paid labor. In the home, cooking has long been the purview of women and is work that is associated with women's unpaid labor. However, there are no other areas of women's domestic work that have experienced this same gender reversal when transferred to a paid or professional arena. For example, women make up the majority of both domestic and paid childcare workers. This is also a low-wage sector largely because of its association with women's unpaid labor and the undervaluing of this work, despite pockets of professionalization. Housecleaning is a similar type of work: most paid workers tend to be women, the work is associated with women's unpaid labor, and it is an unskilled, low-wage job. In housecleaning and childcare, men have never tried to take over and create a separate professional field with exclusionary training requirements and a separate pay scale.

Chapter 3 discusses further the threat of women to the culinary professions. While professional kitchen work has this unique aspect of being tied to unpaid domestic labor, it serves as an exaggerated example of what happens when women's labor is seen as driving wages down. When women are a minority in such sectors, the wage gap is usually greatest and the undervaluing of female labor can often go unnoticed. In these discourses, we can see the way in which women's skill and the value of their work is demeaned. These types of discourses are often couched in defenses of masculinity, which is conflated with professionalism. Here the gendered nature of organizations and work is clear—whether it is professional cooking or trading on the stock exchange floor (Allon 2014), this work is clearly articulated as men's work. These discourses produce value judgments that are not based on an analysis of skill or performance; rather, they are discourses that reproduce stereotypes that function to exclude women from specific types of work and economic parity.

Women continue to persevere, but as with the case of culinary professions, there are often attempts to sideline women and relegate them to their own separate category. This is the case with the World's Best Female Chef award (chapter 4). Such awards and news coverage place an emphasis on women being an exception, and they also draw into question whether women are able to compete alongside men. Haute cuisine is not the only elite arena where women face exclusion: a 2019 *New York Times Magazine* article focused on women's fight for gender equity in big-wave surfing (Duane 2019). In this case, arguments about strength and safety were deployed. Ultimately, the case of surfing reveals the ways in which governing bodies can systematically exclude women from the highest ranks of a sport. With haute cuisine and culinary professions, the exclusion is less blatant and the enforcement is more structural. The Meilleur ouvrier de France competition is an excellent example of the ways in which the French culinary establishment reproduces male dominance and systematically excludes women. There has been resistance within these establishments to try to understand and resolve the issue of women's underrepresentation. Studying professional kitchens can reveal a great deal about gatekeeping and the role of professional organizations in policing the field.

Looking to Lyon to Lead

This book focuses on Lyon because of its long history of prominent female chefs. Despite the prominence of women like Eugénie Brazier and her mentor Françoise Fillioux, there is no monument to their achievements. The corridors of the Halles Bocuse, a large covered market in Lyon's Third Arrondissement, have been named for the mères lyonnaises, but this is an obscure nod to women's culinary excellence that is housed under the larger structure that trumpets Bocuse's achievements. Rather than another wall mural featuring Bocuse and his band of boys, it is time for Lyon to recognize women's contribution to local culinary excellence in the past and now.

Celebrating this history and allowing women to claim their place in the city's kitchens can help Lyon remain a national and international center for the culinary arts. The many culinary training programs in and around Lyon have a strong population of female students—many of whom are foreign women who have come to Lyon because of its history of culinary excellence. With Jacotte Brazier's scholarships starting to play an important role in supporting young women as they work their way through culinary school, we will hopefully see more graduates take their places in the industry.

There is still a gap in early and mid-career support for women, and this is when they are most likely to drop out. Not every cook is destined to be a chef de cuisine or a Michelin-starred chef, but those who choose to cook should be able to do so without having to sacrifice family, health, and general well-being. It is here that Lyon can be a leader in culinary innovation—finding a solution for how to keep women in kitchens will ensure that Lyon remains a leader in the culinary arts. Women's ways of doing, creativity, and the balanced dynamic they offer to kitchen work are already starting to change daily work practices and the field of professional cooking.

The impact of the COVID-19 pandemic on restaurants around the world has been devastating. In France, numerous lockdowns have caused restaurants to close completely, some of them for good, and others have been able to move to serving takeout to get by. The closure of restaurants has gone on longer than expected, but the French government has continued to offer aid in the form of extending short-term unemployment payments, postponing tax payments, and providing emergency assistance to small and independently owned bars and restaurants. Many of the participants in this research told me that this was the only thing keeping them in business. However, groups like the Conféderation des petites et moyennes enterprises (PME, Confederation of small and medium businesses) have argued that this assistance is not enough (C. Cohen 2020). In September 2020, when further closures were announced, restaurant and bar owners and workers took to the streets to protest. The closures were considered the last straw in the challenges that this industry has been facing. Many bars and restaurants will not survive the pandemic.

When fewer restaurants reopen after this global health crisis, there will be more competition than ever within the workforce. It is likely fewer women will return to restaurant work. During the pandemic, women more often than men left their jobs to take care of children when schools closed. For households with children, family coping strategies tended to lean heavily on women's unpaid labor in the home. The pandemic is expected to undo the progress that women were making with regards to equal pay (Makooi 2020).

Women in the restaurant industry have certainly suffered, but those who remain when restaurants reopen will be the survivors who have the potential to reshape the industry. There has been speculation that the pandemic has disrupted the restaurant industry, particularly in the United States, to the point where the industry could undergo a drastic change in the way businesses are organized and run (Krishna 2020).

The lower overhead of restaurants in Lyon, compared with Paris, could mean that more restaurants will survive. In addition, many of the more established restaurants that own their commercial space will have a better chance of reopening. It is hard to say what the restaurant landscape will look like when the dust settles, but it is likely that food and fine dining will remain central to Lyonnais culture and the city's economy.

What role will women play in the rebuilding and in the future of this gastronomic city? Lyon has shown openness to women in the past, and it is proving to be a place where women in the culinary arts can thrive. For the gastronomic capital of France, the future is quite possibly female.

NOTES

Prologue

1. It was not an uncommon practice for rural and working-class urban women to leave their children with wet nurses in the countryside. The cost of wet nursing was cheaper in rural areas, and so affordable for women earning city wages for work as laborers or domestic servants.

2. In Varille 1928 and in Curnonsky and Grancher's accounts of popular eateries in Lyon during the interwar period, it is clear that many establishments were run by a husband-wife team (Curnonsky and Grancher, 1935).

3. *Poularde en demi-deuil* is a boiled Bresse chicken with thin slices of black truffle tucked under the skin. It is in "half mourning" because only half of its body is covered in black truffles. Fillioux claimed that the secret to her dish was cooking at least ten chickens at once in a big pot.

Introduction

1. In 2017, 41.5 percent of students enrolled in the CAP cuisine were women, 35.4 percent in the BAC Pro and 61 percent in the BTS. In the BTS, women had a success rate if 85.9 percent, compared with 77.7 percent of men. Ministère de l'éducation nationale, 2018.

2. When I returned to my field in Lyon in 2019, I discovered that Catherine Simon's *Mangées: Une histoire des mères lyonnaises* (2018) had angered many of the participants in my research. They did not feel that they had been represented correctly, and they felt that the book sensationalized the lives of the mères lyonnaises, muddying their memory.

3. In March 2018, *Télérama* published a map created by Vérane Frédiani and Estérelle Payany noting all the establishments with female chefs. This was one of the grassroots initiatives that came at the height of the #MeToo movement (Frédiani and Payany 2018).

Chapter 1

1. "Charles" is a familiar term for "male companion" or "boyfriend."

2. Studies of the technical school L'École de la Martinière in Lyon indicate a rise in the number of young women being trained for domestic service (Audet 1998; Pandraud 1997; Thivend and Schweitzer 2005).

3. The *pébrine* epidemic in the last half of the nineteenth century was the hardest to hit the silk industry.

4. Until 1965, women could not open their own bank accounts or access many forms of professional training and higher postsecondary schooling. In 1965, the Réforme des régimes matrimoniaux de 1804 made it possible for women to manage their own financial affairs and pursue professional careers without consent from their husbands. (Terréand and Simler 2011, 36–41).

5. The *Guide Michelin* was first published in 1900.

6. The sauce in Brazier's *quenelles financière* is made from reduced meat stock, butter, Madeira, and mushrooms. Fillioux's dishes were truffled poultry, quenelles with a crayfish butter gratin, and artichoke hearts with foie gras. Quenelles are a Lyonnais specialty usually made with pike that is processed with flour, egg, and butter. They are rarely made in house in restaurants. Most restaurants bought from the handful of caterers specialized in making quenelles. The dishes listed above are from the *Guide Michelin*, France, 1933.

7. "Madame Brazier est une très grande cuisinière—l'une des plus grandes que nous ayons eues, de toute notre tradition culinaire." Here Grancher uses "cuisinière" and not "chef de cuisine," still differentiating between men's (chefs') and women's (cooks') labor in the kitchen.

8. Again, Grancher refers to Madame Bigot as a cook, also using the title cordon-bleu, which specifically applies to talented female cooks, particularly those working in the domestic sphere. We can see how already women have separate categories early on in gastronomic criticism.

9. Referring to Toussaint-Samat's *Histoire de la cuisine bourgeoise* (2001), Ferguson states that "the term cordon bleu dates back to 1814, taken from the *Cordon bleu* (blue sash) worn by members of the royal Order of the Holy Spirit. Irony surely played an important part in the promotion of the lowly cook to an exalted status to which no woman, much less a cook, could aspire" (2004, 229–30n29). The members of this order held gourmet gatherings, and this is how the blue sash became associated with good cooking. During the French Revolution, this order was abolished but the expression "cordon bleu" continued to be used to designate a person as an excellent cook. In the late nineteenth century, the term came to mainly designate female cooks.

10. This idea of honesty comes partly from the government's recent creation of the *fait maison* certification, which helps to differentiate cooking from scratch versus reheating prepared foods in restaurants. During the period when I conducted this interview, the French press and consumers were discussing the matter of transparency in restaurant cooking and the quality of food ("Le décret" 2015).

Chapter 2

1. Dominique Brunet (1997, 48) notes that the proximity of the *piano* to the dining room was strategic—it made people hungry.

2. Beaujolais-loving Gnafron is a puppet that is friends with Guignol, perhaps the most well-known Lyonnais marionette. Laurent Mourget created these figures in the early nineteenth century and they have become symbols of the city (Fournel 1981).

3. "L'association a mis en place le label pour garantir à la clientèle le respect d'une tradition culinaire lyonnaise, et aussi la qualité et l'origine des produits locaux, une cuisine familiale maison faite sur place, un accueil chaleureux, et une ambiance typique lyonnaise dans un cadre historique."

4. Harris and Giuffre talk extensively about what happens to women in kitchens who choose to "act like 'one of the guys' and adopted a leadership style marked by masculine qualities" (2015, 137). Adopting a masculine style of leadership, yelling, cursing, and making sexualized jokes allowed some women in U.S. kitchens to affirm their position of power (138). Men often branded these women as "bitches," a label that the women either owned or rejected. In France, there was some negative name calling, but there was not the same categorical dismissal or condemnation of women who decided to take a tough leadership stance.

5. Sixteen weeks is the legal length of maternity leave in France for the first and second children. It is twenty-six weeks for the third child, thirty-four weeks for twins, and forty-six weeks for triplets. "La durée du congé maternité d'une salariée," L'Assurance Maladie, August 20, 2020, https://www.ameli.fr/assure/droits-demarches/famille/maternite-paternite-adoption/conge-maternite.

6. The memory of his grandmother's cooking was one of the reasons that Christian Têtedoie gave for buying La Voûte. He was nostalgic for the first meal that he had in Lyon at this historic restaurant. He claimed that it had reminded him of his grandmother's cooking (Faus n.d.). Also, when I interviewed Alain Alexanian, he talked extensively about the influence his grandmother's cooking and garden had on his culinary career.

7. Plum Lyon received glowing reviews on Trip Advisor, https://www.tripadvisor.com/Attraction_Review-g187265-d3928744-Reviews-Plum_Lyon_Teaching_Kitchen-Lyon_Rhone_Auvergne_Rhone_Alpes.html, accessed January 17, 2020.

Chapter 3

1. According to Lave and Wenger, "learning is not merely situated in practice—as if it were some independently reifiable process that just happened to be located somewhere; learning is an integral part of generative social practice in the lived-in world" (1991, 35).

2. Having apprentices observe and only do menial tasks is quite common in this form of learning. The initial period of apprenticeship serves to bring the novice into the culture of work and to establish the hierarchy of the workplace—socialization and control (Goody 1989).

Chapter 4

1. Given the lack of specific literature on gender and mentorship in the culinary arts, I have drawn here on the extensive research from the business world and the role of mentorship in women's success as managers and leaders in business. See Ochberg, Barton, and West 1989 and Schwiebert et al. 1999.

2. In 2012, Nicholas Le Bec's restaurant Rue Le Bec closed abruptly. After nearly twelve years in Lyon, Le Bec fled the country: his businesses were nearly 5 million euros in debt (Lagrange and Thibaut, 2012).

3. The menu notes that Audrey Jacquier won fourth place for pâté en croûte in the 2013 World Championship, an important culinary competition in the eyes of the Lyonnais culinary community.

4. *Télérama* started as a television guide and has become an important weekly for entertainment and cultural news. It is distributed at most newsstands throughout France. In 2019, *Télérama* had a weekly circulation of 485,657 (ACPM n.d.).

5. *L'Obs* was formerly known as *Le Nouvel observateur* (1964–2014) and is a French weekly newsmagazine. Historically, *L'Obs* has been a left-leaning publication. It has one of the highest circulation rates of weekly newsmagazines in France (222,470 in 2019) (ACPM n.d.).

Conclusion

1. At the time of this writing, men get eleven days of paternity leave for their first child and eighteen days for their second (Pailhé, Solaz, and Tô 2018).

2. This would be a reversal of the shift during the Industrial Revolution that Sheila Cooper describes as "service to servitude": there was no place for institutions and systems that reinforced social networks and family ties (2005, 383).

BIBLIOGRAPHY

Abarca, Meredith E. 2006. *Voices in the Kitchen: Views of Food and the World from Working-Class Mexican and Mexican American Women.* College Station: Texas A & M University Press.

———. 2007. "Charlas Culinarias: Mexican Women Speak from the Public Kitchens." *Food and Foodways* 15, no. 3–4 (October): 183–212.

Académie française. 2014. "La féminisation des noms de métiers, fonctions, grades ou titres—Mise au point de l'Académie française." Académie française. http://www.academie-francaise.fr/actualites/la-feminisation-des-noms-de-metiers-fonctions-grades-ou-titres-mise-au-point-de-lacademie. Accessed December 30, 2020.

Acker, Joan. 1990. "Hierarchies, Jobs, Bodies: A Theory of Gendered Organizations." *Gender and Society* 4, no. 2: 139–58.

———. 2006. "Inequality Regimes: Gender, Class, and Race in Organizations." *Gender and Society* 20, no. 4: 441–64.

ACPM. N.d. "L'Obs." Alliance pour les Chiffres de la Presse et des Médias. https://www.acpm.fr/Support/l-obs. Accessed January 23, 2021.

———. N.d. "Télérama." Alliance pour les Chiffres de la Presse et des Médias. https://www.lepoint.fr/societe/l-etrange-fuite-du-chef-etoile-18-10-2012-1695718_23.php. Accessed January 23, 2021.

Adapon, Joy. 2008. *Culinary Art and Anthropology.* New York: Berg.

Adkins, Lisa. 2001. "Cultural Feminization: 'Money, Sex and Power' for Women." *Signs: Journal of Women in Culture and Society* 26, no. 3 (April): 669–95.

Agence France-Presse. 2020. "'Food Traboule' et suites connectées pour faire revivre une icône du Vieux Lyon." *Le Point*, January 13, 2020.

Allen, Patricia, and Carolyn Sachs. 2012. "Women and Food Chains: The Gendered Politics of Food," in *Taking Food Public: Redefining Foodways in a Changing World*, edited by Psyche Williams-Forson and Carole Counihan, 23–40. New York: Routledge.

Allon, Fiona. 2014. "The Feminisation of Finance: Gender, Labour and the Limits of Inclusion." *Australian Feminist Studies* 29, no. 79 (May): 12–30.

Anonymous. 2012. *Cuisinière lyonnaise*. Lyon: Les cuisinières-Sobbollire.

Audet, Fabrice. 1998. *Enseignement technique et bassin industriel: L'école la Martinière de Lyon, 1830–1965*. PhD diss., Université Lumière Lyon 2.

Auslander, Leora. 1996. *Taste and Power: Furnishing Modern France*. Berkeley: University of California Press.

Avakian, Arlene Voski. 2005. *Through the Kitchen Window: Women Explore the Intimate Meanings of Food and Cooking*. Oxford: Berg.

Avakian, Arlene Voski, and Barbara Haber, eds. 2005. *From Betty Crocker to Feminist Food Studies: Critical Perspectives on Women and Food*. Amherst: University of Massachusetts Press.

Baranowski, Shelley, and Ellen Furlough. 2001. *Being Elsewhere: Tourism, Consumer Culture, and Identity in Modern Europe and North America*. Ann Arbor: University of Michigan Press.

Barre, Josette. 2001. *La colline de la Croix-Rousse*. Lyon: Éditions Lyonnaises d'Art et d'Histoire.

Bascom, William. 1965. "The Forms of Folklore: Prose Narratives." *Journal of American Folklore* 78, no. 307 (January): 3–20.

Baudelot, Christian. 2000. "The Future Remains Open." In *The Gendering of Inequalities: Women, Men and Work*, edited by Jane Jenson, Jacqueline Lauffer, and Margaret Maruani, 313–19. Translated by Helen Arnold. Aldershot, UK: Ashgate.

Béja, Alice. 2014. "Top chef, l'excellence à la française?" *Esprit* 3 (March/April): 214–18.

Black, Rachel Eden. 2005. "The Porta Palazzo Farmers' Market: Local Food, Regulations and Changing Traditions." *Anthropology of Food* 4 (May). https://journals.openedition.org/aof/157. Accessed February 1, 2021.

———. 2018. "Gastronomie, Inégalité, Fraternité." *Anthropology News*, May 10, 2018. https://anthrosource.onlinelibrary.wiley.com/doi/10.1111/AN.858. Accessed February 2, 2021.

Bleich, Erik. 2001. *Race Policy in France*. Brookings Institution, May 1, 2001. https://www.brookings.edu/articles/race-policy-in-france/. Accessed February 23, 2020.

Bocuse d'Or. n.d. "History." Bocuse d'Or. https://www.bocusedor.com/en/the-contest/history/. Accessed December 20, 2020.

Bourdain, Anthony. 2000. *Kitchen Confidential: Adventures in the Culinary Underbelly*. New York: Bloomsbury.

Bourelly, Martine. 2010. "Cheffe de cuisine: Le coût de la transgression." *Cahiers du genre* 48, no. 1: 127–48. doi:10.3917/cdge.048.0127.

Brazier, Eugénie, with Roger Moreau and Jacotte Brazier. 1992. *Les secrets de la Mère Brazier*. 2d ed. Paris: Solar.

Brewis, Joanna. 2000. "'When a Body Meet a Body . . . ': Experiencing the Female Body at Work." In *Organizing Bodies: Policy, Institutions and Work*, edited by Linda McKie and Nick Watson, 166–84. New York: St. Martin's.

Britton, Dana M. 2000. "The Epistemology of the Gendered Organization." *Gender and Society* 14, no. 3: 418–34.

Brooks, David. 2000. *Bobos in Paradise: The New Upper Class and How They Got There*. New York: Simon and Schuster.

Brunet, Dominique. 1997. *Les mères lyonnaises*. Master's thesis, Université Jean Moulin Lyon III.

Buford, Bill. 2020. *Dirt: Adventures in Lyon as a Chef in Training, Father, and Sleuth Looking for the Secret of French Cooking*. New York: Knopf.

Burrow, Robin, John Smith, and Christalla Yakinthou. 2015. "'Yes Chef': Life at the Vanguard of Culinary Excellence." *Work, Employment and Society* 29, no. 4 (April): 673–81.

Butin, Jean. 1999. *Ces lyonnaises qui ont marqué leurs temps: Passionnées, fascinantes, légendaires*. Lyon: Éditions lyonnaises d'art et d'histoire.

Butler, Judith. 1999. *Gender Trouble: Feminism and the Subversion of Identity*. 2d ed. New York: Routledge.

Byrd, Barbara. 1999. "Women in Carpentry Apprenticeship: A Case Study." *Labor Studies Journal* 24, no. 3 (September): 3–22. https://doi.org/10.1177/0160449X9902400301.

Cairns, Kate, and Josée Johnston. 2015. *Food and Femininity*. London: Bloomsbury.

Cairns, Kate, Josée Johnston, and Shyon Baumann. 2010. "Caring about Food: Doing Gender in the Foodie Kitchen." *Gender and Society* 24, no. 5: 591–615.

Caldwell, Melissa. 2006. "Tasting the Worlds of Yesterday and Today: Culinary Tourism and Nostalgia Foods in Post-Soviet Russia." In *Fast Food/Slow Food: The Cultural Economy of the Global Food System*, edited by Richard Wilk, 97–114. Lanham, MD: Alta Mira.

Cammas, Alexandre. 2012. "Le guide Michelin doit se libérer de l'influence des grands chefs." *Le Monde*, March 5, 2012. https://www.lemonde.fr/idees/article/2012/03/05/le-guide-michelin-doit-se-liberer-de-l-influence-des-grands-chefs_1651980_3232.html.

Cappellini, Benedetta, and Elizabeth Parsons. 2012. "Practising Thrift at Dinnertime: Mealtime Leftovers, Sacrifice and Family Membership." *Sociologi-*

cal Review 60, no. 2 supplement: 121–34. https://doi.org/10.1111/1467-954X.12041

Chauvel, Louis. 2006. *Les Classes moyennes à la dérive.* Paris: Le Seuil.

Cheshes, Jay. 2018. "The Most Innovative Chefs in Lyon, France's Gastronomic Capital." *Wall Street Journal,* July 24, 2018. https://www.wsj.com/articles/the-4-most-innovative-restaurants-in-lyon-frances-gastronomic-capital-1532459914. Accessed February 29, 2020.

Chevallier, Jim. 2018. *A History of the Food of Paris: From Roast Mammoth to Steak Frites.* Lanham, MD: Rowman and Littlefield.

Child, Julia, and Alex Prud'homme. 2006. *My Life in France.* New York: Anchor.

Chrisafis, Angelique. 2020. "French Chefs Stew over Renowned Restaurant's Loss of Michelin Star." *Guardian,* January 17, 2020. https://www.theguardian.com/world/2020/jan/17/french-chefs-stew-over-renowned-restaurants-loss-of-michelin-star. Accessed February 29, 2020.

Cohen, Claudia. 2020. "Covid-19: De nouvelles aides financières pour les bars, restaurants et salles de sport." *Le Figaro,* September 25, 2020. https://www.lefigaro.fr/conjoncture/covid-19-de-nouvelles-aides-financieres-pour-les-bars-restaurants-et-salles-de-sport-20200925. Accessed February 3, 2021.

Cohen, Évelyne. 2015. "Les émissions culinaires à la télévision française (1954–2015)." *Le temps des médias* 24, no. 1 (March): 165–79.

Cohen, Philip N., and Matt L. Huffman. 2007. "Working for the Woman? Female Managers and the Gender Wage Gap." *American Sociological Review* 72, no. 5 (October): 681–704.

Conrick, Maeve. 2009. "Representations of Gender in the Francophone Context of Québec and Canada: The Experience of 'La Féminisation Linguistique' in Principle and Practice." *Québec Studies* 48, no. 1 (December): 121–34. doi:10.3828/QS.48.1.121.

Cooper, Melinda. 2017. *Family Values: Between Neoliberalism and the New Social Conservatism.* New York: Zone Books.

Cooper, Sheila McIsaac. 2005. "Service to Servitude? The Decline and Demise of Life-Cycle Service in England." *History of the Family* 10, no. 4 (January): 367–86. https://doi.org/10.1016/j.hisfam.2005.09.003.

Counihan, Carole. 1999. *The Anthropology of Food and Body: Gender, Meaning, and Power.* New York: Routledge.

———. 2004. *Around the Tuscan Table: Food, Family, and Gender in Twentieth-Century Florence.* New York: Routledge.

———. 2009. *A Tortilla Is Like Life: Food and Culture in the San Luis Valley of Colorado.* Austin: University of Texas Press.

———. 2018. *Italian Food Activism in Urban Sardinia: Place, Taste, and Community.* New York: Bloomsbury.

Coy, Michael W. 1989. "Part 1: From Theory." In Coy, *Apprenticeship,* 1–12.

———, ed. 1989. *Apprenticeship: From Theory to Method and Back Again.* Albany: State University of New York Press.

Crenshaw, Kimberlé. 1995. "Mapping the Margins: Intersectionality, Identity Politics, and Violence against Women of Color." In *Critical Race Theory: The Key Writings that Formed the Movement,* edited by Kimberlé Crenshaw, Neil Gotanda, Gary Peller, and Kendall Thomas, 357–84. New York: New Press.

Csergo, Julia. 1996. "L'émergence des cuisines régionales." In *Histoire de l'alimentation,* edited by Jean-Louis Flandrin and Massimo Montanari, 823–41. Paris: Arthème Fayard.

———. 2008. "Lyon, première 'capitale mondiale de la gastronomie' 1925–1935." In *Voyages en gastronomies: L'invention des capitales et des régions gourmands,* edited by Julia Csergo and Jean-Pierre Lemasson, 33–49. Paris: Autrement.

Curnonsky, and Marcel E. Grancher. 1935. *Lyon, capitale mondiale de la gastronomie.* Lyon: Les éditions Lugdunum.

Curnonsky, and Marcel Rouff. 1925. *La France gastronomique.* Vols. 1 and 2, *Lyon et le lyonnais,* edited by Marcel Rouff. Paris: F. Rouff.

Curnutt, Hugh. 2016. "Cooking on Reality TV: Chef-Participants and Culinary Television." In *Food, Media and Contemporary Culture: The Edible Image,* edited by Peri Bradley, 144–63. New York: Palgrave Macmillan.

Daudet, Léon. 1927. *À boire et à manger.* Saint-Félicien-en-Vivarais: Au Pigeonnier.

Daune-Richard, Anne-Marie. 2000. "The Social Construction of Skill." In *The Gendering of Inequalities: Women, Men, and Work,* edited by Jane Jenson, Jacqueline Laufer, and Margaret Maruani, 111–23. Translated by Helen Arnold. Aldershot, UK: Ashgate.

Dégh, Linda, and Andrew Vázsonyi. 1974. "The Memorate and the Proto-Memorate." *Journal of American Folklore* 87, no. 345 (July–September): 225–39.

Denner, Jill, Linda Werner, Steve Bean, and Shannon Campe. 2005. "The Girls Creating Games Program: Strategies for Engaging Middle-School Girls in Information Technology." *Frontiers: A Journal of Women Studies* 26, no. 1: 90–98. doi:10.1353/fro.2005.0008.

Deutsch, Francine M. 2007. "Undoing Gender." *Gender and Society* 21, no. 1 (February): 106–27. doi:10.1177/0891243206293577.

DeVault, Marjorie L. 1991. *Feeding the Family: The Social Organization of Caring as Gendered Work.* Chicago: University of Chicago Press.

Devetter, François-Xavier, and Sandrine Rousseau. 2011. *Du balai: Essai sur le ménage à domicile et le retour de la domesticité.* Paris: Raisons d'agir.

Direction de l'animation de recherche, des études et des statistiques (DARES). 2016. *Cuisiniers—Portraits Statistiques Des Métiers, 1982–2014.*

April 7, 2016. https://dares.travail-emploi.gouv.fr/sites/default/files/8f4d553d39fef2cc6bd54b982867e6d8/S1Z%20-%20Cuisiniers.pdf. Accessed February 2, 2021.

Donadio, Rachel. 2018. "France, Where #MeToo Becomes #PasMoi." *Atlantic*, January 9, 2018. https://www.theatlantic.com/international/archive/2018/01/france-me-too/550124/. Accessed February 29, 2020.

Donovan, Lisa. 2020. *Our Lady of Perpetual Hunger: A Memoir*. New York: Penguin.

D'Oriola, Paulina. 2017. "Tabata Mey: 'Il n'y a que la passion qui nous permette de tenir.'" *Business o féminin*, January 25, 2017. https://www.businessofeminin.com/tabata-mey-il-ny-que-la-passion-qui-nous-permette-de-tenir/. Accessed December 29, 2020.

Dornenburg, Andrew, and Karen Page. 2003. *Becoming a Chef*. Rev. ed. Hoboken, NJ: Wiley.

Drouard, Alain. 2004. *Histoire des cuisiniers en France XIX–XXe siècle*. Paris: CNRS éditions.

———. 2007. *Histoire des innovations alimentaires: XIXe et XXe siècles*. Paris: Éditions L'Harmattan.

———. 2017. "Cuisiniers et cuisinières de maison bourgeoise (France, XIXe–XXe siècle)." *Food and History* 15, no. 1–2 (January): 255–72. https://doi.org/10.1484/J.FOOD.5.116341.

Druckman, Charlotte. 2010. "Why Are There No Great Women Chefs?" *Gastronomica* 10, no. 1 (February): 24–31. https://doi.org/10.1525/gfc.2010.10.1.24.

Duane, Daniel. 2019. "The Fight for Gender Equality in One of the Most Dangerous Sports on Earth." *New York Times Magazine*, February 7, 2019. https://www.nytimes.com/interactive/2019/02/07/magazine/women-surf-big-wave.html. Accessed February 29, 2020.

Duffy, Mignon. 2005. "Reproducing Labor Inequalities: Challenges for Feminists Conceptualizing Care at the Intersections of Gender, Race, and Class." *Gender and Society* 19, no. 1 (February): 66–82. doi:10.1177/0891243204269499.

Dussuet, Annie. 2017. "Le 'travail domestique': Une construction théorique féministe interrompue." *Recherches féministes* 30, no. 2: 101–317.

Éloire, Fabien. 2011. "Capital social et concurrence de statut." *Revue européenne des sciences sociales* 49, no. 2 (December 15): 7–41.

Ely, Robin J. 1995. "The Power in Demography: Women's Social Constructions of Gender Identity at Work." *Academy of Management Journal* 38, no. 3 (June): 589–634. doi:10.2307/256740.

Eymeri-Douzans, Jean-Michel. 2012. "Les concours à l'épreuve." *Revue française d'administration publique* 2, no. 142 (July): 307–25. doi:10.3917/rfap.142.0307.

Ezgulian, Sonia. 2013. *Carnet des mères lyonnaises.* Lyon: Les cuisinières-Sobbollire.

———. 2011. *6m2 de cuisine: Chroniques extraordinaires d'un restaurant ordinaire.* Paris: Les Éditions de l'Epure.

Fantasia, Rick. 2018. *French Gastronomy and the Magic of Americanism.* Philadelphia: Temple University Press.

Fassin, Didier. 2002. "L'intervention française de la discrimination." *Revue française de science politique* 52, no. 4: 403–23.

Faus, Patrick. n.d. "La Voûte—Chez Léa à Lyon (Rhône)." *Gourmets & Co.: Les plaisirs du go, le goût des plaisirs* (blog). http://www.gourmetsandco.com/restaurants/8546-la-voute-chez-lea. Accessed December 29, 2020.

Ferguson, Priscilla Parkhurst. 2004. *Accounting for Taste: The Triumph of French Cuisine.* Chicago: University of Chicago Press.

———. 2014. "The Invention of Modern Cuisine." In *Food in Time and Place: The American Historical Companion to Food History,* edited by Paul Freedman, Joyce E. Chaplin, and Ken Albala, 233–52. Berkeley: University of California Press.

Ferguson, Priscilla Parkhurst, and Sharon Zukin. 1998. "The Careers of Chefs." In *Eating Culture,* edited by Ron Scapp and Brian Seitz, 92–111. Albany: State University of New York Press.

Fine, Gary. 2009 (1996). *Kitchens: The Culture of Restaurant Work.* Berkeley: University of California Press.

Fischler, Claude. 1990. *L'hommivore: Sur les fondamentaux de la biologie et de la philosophie.* Paris: Odile Jacob.

Foor, Cindy, and Susan Walden. 2009. "'Imaginary Engineering' or 'Re-Imagined Engineering': Negotiating Gendered Identities in the Borderland of a College of Engineering." *NWSA Journal* 21, no. 2: 41–64. doi:10.1353/nwsa.0.0078.

Fournel, Paul. 1981. *L'histoire véritable de Guignol.* 2d ed. Genève: Slakine.

Frédiani, Vérane, dir. and writer. 2017. *À la récherché des femmes chefs (The Goddesses of Food).* Documentary film. La Ferme Productions. Distrib. Kino Lorber. 90 min.

Frédiani, Vérane, and Estérelle Payany. 2018. "Où sont les femmes? La carte des 500 cheffes à découvrir dans toute la France." *Télérama,* March 27, 2018. https://www.telerama.fr/monde/gastronomie-la-carte-des-370-cheffes-a-decouvrir-dans-toute-la-france,n5514484.php. Accessed February 29, 2020.

———. 2019. *Cheffes.* Paris: Nouriturfu.

Friedan, Betty. 1963. *The Feminine Mystique.* New York: W. W. Norton.

Gaudry, François-Régis. 2004. "Chef étoilée." *L'Express,* February 9, 2004. https://www.lexpress.fr/styles/saveurs/restaurant/chef-etoilee_490919.html. Accessed February 29, 2020.

———. 2016. "Lyon (Rhône): Les Apothicaires, la sensation de Tabata et Ludovic Mey." *L'Express*, March 17, 2016. https://www.lexpress.fr/styles/saveurs/restaurant/lyon-rhone-les-apothicaires-la-sensation-de-tabata-et-ludovic-mey_1774251.html.

Giard, Luce. 1994. "Faire la cuisine." In *L'invention du quotidien*, vol. 2, *Habiter, cuisiner*, edited by Michel de Certeau, Luce Giard, and Pierre Mayol, 213–352. Paris: Folio.

Gill, Rosalind. 2016. "Post-Postfeminism? New Feminist Visibilities in Postfeminist Times." *Feminist Media Studies* 16, no. 4: 610–30.

Gill, Rosalind, and Christina M. Scharff. 2011. Introduction. In *New Femininities: Postfeminism, Neoliberalism and Subjectivity*, edited by Rosalind Gill and Christina Scharff, 1–17. New York: Palgrave Macmillan.

Gill, Rosalind, Elisabeth K. Kelan, and Christina M. Scharff. 2017. "A Postfeminist Sensibility at Work." *Gender, Work and Organization* 24, no. 3 (May): 226–44.

Ginsburg, Faye, and Rayna Rapp. 1991. "The Politics of Reproduction." *Annual Review of Anthropology* 20 (October): 311–43.

Glenn, Evelyn Nakano. 1992. "From Servitude to Service Work: Historical Continuities in the Racial Division of Paid Reproductive Labor." *Signs* 18, no. 1 (October): 1–43. doi:10.1086/494777.

Goffman, Erving. 1959. *The Presentation of Self in Everyday Life.* Garden City, NY: Anchor.

Goodfellow, Samuel Huston. 2009. "Autonomy or Colony: The Politics of Alsace's Relationship to France in the Interwar Era." In *Views from the Margins: Creating Identities in Modern France*, edited by Kevin J. Callahan and Sarah A. Curtis, 135–57. Lincoln: University of Nebraska Press.

Goody, Esther. 1989. "Learning, Apprenticeship, and the Division of Labor." In Coy, *Apprenticeship*, 233–56.

Granovetter, Mark. 1985. "Economic Action and Social Structure: The Problem of Embeddedness." *American Journal of Sociology* 91, no. 3: 481–510.

Greenfield, Patricia Marks. 2004. *Weaving Generations Together: Evolving Creativity in the Maya of Chiapas.* Santa Fe, NM: School of American Research Press.

Gunther, Scott. 2016. "How and Why 'Bobos' Became French." *French Politics, Culture and Society* 34, no. 3 (December): 105–25.

Gutton, Jean-Pierre. 2000. *Histoire de Lyon et du lyonnais.* Paris: Presses universitaires de France.

Gvion, Liora, and Netta Leedon. 2019. "Incorporating the Home into the Restaurant Kitchen: The Case of Israeli Female Chefs." *Food and Foodways* 27, no. 4 (October): 296–315.

Haas, Jack. 1989. "The Process of Apprenticeship: Ritual Ordeal and the Adoption of a Cloak of Competence." In Coy, *Apprenticeship*, 87–105.

Hamilton, Gabrielle. 2011. *Blood, Bones, and Butter: The Inadvertent Education of a Reluctant Chef.* New York: Random House.

Hansen, Signe. 2008. "Society of the Appetite: Celebrity Chefs Deliver Consumers." *Food, Culture and Society* 11, no. 1 (March): 49–67.

Hargreaves, Alec G. 2004. "Half-Measures: Anti-Discrimination Policy in France from Race in France: Interdisciplinary Perspectives." In *Race in France: Interdisciplinary Perspectives on the Politics of Difference*, edited by Herrick Chapman and Laura L. Frader, 227–45. New York: Berghahn Books.

Harp, Stephen L. 2001. *Marketing Michelin: Advertising and Cultural Identity in Twentieth-Century France.* Baltimore: Johns Hopkins University Press.

Harris, Deborah A., and Patti Giuffre. 2015. *Taking the Heat: Women Chefs and Gender Inequality in the Professional Kitchen.* New Brunswick, NJ: Rutgers University Press.

Harris, Deborah A., and Patti A. Giuffre. 2010. "'Not One of the Guys': Women Chefs Redefining Gender in the Culinary Industry." In *Gender and Sexuality in the Workplace*, edited by Christine L. Williams and Kirsten Dellinger, 59–81. Bingley, UK: Emerald.

Hayes, Shannon. 2010. *Radical Homemakers: Reclaiming Domesticity from a Consumer Culture.* Richmondville, NY: Left to Write.

Herzfeld, Michael. 2004. *The Body Impolitic: Artisans and Artifice in the Global Hierarchy of Value.* Chicago: University of Chicago Press.

Hill, Jacquetta F., and David W. Plath. 1998. "Moneyed Knowledge: How Women Become Commercial Shellfish Divers." In *Learning in Likely Places: Varieties of Apprenticeship in Japan*, edited by John Singleton, 211–25. Cambridge: Cambridge University Press.

Hochschild, Arlie Russell. 1983. *The Managed Heart: Commercialization of Human Feeling.* Berkeley: University of California Press.

Holden, T. J. M. 2005. "The Overcooked and Underdone: Masculinities in Japanese Food Programming." *Food and Foodways* 13, no. 1–2 (March): 39–65. doi:10.1080/07409710590915364.

Hollows, Joanne. 2007. "The Feminist and the Cook: Julia Child, Betty Friedan and Domestic Femininity." In *Gender and Consumption: Domestic Cultures and the Commercialisation of Everyday Life*, edited by Emma Casey and Lydia Martens, 33–48. Burlington, VT: Ashgate.

Holtzman, Jon D. 2006. "Food and Memory." *Annual Review of Anthropology* 35, no. 1 (October): 361–78.

Huffman, Matt. 2013. "Organizations, Managers, and Wage Inequality." *Sex Roles* 68, no. 3–4: 216–22.

Hultin, Mia, and Ryszard Szulkin. 2003. "Mechanisms of Inequality. Unequal Access to Organizational Power and the Gender Wage Gap." *European Sociological Review* 19, no. 2 (April): 143–59. doi:10.1093/esr/19.2.143.

Hutchins, Edwin. 1993. "Learning to Navigate." In *Understanding Practice: Perspectives on Activity and Context*, edited by Seth Chaiklin and Jean Lave, 35–63. Cambridge: Cambridge University Press.

Ingold, Tim, and Elizabeth Hallam. 2007. "Creativity and Cultural Improvisation: An Introduction." In *Creativity and Cultural Improvisation*, edited by Tim Ingold and Elizabeth Hallam, 1–24. London: Routledge.

James, Joanna, dir. 2020. *A Fine Line: A Woman's Place Is in the Kitchen.* Documentary film. Zoel Productions. 70 min.

Jefferson, Laura, Karen Bloor, and Alan Maynard. 2015. "Women in Medicine: Historical Perspectives and Recent Trends." *British Medical Bulletin* 114, no. 1 (June): 5–15. doi:10.1093/bmb/ldv007.

Johnston, Josee, and Shyon Baumann. 2010. *Foodies: Democracy and Distinction in the Gourmet Foodscape.* New York: Routledge.

Judkis, Maura. 2018a. "In the Midst of Restaurants' Me Too Reckoning, Female Chefs Grapple with What Comes Next." *Washington Post*, June 12, 2018. https://www.washingtonpost.com/lifestyle/food/in-the-midst-of-restaurants-me-too-reckoning-female-chefs-grapple-with-what-comes-next/2018/06/11/110789fe-5304-11e8-abd8–265bd07a9859_story.html. Accessed March 2, 2020.

———. 2018b. "The Title of World's Best Female Chef Is 'Stupid.' Just Ask a Woman Who Won it." *Washington Post*, April 26, 2018. https://www.washingtonpost.com/news/food/wp/2018/04/26/the-title-of-worlds-best-female-chef-is-stupid-just-ask-a-woman-who-won-it/. Accessed March 2, 2020.

Kanter, Rosabeth Moss. 1977. *Men and Women of the Corporation.* New York: Basic Books.

Karpik, Lucien. 2000. "Le Guide Rouge Michelin." *Sociologie du travail* 42, no. 3 (July): 369–89. doi:10.1016/S0038-0296(00)01086-4.

Kelan, Elisabeth. 2009. *Performing Gender at Work.* New York: Springer.

Kludt, Amanda. 2019. "We Once Again Ask Why There Is a 'Best Female Chef' Award—Eater." *Eater*, March 1, 2019. https://www.eater.com/2017/1/25/14371688/best-female-chef-award-insulting. Accessed March 2, 2020.

Konkol, Stephanie. 2013. "Someone's in the Kitchen, Where's Dinah? Gendered Dimensions of the Professional Culinary World." PhD diss., DePaul University. https://via.library.depaul.edu/soe_etd/68.

Krishna, Priya. 2020. "How to Save Restaurants: Rebuilding the Restaurant Business Requires a New Model for Its Labor." *New York Times*, September 10, 2020. https://www.nytimes.com/2020/09/10/opinion/sunday/restaurants-indoor-dining.html. Accessed February 3, 2021.

Labbas, Assia. 2018. "France's New Michelin Guide: More Fraternité than Égalité." *New York Times*, February 23, 2018. https://www.nytimes.com/2018/02/23/world/europe/michelin-guide-france-women-chefs.html. Accessed March 2, 2020.

Lagrange, Catherine, and Thibaut Danancher. 2012. "L'étrange fuite du chef étoilé." *Le Point*, October 18, 2012. https://www.lepoint.fr/societe/l-etrange-fuite-du-chef-etoile-18–10–2012–1695718_23.php. Accessed January 23, 2021.

Lamamra, Nadia, Farinaz Fassa, and Martine Chaponnière. 2014. "Formation professionnelle: L'apprentissage des normes de genre." *Nouvelles questions féministes* 33, no. 1 (October): 8–14. doi:10.3917/nqf.331.0008.

Lamont, Michèle. 2004. "Immigration and the Salience of Racial Boundaries among French Workers." In *Race in France: Interdisciplinary Perspectives on the Politics of Difference,* edited by Laura L. Frader, and Herrick Chapman, 141–61. New York: Berghahn Books.

Lamy, Guillaume. 2012. "Du rififi dans les bouchons de Lyon." *Lyon capitale,* December 1, 2012. https://www.lyoncapitale.fr/a-table/du-rififi-dans-les-bouchons-de-lyon/.

Lane, Christel. 2014. *The Cultivation of Taste: Chefs and the Organization of Fine Dining.* Oxford: Oxford University Press.

L'association les bouchons lyonnais. n.d. "Garants de la tradition culinaire française." Les bouchons lyonnais. http://lesbouchonslyonnais.org/garants-de-la-tradition-culinaire-francaise/. Accessed March 27, 2017.

Lave, Jean, and Etienne Wenger. 1991. *Situated Learning: Legitimate Peripheral Participation.* Cambridge: Cambridge University Press.

"Le décret qui simplifie et renforce le dispositif 'Fait maison' est publié." 2015. Ministère de l'économie des finances et de la relance. May 7, 2015. http://www.economie.gouv.fr/dispositif-fait-maison-est-simplifie. Accessed February 2, 2021.

Le Monde and Agence France-Presse. 2017. "Sébastien Bras Renonce à figurer au Guide Michelin." *Le Monde,* September 20, 2017. https://www.lemonde.fr/m-gastronomie/article/2017/09/20/sebastien-bras-renonce-a-figurer-au-guide-michelin_5188474_4497540.html. Accessed February 2, 2021.

Le Monde and Agence France-Presse. 2019. "Le chef Marc Veyrat perd le procès intenté contre le Guide Michelin après la perte de sa troisième étoile." *Le Monde,* December 31, 2019. https://www.lemonde.fr/m-gastronomie/article/2019/12/31/le-chef-marc-veyrat-perd-le-proces-intente-contre-le-guide-michelin-apres-la-perte-de-sa-3e-etoile_6024499_4497540.html. Accessed February 2, 2021.

Lequin, Yves. 1986. "Apprenticeship in Nineteenth-Century France: A Continuing Tradition or a Break with the Past?" In *Work in France: Representations, Meaning, Organization, and Practice,* edited by Steven L. Kaplan and Cynthia J. Koepp, 457–74. Ithaca, NY: Cornell University Press.

Les Toques Blanches lyonnaises. n.d. "Our History." Les Toques blanches lyonnaises. https://www.toques-blanches-lyonnaises.com/en/history/. Accessed December 29, 2020.

Lewis, Patricia. 2014. "Postfeminism, Femininities and Organization Studies: Exploring a New Agenda." *Organization Studies* 35, no. 12 (August): 1845–66. doi:10.1177/0170840614539315.

Lewis, Patricia, Yvonne Benschop, and Ruth Simpson. 2017. "Postfeminism, Gender and Organization." *Gender, Work and Organization* 24, no. 3: 213–25.

MacCannell, Dean. 1973. "Staged Authenticity: Arrangements of Social Space in Tourist Settings." *American Journal of Sociology* 79, no. 3 (November): 589–603. doi:10.1086/225585.

Makooi, Bahar. 2020. "Pauvreté, tâches parentales, promotions: le prix payé par les femmes à la crise du Covid-19." France24, July 23, 2020. https://www.france24.com/fr/20200723-pauvret%C3%A9-t%C3%A2ches-parentales-promotions-le-prix-pay%C3%A9-par-les-femmes-%C3%A0-la-crise-du-covid-19. Accessed February 3, 2021.

Marie, Patricia. 2014. *Hommes et femmes dans l'Apprentissage et la transmission de "l'art culinaire."* Paris: L'Harmattan.

Martens, Albert, and Luc Denolf. 1993. "Inégalité sociale sur le marché de l'emploi: Le déterminant ethnique." *Critique régionale* 19: 39–55.

Martin, Brett. 2018. "Lyon Is the Real Capital of French Food." *GQ*, March 12, 2018. https://www.gq.com/story/lyon-french-food-travel-guide. Accessed January 9, 2020.

Matchar, Emily. 2013. *Homeward Bound: Why Women Are Embracing the New Domesticity*. New York: Simon and Schuster.

Mauss, Marcel. 2002 (1954). *The Gift: The Form and Reason for Exchange in Archaic Societies*. London: Routledge.

Mayol, Pierre. 1994. "Habiter." In *L'invention du quotidien 2: Habiter, cuisiner*, edited by Michel de Certeau, Luce Giard and Pierre Mayol, 15–189. Paris: Folio.

Mazet-Delpeuch, Danièle. 2012. *Carnets de cuisine: Du Périgord à l'Elysée*. Paris: Bayard Culture.

McCoy, Leah. 2001. "Remarkable Women in Mathematics and Science." In *Changing the Faces of Mathematics: Perspectives on Gender*, edited by Judith E. Jacobs, Joanne Rossi Becker, and Gloria F. Gilmer, 125–32. Reston, VA: National Council of Teachers of Mathematics.

Méjanès, Stéphane. 2020. "'Food Traboule,' le temple lyonnais de la street food." *L'Obs*, January 16, 2020. https://www.nouvelobs.com/food/20200116.OBS23568/food-traboule-le-temple-lyonnais-de-la-street-food.html. Accessed January 20, 2020.

Menon. 1822. *La cuisinière bourgeoise*. Paris: Éditions du Bastion.

Mériot, Sylvie-Anne. 2002. *Le cuisinier nostalgique: Entre restaurant et cantine*. Paris: CNRS éditions.

Mesplède, Jean-François. 2001. *Eugénie Brazier: Un heritage gourmand*. Lyon: Page d'écriture.

———. 2010. *Dictionnaire des cuisiniers*. Lyon: Page d'écriture.

Ministère de l'éducation nationale, de la jeunesse et des sports. 2019. *Repères et références statistiques sur les enseignements, la formation et la recherche 2019*. https://www.education.gouv.fr/reperes-et-references-statistiques-sur-les-enseignements-la-formation-et-la-recherche-2019-3806. Accessed February 2, 2021.

Mintz, Sidney W. 1989. "Cuisine and Haute Cuisine: How Are They Linked?" *Food and Foodways* 3, no. 3 (January): 185–90.

———. 1996. *Tasting Food, Tasting Freedom: Excursions into Eating, Culture, and the Past.* Boston: Beacon.

Motoyama, Sono. 2018. "Inside the French Culinary Competition that Drives Chefs to Tears." Eater, November 30, 2018. https://www.eater.com/2018/11/30/18118337/mof-meilleur-ouvrier-de-france-french-chef. Accessed July 12, 2019.

Murphy, John P. 2018. "Foie Gras in the Freezer: Picard Surgelés and the Branding of French Culinary Identity." *Food and Foodways* 26, no. 2 (April): 146–69. doi:10.1080/07409710.2018.1454774.

Nader, Laura. 2018. "Up the Anthropologist: Perspectives Gained from Studying Up." In *Contrarian Anthropology: The Unwritten Rules of Academia,* 12–32. New York: Berghahn Books.

Naulin, Sidonie. 2012. "Le repas gastronomique des français: Génèse d'un nouvel objet culturel." *Sciences de la société* 87: 8–25. doi:10.4000/sds.1488.

Ochberg, R. L., G. M. Barton, and A. N. West. 1989. "Women Physicians and Their Mentors." *Journal of the American Medical Women's Association* 44, no. 4 (July): 123–26.

Oldenburg, Ray. 1989. *The Great Good Place: Cafés, Coffee Shops, Community Centers, Beauty Parlors, General Stores, Bars, Hangouts and How They Get You through the Day.* New York: Paragon House.

O'Meara, Kerry Ann, and Nelly P. Stromquist. 2015. "Faculty Peer Networks: Role and Relevance in Advancing Agency and Gender Equity." *Gender and Education* 27, no. 3 (April): 338–58. doi:10.1080/09540253.2015.1027668.

Oren, Tasha. 2013. "On the Line: Format, Cooking and Competition as Television Values." *Critical Studies in Television: The International Journal of Television Studies* 8, no. 2: 20–35.

Orenstein, Peggy. 2010. "The Femivore's Dilemma." *New York Times Magazine,* March 11, 2010. https://www.nytimes.com/2010/03/14/magazine/14fob-wwln-t.html. Accessed March 2, 2020.

Padavic, Irene. 1991. "The Re-Creation of Gender in a Male Workplace." *Symbolic Interaction* 14, no. 3: 279–94.

Pailhé, Ariane. 2008. "Inégalités racistes et sexistes dans l'accès à l'emploi en France." *Nouvelles questions féministes* 27, no. 1 (January): 92–112. doi:10.3917/nqf.271.0092.

Pailhé, Ariane, Anne Solaz, and Maxime Tô. 2018. *Can Daddies Learn How to Change Nappies? Evidence from a Short Paternity Leave Policy.* Documents de travail 240, INED éditions. https://www.ined.fr/en/publications/editions/document-travail/can-daddies-learn-how-to-change-nappies/. Accessed February 2, 2021.

Pandraud, Cyrille. 1997. "La formation et les élèves de l'école la Martinière À Lyon: 1826–1841." Master's thesis, Université Lumière Lyon II.

Parker, Thomas. 2015. *Tasting French Terroir: The History of an Idea.* Berkeley: University of California Press.

Parkins, Wendy, and Geoffrey Craig. 2006. *Slow Living.* Oxford: Berg.

Paxson, Heather. 2012. *The Life of Cheese: Crafting Food and Value in America.* Berkeley: University of California Press.

Payany, Estérelle. 2019. "En 2020, le restaurant traditionnel va disparaître (et c'est inéluctable)." *Télérama,* September 8, 2019. https://www.telerama.fr/sortir/en-2020,-le-restaurant-traditionnel-va-disparaitre-et-cest-ineluctable,n6401822.php. Accessed March 2, 2020.

Perrot, Michelle. 1978. "De la nourrice à l'employée: Travaux de femmes dans la France du XIXe Siècle." *Le mouvement social* 105 (October–December): 3–10. https://doi.org/10.2307/3777547.

Peterson, T. Sarah. 1994. *Acquired Taste: The French Origins of Modern Cooking.* Ithaca, NY: Cornell University Press.

"Pierre Grison: Le prix des bouchons lyonnais a pris du ventre." 2012. *Lyon Mag,* March 5, 2012. https://www.lyonmag.com/article/37110/pierre-grison-8220-le-prix-des-bouchons-lyonnais-a-pris-du-ventre-8221. Accessed December 20, 2019.

Piketty, Thomas, Gilles Postel-Vinay, and Jean-Laurent Rosenthal. 2006. "Wealth Concentration in a Developing Economy: Paris and France, 1807–1994." *American Economic Review* 96, no. 1 (March): 236–56. doi:10.1257/000282806776157614.

Pini, Barbara. 2005. "The Third Sex: Women Leaders in Australian Agriculture." *Gender, Work and Organization* 12, no. 1 (January): 73–88. doi:10.1111/j.1468-0432.2005.00263.x.

Piser, Karina. 2018. "In France, Is the #MeToo Movement Passé?" *Nation,* November 2, 2018. https://www.thenation.com/article/archive/france-metoo-balancetonporc/. Accessed March 2, 2020.

Plessy, Bernard, and Louis Challet. 1987. *Des canuts passementiers et moulinières au XIXe siècle.* Paris: Hachette.

Postec, Vanessa. 2012. *Le goût des femmes à table.* Paris: Presses universitaires de France.

Powell, Abigail, Barbara Bagilhole, and Andrew Dainty. 2009. "How Women Engineers Do and Undo Gender: Consequences for Gender Equality." *Gender, Work and Organization* 16, no. 4 (June): 411–28. doi:10.1111/j.1468-0432.2008.00406.x.

Rambourg, Patrick. 2005. *De la cuisine à la gastronomie: Histoire de la table française.* Paris: Louis Audibert.

Ray, Krishnendu. 2007. "Domesticating Cuisine: Food and Aesthetics on American Television." *Gastronomica* 7, no. 1: 50–63.

———. 2016. *The Ethnic Restaurateur.* London: Bloomsbury Academic.

Regan, Iliana. 2019. *Burn the Place: A Memoir.* Evanston, IL: Agate Midway.

"Restaurant Les Apothicaires—Lyon." N.d. Les Apothicaires. https://lesapothicairesrestaurant.com/. Accessed December 19, 2019.

Reynaud, Christel. 2016. "Bande de gourmands, des potes au service d'une cuisine en liberté." *Le Progrès*, February 5, 2016. https://www.leprogres.fr/lyon/2016/02/05/bande-de-gourmands-des-potes-au-service-d-une-cuisine-en-liberte. Accessed January 27, 2021.

Reynolds, Deirdre. 2018. "'I Can Never Fully Understand Why Women Are Just Dismissed by Michelin'—Why Chefs Are Saying #MichelinToo." *Independent*, March 1, 2018. https://www.independent.ie/life/food-drink/food-news/i-can-never-fully-understand-why-women-are-just-dismissed-by-michelin-why-chefs-are-saying-michelintoo-36650724.html. Accessed March 2, 2020.

Riatto, Laurence. 2014. "Tabata Bonardi de Top Chef, 1e femme à diriger un restaurant Bocuse." Elle à Table. https://www.elle.fr/Elle-a-Table/Les-dossiers-de-la-redaction/News-de-la-redaction/Tabata-Bonardi-de-Top-Chef-1e-femme-a-diriger-un-restaurant-Bocuse-2680647. Accessed February 28, 2020.

Ridgeway, Ceclia. 2011. *Framed by Gender: How Gender Inequality Persists in the Modern World.* Oxford: Oxford University Press.

Risman, Barbara. 2009. "From Doing to Undoing: Gender as We Know It." *Gender and Society* 23, no. 1 (February 1): 81–84. https://doi.org/10.1177/0891243208326874.

Rodriguez, Cecilia. 2017. "Top 100 Bistros in Paris: New Gastronomic Stars at Affordable Prices." *Forbes*, April 29, 2017. https://www.forbes.com/sites/ceciliarodriguez/2017/04/29/top-100-bistros-in-paris-the-new-gastronomic-stars-at-affordable-prices/#a0950d7370b9. Accessed March 2, 2020.

Roosth, Sophia. 2013. "Of Foams and Formalisms: Scientific Expertise and Craft Practice in Molecular Gastronomy." *American Anthropologist* 115, no. 1 (March): 4–16.

Rouèche, Yves. 2018. *Histoire(s) de la gastronomie lyonnaise.* Lyon: Libel.

Ruhlman, Michael. 2006. *The Reach of a Chef: Professional Cooks in the Age of Celebrity.* New York: Penguin.

Safranova, Valeriya. 2018. "Catherine Deneuve and Others Denounce the #MeToo Movement." *New York Times*, January 9, 2018. https://www.nytimes.com/2018/01/09/movies/catherine-deneuve-and-others-denounce-the-metoo-movement.html. Accessed March 2, 2020.

Sage, Alexandria. 2014. "Kebabs Are Causing an Identity Crisis in France." Business Insider, October 28, 2014. https://www.businessinsider.com/r-in-france-kebabs-get-wrapped-up-in-identity-politics-2014–10. Accessed September 24, 2019.

Saltzman Chafetz, Janet. 1991. "The Gender Division of Labor and the Reproduction of Female Disadvantage: Toward an Integrated Theory."

In *Gender, Family and Economy: The Triple Overlap,* edited by Rae Lesser Blumberg, 74–94. Newbury Park, CA: Sage.

Samuelsson, Marcus. 2012. *Yes, Chef: A Memoir.* New York: Random House.

Sarmiento-Mirwaldt, Katja, Nicholas Allen, and Sarah Birch. 2014. "No Sex Scandals Please, We're French: French Attitudes Towards Politicians' Public and Private Conduct." *West European Politics* 37, no. 5 (September): 867–85.

Schweitzer, Sylvie. 2002. *Les femmes ont toujours travaillé: Une histoire du travail des femmes aux XIXe et XXe siècles.* Paris: Odile Jacob.

Schwiebert, Valerie L., Mary D. Deck, Monica L. Bradshaw, Pamela Scott, and Melanie Harper. 1999. "Women as Mentors." *Journal of Humanistic Counseling, Education and Development* 37, no. 4 (June): 241–53.

Shapiro, Laura. 2009. *Perfection Salad: Women and Cooking at the Turn of the Century.* Berkeley: University of California Press.

Shapiro, Mary, Cynthia Ingols, and Stacy Blake-Beard. 2008. "Confronting Career Double Binds: Implications for Women, Organizations, and Career Practitioners." *Journal of Career Development* 34, no. 3: 309–33. doi:10.1177/0894845307311250.

Simon, Catherine. 2018. *Mangée: Une histoire des mères lyonnaises.* Paris: Sabine Wespieser éditeur.

Simon, Patrick, and Mohamed Madoui. 2011. "Le marché du travail à l'épreuve des discriminations." *Sociologies pratiques* 23, no. 2 (October): 1–7.

Sims, Rebecca. 2009. "Food, Place and Authenticity: Local Food and the Sustainable Tourism Experience." *Journal of Sustainable Tourism* 17, no. 3 (May): 321–36. doi:10.1080/09669580802359293.

Smart, Barry. 1994. "Digesting the Modern Diet." In *The Flâneur,* edited by Keith Tester, 158–81. New York: Routledge.

Smith, Tony. 1975. *The End of the European Empire: Decolonization After World War II.* Lexington, MA: Heath.

Spongberg, Mary. 2002. *Writing Women's History since the Renaissance.* New York: Palgrave Macmillan.

Stainback, Kevin, Sibyl Kleiner, and Sheryl Skaggs. 2016. "Women in Power: Undoing or Redoing the Gendered Organization?" *Gender and Society* 30, no. 1: 109–35.

Stotsky, Janet G., Sakina Shibuya, Lisa Kolovich, and Suhaib Kebhaj. 2016. *Trends in Gender Equality and Women's Advancement.* N.p.: International Monetary Fund.

Sussman, George D. 1975. "The Wet-Nursing Business in Nineteenth-Century France." *French Historical Studies* 9, no. 2 (Autumn): 304–28.

Sutton, David E. 2014. *Secrets from the Greek Kitchen: Cooking, Skill, and Everyday Life on an Aegean Island.* Oakland: University of California Press.

Swinbank, Vicki A. 2002. "The Sexual Politics of Cooking: A Feminist Analysis of Culinary Hierarchy in Western Culture." *Journal of Historical Sociology* 15, no. 4 (December): 464–94.

Tangherlini, Timothy R. 1990. "'It Happened Not Too Far from Here . . .': A Survey of Legend Theory and Characterization." *Western Folklore* 49, no. 4 (October): 371–90.

Terré, François, and Philippe Simler. 2011. *Droit civil: Les régimes matrimoniaux*. 6th ed. Paris: Dulluz.

Terrio, Susan Jane. 2000. *Crafting the Culture and History of French Chocolate*. Berkeley: University of California Press.

Thivend, Marianne. 2010. "Les formations techniques et professionnelles entre l'état, la ville et le patronat: L'emploi de la taxe d'apprentissage à lyon dans l'entre-deux-guerres." *Le Mouvement Social* 232, no. 3: 9–27.

Thivend, Marianne, and Sylvie Schweitzer. 2005. "Etat des lieux des formations techniques et professionnelles dans l'agglomération lyonnaise: XIXe Siècle—Années 1960." Historie de L'École centrale de Lyon. https://histoire.ec-lyon.fr/docannexe/file/1398/larhra0001.pdf. Accessed February 12, 2021.

Thompson, E. P. 1991 (1963). *The Making of the English Working Class*. Toronto: Penguin Books.

Thompson, Paul, and Joanna Bornat. 2017. *The Voice of the Past: Oral History*. 4th ed. Oxford: Oxford University Press.

Timsit, Annabelle. 2017. "The Push to Make French Gender-Neutral." *Atlantic*, November 24, 2017. Accessed March 2, 2020. https://www.theatlantic.com/international/archive/2017/11/inclusive-writing-france-feminism/545048/. Accessed March 2, 2020.

Toussaint-Samat, Maguelonne. 2001. *Histoire de la cuisine bourgeoise: Du moyen âge à nos jours*. Paris: Editions Albin Michel.

Tronto, Joan C. 2002. "The 'Nanny' Question in Feminism." *Hypatia* 17, no. 2: 34–51. doi:10.1111/j.1527-2001.2002.tb00764.x.

Trubek, Amy B. 2000. *Haute Cuisine: How the French Invented the Culinary Profession*. Philadelphia: University of Pennsylvania Press.

Tucker, Robert C. 1978. *The Marx-Engels Reader*. 2d ed. New York: Norton.

UNESCO. N.d. "Gastronomic Meal of the French." Intangible Cultural Heritage, UNESCO. https://ich.unesco.org/en/RL/gastronomic-meal-of-the-french-00437. Accessed January 21, 2021.

Van Compernolle, Rémi Adam. 2007. "'Une pompière? C'est affreux!': Étude lexicale de la féminisation des noms de métiers et grades en France." *Langage et société* 120 (June): 107–26.

Varille, Mathieu. 1928. *La cuisine lyonnaise*. Lyon: P. Masson.

Verdier, Yvonne. 1979. *Façons de dire, façons de faire: La laveuse, la couturière, la cuisinière*. Paris: Gallimard.

Vergopoulos, Hécate. 2014. "Mise en marché et industrialisation des patrimoines." *Culture et musées* 23, no. 1 (July): 139–63. https://doi.org/10.3406/pumus.2014.1773.

Vincent, Christian, dir. 2012. *Les saveurs du Palais (Haute Cuisine)*. Armada Films and Vendôme Production. 95 min.

Voici. 2016. "Tabata Bonardi (Top Chef) s'est remariée et a ouvert un restaurant avec son époux." *Voici*, March 14, 2016. https://www.voici.fr/news-people/actu-people/tabata-bonardi-top-chef-s-est-remariee-et-a-ouvert-un-restaurant-avec-son-epoux-587736. Accessed January 21, 2021.

West, Candace, and Don H. Zimmerman. 1987. "Doing Gender." *Gender and Society* 1, no. 2 (June): 125–51. doi:10.1177/0891243287001002002.

White, Marco Pierre, with James Steen. 2007. *The Devil in the Kitchen: Sex, Pain, Madness, and the Making of a Great Chef*. New York: Bloomsbury.

White, Paul. 1989. "Internal Migration in the Nineteenth and Twentieth Centuries." In *Migrants in Modern France Population Mobility in the Later Nineteenth and Twentieth Centuries*, edited by Philip E. Ogden and Paul White, 13–33. London: Unwin Hyman.

Wiest, Lynda R. 2009. "Female Mathematicians as Role Models for All Students." *Feminist Teacher* 19, no. 2: 162–67. doi:10.1353/ftr.0.0039.

Wilk, Richard R. 2006. *Fast Food/Slow Food: The Cultural Economy of the Global Food System*. Lanham, MD: Altamira.

Williams-Forson, Psyche, and Abby Wilkerson. 2011. "Intersectionality and Food Studies." *Culture and Society* 14, no. 1 (March): 7–28. doi:10.2752/175174411X12810842291119.

Wilson, Eli Revelle Yano. 2021. *Front of the House, Back of the House: Race and Inequality in the Lives of Restaurant Workers*. New York: New York University Press.

Winchester, Hillary P. M. 1986. "Agricultural Change and Population Movements in France, 1892–1929." *Agricultural History Review* 34, no. 1: 60–78.

Windebank, Jan. 2012. "Social Policy and Gender Divisions of Domestic and Care Work in France." *Modern and Contemporary France* 20, no. 1 (February): 21–35. doi:10.1080/09639489.2011.631699.

The World's 50 Best Restaurants. 2019. "The World's Best Female Chef 2019." The World's 50 Best Restaurants. https://www.theworlds50best.com/awards/best-female-chef. Accessed December 23, 2020.

Zancarini-Fournel, Michelle. 2005. *Histoire des femmes en France: XIXe–XXe siècle*. Paris: Presses universitaires de Rennes.

INDEX

RACHEL E. BLACK is an associate professor of anthropology at Connecticut College. She is the author of *Porta Palazzo: The Anthropology of an Italian Market* and coeditor of *Wine and Culture: Vineyard to Glass.*

The University of Illinois Press
is a founding member of the
Association of University Presses.

University of Illinois Press
1325 South Oak Street
Champaign, IL 61820-6903
www.press.uillinois.edu